Strange Alchemy

Strange Alchemy

An Introduction to Weird Literature

⁂

Edited by

tammy lynne stoner

Chemeketa Press | Salem, Oregon

Strange Alchemy: An Introduction to Weird Literature

ISBN13: 978-1-955499-50-7

Chemeketa Press
Chemeketa Community College
4000 Lancaster Dr NE
Salem, Oregon 97305
collegepress@chemeketa.edu
chemeketapress.org

Cover design by Jaiden Collazo
Interior design by Ronald Cox

Text acknowledgments appear on pages 333 to 336 and constitute an extension of the copyright page.

Printed in the United States of America.

Land Acknowledgment
Chemeketa Press is located on the land of the Kalapuya, who today are represented by the Confederated Tribes of the Grand Ronde and the Confederated Tribes of the Siletz Indians, whose relationship with this land continues to this day. We offer gratitude for the land itself, for those who have stewarded it for generations, and for the opportunity to study, learn, work, and be in community on this land. We acknowledge that our College's history, like many others, is fundamentally tied to the first colonial developments in the Willamette Valley in Oregon. Finally, we respectfully acknowledge and honor past, present, and future Indigenous students of Chemeketa Community College.

Dedication

For my children, Oliver, Cedar, and Rosie,
who are all weird in their own strange, lovable ways.
Always be you.

Contents

Publisher's Note viii

Introduction: Why Weird Matters ix

Bibliography xvii

Part 1 | Weird Feminism

Carmen Maria Machado | *The Husband Stitch* 3

Chrys Tobey | *Ms. Bovary Goes House Hunting in 2014* 33

My Alter Egos Ran Off With This Poem 35

Alice W. Fuller | *A Wife Manufactured to Order* 39

Alice Gerstenberg | *Overtones: A One-Act Play* 51

Charlotte Perkins Gilman | *The Yellow Wallpaper* 69

Why I Wrote "The Yellow Wallpaper" 90

Part 2 | Weird Environmentalism

Talia Lakshmi Kolluri | *What We Fed to the Manticore* 97

Jane Hirshfield | *Common Pigeon* 113

Louisa May Alcott | *Lost in a Pyramid, or the Mummy's Curse* 119

Edgar Allan Poe | *The City in the Sea* 133

H. P. Lovecraft | *The Colour Out of Space* 139

Natalie Diaz | From *exhibits from The American Water Museum* 177

Alissa Hattman | From *Sift* 183

Brittney Corrigan | *The Last* 191

Part 3 | Weird Transhumanism

Philip K. Dick | *Second Variety* 199

Ray Bradbury | *Lazarus Come Forth* 257

Ambrose Bierce | *Moxon's Monster* 275

Ryan McCarty | *Why Wouldn't Autonomous Cars Cry at Night* 289

Matthea Harvey | *The Future of Terror* 293

Dashka Slater | *The Jeanines of Summer* 297

Rosebud Ben-Oni | *Poet Wrestling with the Possibility She's Living in a Simulation* 327

Credits 333

Publisher's Note

Disturbing the norm is a defining feature of weird literature. The works included in this anthology have been selected for their strange reflections on feminism, environmentalism, and transhumanism. Because of this focus, readers will encounter misogyny, environmental destruction, animal death, and body horror, with references to blood and gore, sexual content and questionable consent, psychological and emotional abuse, suicide, and graphic violence. We offer this note to prepare readers to engage critically and mindfully with challenging material, which is one of the many rewards of reading. In literature, the representation of these subjects is not an endorsement but rather an opportunity to confront, question, and explore the bizarre edges of the human and more-than-human worlds.

Introduction: Why Weird Matters

tammy lynne stoner

As a teenager, I escaped into my messy room, wooden closet doors covered in The Cure, Bow Wow Wow, and The Smiths stickers, to read Gabriel García Márquez, a Colombian journalist who became one of the most beloved and acclaimed writers of the twentieth century. His magical realist narratives didn't just tell stories; they invited me into worlds where the fantastical became ordinary as a way to address issues of humanity. A tattered angel falling from the sky and a plague of insomnia transforming an entire community weren't just plot points; they were invitations to see the world in a new and strange way.

After reading García Márquez, I devoured other "weird" writing that challenged narrative boundaries, books by US writers like Katherine Dunn's *Geek Love*, with its carnival of genetic mutations, and Karen Russell's short stories in *St. Lucy's Home for Girls Raised by Wolves* with their surreal landscapes of half-werewolf girls. I loved stories that led me to question perception, humanity, and even reality. A membrane that has, at least for me, nearly evaporated over the years.

So that brings us to this peculiar collection.

In our ever-evolving world, we are in many ways already living the weird. Botanists have discovered that plant roots can "think." Government agencies are declassifying UFO records. Physicists are wrestling with Unified Field Theory, an attempt to describe the fundamental forces of the physical world in a single theoretical framework. People are falling in love with

AI-powered chatbots. Evidence mounts proving the presence of microplastics in most living beings. The highest temperatures on record are leading to wildfires and extreme weather events, like fire tornadoes.

The pieces you'll read in this anthology uncover moments of the strange that are, oftentimes, also moments of the most profound truth. They don't ask you to believe in the unbelievable; they ask you to recognize that we've been living in the unbelievable and the potential of the unbelievable all along.

The Evolution of "Weird" in Literature

The term "weird literature" emerged in the 1930s as writers and critics sought to distinguish a particular kind of fantastic fiction from traditional gothic horror. American author H. P. Lovecraft (featured also in this collection), popularized the term in his essay "Supernatural Horror in Literature," when he argued that weird fiction differed from conventional horror by requiring "a certain atmosphere of breathless and unexplainable dread of outer, unknown forces" and "a malign and particular suspension or defeat of those fixed laws of Nature which are our only safeguard against the assaults of chaos."

What made weird fiction revolutionary was its rejection of familiar supernatural antagonists—vampires, ghosts, werewolves—in favor of cosmic uncertainties that challenged human understanding itself.

The New Weird movement in literature of the 1990s and 2000s further evolved these concepts mainly by blending genres—science fiction, fantasy, and horror—to address contemporary political and social concerns. US writers of the New Weird include Jeff VanderMeer, Kelly Link, Brian Evenson, Caitlín R. Kiernan, Carmen Maria Machado (more on her later), and Livia Llewellyn, although there are hundreds more!

What does it mean to call literature "strange" or "weird" today? This collection encourages readers to think of strangeness as literature's capacity to defamiliarize the familiar—to make us see our own world with fresh eyes by presenting it through radically different lenses.

The weird, as defined for this collection, operates through "strange alchemy"—the transformation of the bizarre into the profound. It's literature that invites readers into worlds that initially seem foreign or impossible, then reveals those worlds as mirrors reflecting often urgent truths about our own reality. Weird literature isn't escapism; it's a form of critical engagement that allows us to examine difficult topics—gender inequality, ecological collapse, technological transformation—through metaphorical distance that paradoxically brings us closer to understanding.

Our Trifecta of American Strange

Strange Alchemy is organized around three categories of weird literature:

» **Feminism,** with selections that interrogate how gendered power structures distort identity and agency.
» **Environmentalism,** with works that confront humanity's relationship with the natural world.
» **Transhumanism,** with pieces that grapple with technology's promise to fundamentally alter what it means to be human.

This collection deliberately focuses on voices from the United States because the strange emerges differently within each cultural context, and we wanted to explore how uniquely American anxieties manifest through weird literature.

Weird Feminism

In our first section, we examine literature that uses strange or surreal elements to expose and examine gender-based power structures.

Writers like Carmen Maria Machado show us the quiet horror embedded in ordinary marital dynamics, while poet Chrys Tobey's persona poems reimagine historical figures like Queen Elizabeth, Cleopatra, and Marie Antoinette setting the historical record straight. Alice Gerstenberg's one-act play, written in 1913, allows two women to interact as they appear in real life alongside their feisty, truthful inner selves. In all of these examples, women are given voices formally controlled by men, or a society run by men.

The feminist weird thrives on this tension between surface propriety and underlying truth, recognizing that women's lived experiences often feel so surreal that realist fiction cannot contain them.

These stories embrace the weird not as escape from reality but as the only honest way to represent realities that patriarchal culture has rendered invisible or unspeakable.

Weird Environmentalism

This next section employs weird or fantastical elements to help us process the environmental crisis and our relationship with the natural world. As literary scholar Rob Nixon argues in *Slow Violence and the Environmentalism of the Poor*, many environmental disasters happen too slowly and invisibly for people to notice or care about—like toxic pollution that takes decades to kill or climate change that unfolds over generations. Weird literature offers unique tools for making these environmental crises imaginatively visible and urgent, transforming abstract data into visceral, emotional experiences that can motivate understanding and action. By defamiliarizing our relationship with nature through surreal and fantastical elements, writers of the weird help readers grasp the magnitude of ecological loss while avoiding the paralysis that often accompanies environmental despair.

In this section, you'll find pieces that are "weird" in their storylines and settings, but also sometimes in their writing style. For example, Mojave American writer Natalie Diaz's poem "*exhibits from* the American Water Museum" imagines a bizarre museum displaying America's destruction of water and Indigenous communities. Diaz's poem offers fragmented, numbered exhibits where visitors become exhibits themselves. This tactic demonstrates a common occurrence in weird literature: the breakdown of boundaries between observer and observed that forces readers to experience being the subject rather than simply witnessing it.

The works in this section demonstrate how weird literature can reimagine ecological grief in ways that are both approachable and beautiful, offering new frameworks for processing environmental crises without surrendering to hopelessness.

Weird Transhumanism

Literature has been wrestling with the promise and peril of human enhancement long before we had fancy terms like "transhumanism." English novelist Mary Shelley kicked off this conversation in 1818 when Victor Frankenstein decided that death was more of a suggestion than a rule. Shelley's monster serves as one of literature's first cautionary tales about what happens when brilliant people get a little too confident around improving on the original human design.

A few decades later, in 1897, English writer H. G. Wells gave us *The Invisible Man*, who couldn't figure out how to become visible again. These stories established a pattern. The problem isn't usually the technology itself, but the humans who assume they're wise enough to redesign existence.

The transhumanist themes that Shelley and Wells explored became central to mid-twentieth-century science fiction for authors like writer and biochemistry professor Isaac Asimov. His *Foundation* novel series (1940s–50s) is an example of transhumanist storytelling that has been reimagined in the television series (2021–) by the same name.

By the 1970s and 80s, feminist science fiction writers in the United States really shook it up. Ursula K. Le Guin questioned whether technological enhancement was progress or just another form of domination, while Octavia Butler's *Xenogenesis* trilogy (1987–89) explored genetic engineering and human-alien hybridity.

By the 1980s, writers like Philip K. Dick had already been exploring what happens when the line between human and machine gets blurry. Novelist William Gibson's *Neuromancer* exploded onto the scene in 1984, completely redefining what science fiction could do with language and imagination. Gibson didn't just describe cyberspace—he made readers feel the electric rush of diving into data streams, the disorienting beauty of information made tangible. His world-building was so radical and complete that it essentially invented the internet in fiction before most people had ever touched a computer. The novel's poetic intensity proved that cyberpunk could be both philosophically complex and aesthetically stunning—and squarely transhumanist. (Go read it!)

Transhumanism explores the increasingly blurred boundaries between human consciousness, technology, and identity. The pieces in this collection examine how digital technology, artificial intelligence, biotechnology, and cybernetic enhancement are reshaping fundamental questions about what it means to be human—as true transhumanism should!

When you read Philip K. Dick's 1953 story "Second Variety" in this collection, you'll see how it remains startlingly relevant—and prescient—as it demonstrates the ever-vanishing lines between robot and human. Dashka Slater's "The Jeanines of Summer," written seventy years later, takes this a step further with a personal robot completing a polyamorous marriage.

Today, out of fictional environments and into the "real" world, let's see if the warnings of transhumanist writing come true!

The Purpose (other than to blow your mind)

Strange Alchemy is here to serve as an intellectual provocation. These pieces are not meant to provide answers; they're meant to expand the questions we're capable of asking.

Each selection comes with a Reader's Guide. For instructors, these sections provide structured yet flexible assignment suggestions that can spark deeper dives into the meaning of the work, generate writing exercises, and encourage workshop discussions. For readers, hopefully, these additions give you a moment of pause.

In a world that often demands simple, straightforward stories, weird literature argues for complexity, for nuance, for the power of imagination to reveal truths that direct statements often cannot. My hope is that these pages will be a starting point—or perhaps a continuation point for folks who already love the weird—showing us unique ways of thinking, writing, and maybe even *being* in this strange world of ours.

▪

Bibliography

Asimov, Isaac. *Foundation Trilogy*. Ballantine Books, 1986. Originally published as *Foundation* (1951), *Foundation and Empire* (1952), and *Second Foundation* (1953).

Butler, Octavia E. *Lilith's Brood: The Xenogenesis Trilogy*. Library of America, 2025. Originally published as *Dawn* (1987), *Adulthood Rites* (1988), and *Imago* (1989).

Dunn, Katherine. *Geek Love*. Alfred A. Knopf, 1989.

García Márquez, Gabriel. *Love in the Time of Cholera*. Translated by Edith Grossman. Alfred A. Knopf, 1988. Originally published 1985.

García Márquez, Gabriel. "A Very Old Man with Enormous Wings." In *Leaf Storm and Other Stories*, translated by Gregory Rabassa, 203–208. Harper & Row, 1972. Originally published 1968.

Gibson, William. *Neuromancer*. Ace Books, 1984.

Lovecraft, H. P. "Supernatural Horror in Literature." *The Recluse* 1, no. 2 (1927): 23–50.

Nixon, Rob. *Slow Violence and the Environmentalism of the Poor*. Harvard University Press, 2011.

Russell, Karen. *St. Lucy's Home for Girls Raised by Wolves*. Alfred A. Knopf, 2006.

Shelley, Mary. *Frankenstein; or, The Modern Prometheus*. Lackington, Hughes, Harding, Mavor & Jones, 1818.

Wells, H. G. *The Invisible Man*. C. Arthur Pearson, 1897.

Part 1

Weird Feminism

The Husband Stitch

Carmen Maria Machado

This short story, first published in 2014, weaponizes a classic children's tale to expose the dark underbelly of some conventional marriages. Using the central image of a mysterious green ribbon that must never be untied, Carmen Maria Machado examines how women's bodies can become contested territory when they enter into romantic relationships. The story refuses to separate the fantastical from the mundane: the ribbon is both supernatural mystery and perfect metaphor for the ways women are expected to remain partially unknowable while simultaneously offering complete access to their bodies. A feminist fairy tale.

(If you read this story out loud, please use the following voices:
ME: as a child, high-pitched, forgettable; as a woman, the same.
THE BOY WHO WILL GROW INTO A MAN, AND BE MY SPOUSE: robust with serendipity.
MY FATHER: kind, booming; like your father, or the man you wish was your father.
MY SON: as a small child, gentle, sounding with the faintest of lisps; as a man, like my husband.
ALL OTHER WOMEN: interchangeable with my own.)

In the beginning, I know I want him before he does. This isn't how things are done, but this is how I am going to do them. I am at a neighbor's party with my parents, and I am seventeen. I drink half a glass of white wine in the kitchen with the neighbor's teenage daughter. My father doesn't notice. Everything is soft, like a fresh oil painting.

The boy is not facing me. I see the muscles of his neck and upper back, how he fairly strains out of his button-down shirts, like a day laborer dressed up for a dance, and I run slick. And it isn't that I don't have choices. I am beautiful. I have a pretty mouth. I have breasts that heave out of my dresses in a way that seems innocent and perverse at the same time. I am a good girl, from a good family. But he is a little craggy, in that way men sometimes are, and I want. He seems like he could want the same thing.

I once heard a story about a girl who requested something so vile from her paramour that he told her family and they had her hauled off to a sanatorium. I don't know what deviant pleasure she asked for, though I desperately wish I did. What magical thing could you want so badly they take you away from the known world for wanting it?

The boy notices me. He seems sweet, flustered. He says hello. He asks my name.

I have always wanted to choose my moment, and this is the moment I choose.

On the deck, I kiss him. He kisses me back, gently at first, but then harder, and even pushes open my mouth a little with his tongue, which surprises me and, I think, perhaps him as well. I have imagined a lot of things in the dark, in my bed, beneath the weight of that old quilt, but never this, and I moan. When he pulls away, he seems startled. His eyes dart around for a moment before settling on my throat.

"What's that?" he asks.

"Oh, this?" I touch the ribbon at the back of my neck. "It's just my ribbon."[1] I run my fingers halfway around its green and glossy length, and bring them to rest on the tight bow that sits in the front. He reaches out his hand, and I seize it and press it away.

"You shouldn't touch it," I say. "You can't touch it."

Before we go inside, he asks if he can see me again. I tell him that I would like that. That night, before I sleep, I imagine him again, his tongue pushing open my mouth, and my fingers slide over myself and I imagine him there, all muscle and desire to please, and I know that we are going to marry.

We do. I mean, we will. But first, he takes me in his car, in the dark, to a lake with a marshy edge that is hard to get close to. He kisses me and clasps his hand around my breast, my nipple knotting beneath his fingers.

I am not truly sure what he is going to do before he does it. He is hard and hot and dry and smells like bread, and when he breaks me I scream and cling to him like I am lost at sea. His body locks onto mine and he is pushing, pushing, and before the end he pulls himself out and finishes with my blood slicking him down. I am fascinated and aroused by the rhythm, the concrete sense of his need, the clarity of his release. Afterward, he slumps in the seat, and I can hear the sounds of the pond: loons and crickets, and something that sounds like a banjo being plucked. The wind picks up off the water and cools my body down.

I don't know what to do now. I can feel my heart beating between my legs. It hurts, but I imagine it could feel good. I run my hand over myself and feel strains of pleasure from somewhere far off. His breathing becomes quieter and I realize that he is watching me. My skin is glowing beneath the moonlight coming

---

1. "The Husband Stitch" is based on the classic children's horror story "The Green Ribbon" (also called "The Yellow Ribbon"), popularized in Alvin Schwartz's *Scary Stories to Tell in the Dark* (1984) and appearing in various folk tale collections.

through the window. When I see him looking, I know I can seize that pleasure like my fingertips tickling the very end of a balloon's string that has almost drifted out of reach. I pull and moan and ride out the crest of sensation slowly and evenly, biting my tongue all the while.

"I need more," he says, but he does not rise to do anything. He looks out the window, and so do I. *Anything could move out there in the darkness*, I think. A hook-handed man. A ghostly hitchhiker forever repeating the same journey. An old woman summoned from the repose of her mirror by the chants of children.[2] Everyone knows these stories—that is, everyone tells them, even if they don't know them—but no one ever believes them.

His eyes drift over the water and then return to me.

"Tell me about your ribbon," he says.

"There's nothing to tell. It's my ribbon."

"May I touch it?"

"No."

"I want to touch it," he says. His fingers twitch a little, and I close my legs and sit up straighter.

"No."

Something in the lake muscles and writhes out of the water, and then lands with a splash. He turns at the sound.

"A fish," he says.

"Sometime," I tell him, "I will tell you the stories about this lake and her creatures."

He smiles at me, and rubs his jaw. A little of my blood smears across his skin, but he doesn't notice, and I don't say anything.

---

2. Machado weaves numerous folk tales, legends, and fairy tales throughout the story, including a girl pinned to a grave by her skirt (being "right" can be fatal for women), a bride who hides in a trunk and dies ("brides never fare well in stories"), a pioneer girl raised by wolves (female wildness and autonomy), and a woman who steals a corpse's liver (marriage as self-consumption).

"I would like that very much," he says.

"Take me home," I tell him. And like a gentleman, he does.

That night, I wash myself. The silky suds between my legs are the color and scent of rust, but I am newer than I have ever been.

My parents are very fond of him. He is a nice boy, they say. He will be a good man. They ask him about his occupation, his hobbies, his family. He shakes my father's hand firmly, and tells my mother flatteries that make her squeal and blush like a girl. He comes around twice a week, sometimes thrice. My mother invites him in for supper, and while we eat I dig my nails into the meat of his leg. After the ice cream puddles in the bowl, I tell my parents that I am going to walk with him down the lane. We strike off through the night, holding hands sweetly until we are out of sight of the house. I pull him through the trees, and when we find a patch of clear ground I shimmy off my pantyhose, and on my hands and knees offer myself up to him.

I have heard all of the stories about girls like me, and I am unafraid to make more of them. I hear the metallic buckle of his pants and the shush as they fall to the ground, and I feel his half hardness against me. I beg him—"No teasing"—and he obliges. I moan and push back, and we rut in that clearing, groans of my pleasure and groans of his good fortune mingling and dissipating into the night. We are learning, he and I.

There are two rules: he cannot finish inside of me, and he cannot touch my green ribbon. He spends into the dirt, *pat-pat-patt*ing like the beginning of rain. I go to touch myself, but my fingers, which had been curling in the dirt beneath me, are filthy. I pull up my underwear and stockings. He makes a sound and points, and I realize that beneath the nylon, my knees are also caked in dirt. I pull my stockings down and brush, and then up again. I smooth my skirt and repin my hair. A single lock has escaped his slicked-back curls in his exertion, and I tuck it up with the others. We walk down to the stream and I run my hands in the current until they are clean again.

We stroll back to the house, arms linked chastely. Inside, my mother has made coffee, and we all sit around while my father asks him about business.

(If you read this story out loud, the sounds of the clearing can be best reproduced by taking a deep breath and holding it for a long moment. Then release the air all at once, permitting your chest to collapse like a block tower knocked to the ground. Do this again, and again, shortening the time between the held breath and the release.)

I have always been a teller of stories. When I was a young girl, my mother carried me out of a grocery store as I screamed about toes in the produce aisle. Concerned women turned and watched as I kicked the air and pounded my mother's slender back.

"Potatoes!" she corrected when we got back to the house. "Not toes!" She told me to sit in my chair—a child-sized thing, built for me—until my father returned. But no, I had seen the toes, pale and bloody stumps, mixed in among those russet tubers. One of them, the one that I had poked with the tip of my index finger, was cold as ice, and yielded beneath my touch the way a blister did. When I repeated this detail to my mother, something behind the liquid of her eyes shifted quick as a startled cat.

"You stay right there," she said.

My father returned from work that evening, and listened to my story, each detail.

"You've met Mr. Barns, have you not?" he asked me, referring to the elderly man who ran this particular market.

I had met him once, and I said so. He had hair white as a sky before snow, and a wife who drew the signs for the store windows.

"Why would Mr. Barns sell toes?" my father asked. "Where would he get them?"

Being young, and having no understanding of graveyards or mortuaries, I could not answer.

"And even if he got them somewhere," my father continued, "what would he have to gain by selling them amongst the potatoes?"

They had been there. I had seen them with my own eyes. But beneath the sunbeam of my father's logic, I felt my doubt unfurl.

"Most importantly," my father said, arriving triumphantly at his final piece of evidence, "why did no one notice the toes except for you?"

As a grown woman, I would have said to my father that there are true things in this world observed only by a single set of eyes. As a girl, I consented to his account of the story, and laughed when he scooped me from the chair to kiss me and send me on my way.

It is not normal that a girl teaches her boy, but I am only showing him what I want, what plays on the insides of my eyelids as I fall asleep. He comes to know the flicker of my expression as a desire passes through me, and I hold nothing back from him. When he tells me that he wants my mouth, the length of my throat, I teach myself not to gag and take all of him into me, moaning around the saltiness. When he asks me my worst secret, I tell him about the teacher who hid me in the closet until the others were gone and made me hold him there, and how afterward I went home and scrubbed my hands with a steel wool pad until they bled, even though the memory strikes such a chord of anger and shame that after I share this I have nightmares for a month. And when he asks me to marry him, days shy of my eighteenth birthday, I say yes, yes, please, and then on that park bench I sit on his lap and fan my skirt around us so that a passerby would not realize what was happening beneath it.

"I feel like I know so many parts of you," he says to me, knuckle-deep and trying not to pant. "And now, I will know all of them."

There is a story they tell, about a girl dared by her peers to venture to a local graveyard after dark. This was her folly: when they told her that standing on someone's grave at night would cause the inhabitant to reach up and pull her under, she scoffed. Scoffing is the first mistake a woman can make.

"Life is too short to be afraid of nothing," she said, "and I will show you."

Pride is the second mistake.

She could do it, she insisted, because no such fate would befall her. So they gave her a knife to stick into the frosty earth, as a way of proving her presence and her theory.

She went to that graveyard. Some storytellers say that she picked the grave at random. I believe she selected a very old one, her choice tinged by self-doubt and the latent belief that if she were wrong, the intact muscle and flesh of a newly dead corpse would be more dangerous than one centuries gone.

She knelt on the grave and plunged the blade deep. As she stood to run—for there was no one to see her fear—she found she couldn't escape. Something was clutching at her clothes. She cried out and fell to the ground.

When morning came, her friends arrived at the cemetery. They found her dead on the grave, the blade pinning the sturdy wool of her skirt to the earth. Dead of fright or exposure, would it matter when the parents arrived? She was not wrong, but it didn't matter anymore. Afterward, everyone believed that she had wished to die, even though she had died proving that she wanted to live.

As it turns out, being right was the third, and worst, mistake.

My parents are pleased about the marriage. My mother says that even though girls nowadays are starting to marry late, she married my father when she was nineteen, and was glad that she did.

When I select my wedding gown, I am reminded of the story of the young woman who wished to go to a dance with her lover, but could not afford a dress.[3] She purchased a lovely white frock from a secondhand shop, and then later fell ill and passed from this earth. A doctor who examined her in her final days discovered that she had died from exposure to embalming fluid. It turned out that an unscrupulous undertaker's assistant had stolen the dress from the corpse of a bride.

The moral of that story, I think, is that being poor will kill you. I spend more on my dress than I intend, but it is very beautiful, and better than being dead. When I fold it into my hope chest, I think about the bride who played hide-and-go-seek on her wedding day and hid in the attic, in an old trunk that snapped shut around her and did not open. She was trapped there until she died. People thought that she had run away until years later, when a maid found her skeleton, in a white dress, folded inside that dark space. Brides never fare well in stories. Stories can sense happiness and snuff it out like a candle.

We marry in April, on an unseasonably cold afternoon. He sees me before the wedding, in my dress, and insists on kissing me deeply and reaching inside of my bodice. He becomes hard, and I tell him that I want him to use my body as he sees fit. I rescind my first rule, given the occasion. He pushes me against the wall and puts his hand against the tile near my throat, to steady himself. His thumb brushes my ribbon. He does not move his hand, and as he works himself in me he says, "I love you, I love you, I love you." I do not know if I am the first woman to walk up the aisle of St. George's with semen leaking down her leg, but I like to imagine that I am.

---

3. Based on an urban legend about a poisoned dress, a version of this tale appears as "The White Satin Evening Gown" in *Scary Stories to Tell in the Dark* by Alvin Schwartz.

For our honeymoon, we go on a tour of Europe. We are not rich but we make it work. Europe is a continent of stories, and in between consummations, I learn them. We go from bustling, ancient metropolises to sleepy villages to Alpine retreats and back again, sipping spirits and pulling roasted meat from bones with our teeth, eating spaetzle and olives and ravioli and a creamy grain I do not recognize but come to crave each morning. We cannot afford a sleeper car on the train, but my husband bribes an attendant to permit us one hour in an empty room, and in that way we couple over the Rhine, my husband pinning me to the rickety frame and howling like something more primordial than the mountains we cross. I recognize that this is not the entire world, but it is the first part of it that I am seeing. I feel electrified by possibility.

(If you are reading this story out loud, make the sound of the bed under the tension of train travel and lovemaking by straining a metal folding chair against its hinges. When you are exhausted with that, sing the half-remembered lyrics of old songs to the person closest to you, thinking of lullabies for children.)

My cycle stops soon after we return from our trip. I tell my husband one night, after we are spent and sprawled across our bed. He glows with real delight.

"A child," he says. He lies back with his hands beneath his head. "A child." He is quiet for so long that I think that he's fallen asleep, but when I look over his eyes are open and fixed on the ceiling. He rolls on his side and gazes at me.

"Will the child have a ribbon?"

I feel my jaw tighten, and my hand fondles my bow involuntarily. My mind skips between many answers, and I settle on the one that brings me the least amount of anger.

"There is no saying, now," I tell him finally.

He startles me, then, running his hand around my throat. I

put up my hands to stop him but he uses his strength, grabbing my wrists with one hand as he touches the ribbon with the other. He presses the silky length with his thumb. He touches the bow delicately, as if he is massaging my sex.

"Please," I say. "Please don't."

He does not seem to hear. "Please," I say again, my voice louder, but cracking in the middle.

He could have done it then, untied the bow, if he'd chosen to. But he releases me and rolls on his back as if nothing has happened. My wrists ache, and I rub them.

"I need a glass of water," I say. I get up and go to the bathroom. I run the tap and then frantically check my ribbon, tears caught in my lashes. The bow is still tight.

There is a story I love about a pioneer husband and wife killed by wolves. Neighbors found their bodies torn open and strewn around their tiny cabin, but never located their infant daughter, alive or dead. People claimed they saw the girl running with a wolf pack, loping over the terrain as wild and feral as any of her companions.

News of her would ripple through the local settlements upon each sighting. She menaced a hunter in a winter forest—though perhaps he was less menaced than startled at a tiny naked girl baring her teeth and howling so rawly it quaked the skin on his bones. A young woman, on the cusp of marriage age, trying to take down a horse. People even saw her ripping open a chicken in an explosion of feathers.

Many years later, she was said to be seen resting in the rushes along a riverbank, suckling two wolf cubs. I like to imagine that they came from her body, the lineage of wolves tainted human just the once. They certainly bloodied her breasts, but she did not mind, because they were hers and only hers. I believe that when their muzzles and teeth pressed against her she felt a kind of sanctuary, peace she would have found nowhere else. She must have been better among them than she would have been otherwise. Of that, I am certain.

Months pass and my stomach swells. Inside of me, our child is swimming fiercely, kicking and pushing and clawing. In public, I gasp and stagger to the side, clutching my belly and hissing through my teeth to Little One, as I call it, to stop. Once, I stumble on a walk in the park, the same park where my husband had proposed to me the year before, and go to my knees, breathing heavily and near weeping. A woman passing by helps me to sit up and gives me some water, telling me that the first pregnancy is always the worst, but they get better with time.

It is the worst, but for so many reasons besides my altered form. I sing to my child, and think about the old wives' tales of carrying the baby high or low. Do I carry a boy inside of me, the image of his father? Or a girl, a daughter who would soften the sons that followed? I have no siblings, but I know that eldest girls sweeten their brothers and are protected by them from the dangers of the world—an arrangement that buoys my heart.

My body changes in ways I do not expect—my breasts are large and hot, my stomach lined with pale marks, the inverse of a tiger's. I feel monstrous, but my husband seems renewed with desire, as if my novel shape has refreshed our list of perversities. And my body responds: in the line at the supermarket, receiving communion in church, I am marked by a new and ferocious want, leaving me slippery and swollen at the slightest provocation. When he comes home each day, my husband has made a list in his mind of things he desires from me, and I am willing to provide them and more, having been on the edge of coming since that morning's purchase of bread and carrots.

"I am the luckiest man alive," he says, running his hands across my stomach.

In the mornings, he kisses me and fondles me and sometimes takes me before his coffee and toast. He goes to work with a spring in his step. He comes home with one promotion, and then another. "More money for my family," he says. "More money for our happiness."

I go into labor in the middle of the night, every inch of my insides twisting into an obscene knot before release. I scream like I have not screamed since the night by the lake, but for contrary reasons. Now, the pleasure of the knowledge that my child is coming is dismantled by the unyielding agony.

I am in labor for twenty hours. I nearly wrench off my husband's hand, howling obscenities that do not seem to shock the nurse. The doctor is frustratingly patient, peering down between my legs, his white eyebrows making unreadable Morse code across his forehead.

"What's happening?" I ask.

"Breathe," he commands.

I am certain that if any more time passes, I will crush my own teeth to powder. I look to my husband, who kisses my forehead and asks the doctor what's happening.

"I'm not satisfied this will be a natural birth," the doctor says. "We may have to deliver the baby surgically."

"No, please," I say. "I don't want that, please."

"If there's no movement soon, we're going to do it," the doctor says. "It may be best for everyone." He looks up and I am almost certain he winks at my husband, but pain makes the mind see things differently than they are.

I make a deal with Little One, in my mind. *Little One,* I think, *this is the last time that we are going to be just you and me. Please don't make them cut you out of me.*

Little One is born twenty minutes later. They do have to make a cut, but not across my stomach as I had feared. The doctor draws his scalpel down instead, and I feel little, just tugging, though perhaps it is what they have given me. When the baby is placed in my arms, I examine the wrinkled body from head to toe, the color of a sunset sky, and streaked in red.

No ribbon. A boy. I begin to weep, and curl the unmarked baby into my chest. The nurse shows me how to nurse him, and I am so happy to feel him drink, to touch the curls of his fingers, little commas, each of them.

(If you are reading this story out loud, give a paring knife to the listeners and ask them to cut the tender flap of skin between your index finger and thumb. Afterward, thank them.)

There is a story about a woman who goes into labor when the attending physician is tired. There is a story about a woman who herself was born too early. There is a story about a woman whose body clung to her child so hard they cut her to retrieve him. There is a story about a woman who heard a story about a woman who birthed wolf cubs in secret. When you think about it, stories have this way of running together like raindrops in a pond. Each is borne from the clouds separate, but once they have come together, there is no way to tell them apart.

(If you are reading this story out loud, move aside the curtain to illustrate this final point to your listeners. It'll be raining, I promise.)

They take the baby so that they may fix me where they cut. They give me something that makes me sleepy, delivered through a mask pressed gently to my mouth and nose. My husband jokes around with the doctor as he holds my hand.

"How much to get that extra stitch?"[4] he asks. "You offer that, right?"

---

4. The "husband stitch" is a medically unnecessary additional suture sometimes added when repairing vaginal tearing or episiotomy cuts after childbirth, to make the vagina "tighter."

"Please," I say to him. But it comes out slurred and twisted and possibly no more than a small moan. Neither man turns his head toward me.

The doctor chuckles. "You aren't the first—"

I slide down a long tunnel, and then surface again, but covered in something heavy and dark, like oil. I feel like I am going to vomit.

"— the rumor is something like— "

"— like a vir— "

And then I am awake, wide awake, and my husband is gone and the doctor is gone. And the baby, where is—

The nurse sticks her head in the door.

"Your husband just went to get a coffee," she says, "and the baby is asleep in the bassinet."

The doctor walks in behind her, wiping his hands on a cloth.

"You're all sewn up, don't you worry," he said. "Nice and tight, everyone's happy. The nurse will speak with you about recovery. You're going to need to rest for a while."

The baby wakes up. The nurse scoops him from his swaddle and places him in my arms again. He is so beautiful I have to remind myself to breathe.

I recover a small amount every day. I move slowly and ache. My husband moves to touch me and I push him away. I want to return to our life as it was, but such things cannot be helped right now. I am already nursing and rising at all hours to take care of our son with my pain.

Then one day I take him in my hand, and afterward he is so content I realize that I can sate him, even if I remain unsated. Around our son's first birthday, I am healed enough to take my husband back into my bed. I weep with happiness as he touches me, fills me as I have wanted to be filled for so long.

My son is a good baby. He grows and grows. We try to have

another child, but I suspect that Little One did so much ruinous damage inside of me that my body couldn't house another.

"You were a poor tenant, Little One," I say to him, rubbing shampoo into his fine brown hair, "and I shall revoke your deposit."

He splashes around in the sink, cackling with happiness.

My son touches my ribbon, but never in a way that makes me afraid. He thinks of it as a part of me, and he treats it no differently than he would an ear or a finger. It gives him delight in a way that houses no wanting, and this pleases me.

I do not know if my husband is sad that we cannot have another child. He keeps his sorrows as close to himself as he is open with his desires. He is a good father, and he loves his boy. Back from work, they play games of chase and run in the yard. He is too young to catch a ball, still, but my husband patiently rolls it to him in the grass, and our son picks it up and drops it again, and my husband gestures to me and cries, "Look, look! Did you see? He is going to throw it soon enough."

Of all the stories I know about mothers, this one is the most real. A young American girl is visiting Paris with her mother when the woman begins to feel ill. They decide to check into a hotel for a few days so the mother can rest, and the daughter calls for a doctor to assess her.

After a brief examination, the doctor tells the daughter that all her mother needs is some medicine. He takes the daughter to a taxi, gives the driver instructions in French, and explains to the girl that the driver will take her to his residence, where his wife will give her the appropriate remedy. They drive and drive for a very long time, and when the girl arrives, she is frustrated by the unbearable slowness of this doctor's wife, who meticulously assembles the pills from powder. When she gets back into the taxi, the driver meanders down the streets, sometimes doubling back on the same avenue. Frustrated, the girl gets out of the taxi to return to the hotel on foot. When she finally arrives, the hotel clerk tells her that he has never seen her before. When she runs up to the room where her mother had been resting, she finds the walls a different color, the furnishings different than her memory, and her mother nowhere in sight.

There are many endings to the story. In one of them, the girl is gloriously persistent and certain, renting a room nearby and staking out the hotel, eventually seducing a young man who works in the laundry and discovering the truth: that her mother had died of a highly contagious and fatal disease, departing this plane shortly after the daughter was sent from the hotel by the doctor. To avoid citywide panic, the staff removed and buried her body, repainted and refurnished the room, and bribed all involved to deny that they had ever met the pair.

In another version of this story, the girl wanders the streets of Paris for years, believing that she is mad, that she invented her mother and her life with her mother in her own diseased mind. The daughter stumbles from hotel to hotel, confused and grieving, though for whom she cannot say. Each time she is ejected from another posh lobby, she weeps for something lost. Her mother is dead and she does not know it. She won't know it until she, herself, is also dead, assuming that you believe in paradise.

I don't need to tell you the moral of this story. I think you already know what it is.

Our son enters school when he is five, and I remember his teacher from that day in the park, when she had crouched to help me and predicted easy future pregnancies. She remembers me as well, and we talk briefly in the hallway. I tell her that we have had no more children since our son, and now that he has started school, my days will be altered toward sloth and boredom. She is kind. She tells me that if I am looking for a way to occupy my time, there is a wonderful women's art class at a local college.

That night, after my son is in bed, my husband reaches his hand across the couch and slides it up my leg.

"Come to me," he says, and I twinge with pleasure. I slide off the couch, smoothing my skirt very prettily as I shuffle over to him on my knees. I kiss his leg, running my hand up to his belt, tugging him from his bonds before swallowing him whole. He runs his hands through my hair, stroking my head, groaning and pressing into me. And I don't realize that his hand is sliding down the back of my neck until he is trying to loop his fingers through the ribbon. I gasp and pull away quickly, falling back and frantically checking my bow. He is still sitting there, slick with my spit.

"Come back here," he says.

"No," I say. "You'll touch my ribbon."

He stands up and tucks himself into his pants, zipping them up.

"A wife," he says, "should have no secrets from her husband."

"I don't have any secrets," I tell him.

"The *ribbon.*"

"The ribbon is not a secret; it's just mine."

"Were you born with it? Why your throat? Why is it green?"

I do not answer.

He is silent for a long minute. Then,

"A wife should have no secrets."

My nose grows hot. I do not want to cry.

"I've given you everything you have ever asked for," I say. "Am I not allowed this one thing?"

"I want to know."

"You think you want to know," I say, "but you don't."

"Why do you want to hide it from me?"

"I'm not hiding it. It just isn't yours."

He gets down very close to me, and I pull back from the smell of bourbon. I hear a creak, and we both look up to see our son's feet vanishing up the staircase.

When my husband goes to sleep that night, he does so with a

hot and burning anger that falls away as soon as he is truly dreaming. I am up for a long time listening to his breathing, wondering if perhaps men have ribbons that do not look like ribbons. Maybe we are all marked in some way, even if it's impossible to see.

The next day, our son touches my throat and asks about my ribbon. He tries to pull at it. And though it pains me, I have to make it forbidden to him. When he reaches for it, I shake a can full of pennies. It crashes discordantly, and he withdraws and weeps. Something is lost between us, and I never find it again.

(If you are reading this story out loud, prepare a soda can full of pennies. When you arrive at this moment, shake it loudly in the face of the people closest to you. Observe their expression of startled fear, and then betrayal. Notice how they never look at you exactly the same way for the rest of your days.)

I enroll in the art class for women. When my husband is at work and my son is in school, I drive to the sprawling green campus and the squat gray building where the art classes are held.

Presumably, the male nudes are kept from our eyes in some deference to propriety, but the class has its own energy—there is plenty to see on a strange woman's naked form, plenty to contemplate as you roll charcoal and mix paints. I see more than one woman shifting forward and back in her seat to redistribute blood flow.

One woman in particular returns over and over. Her ribbon is red, and is knotted around her slender ankle. Her skin is the color of olives, and a trail of dark hair runs from her belly button to her mons. I know that I should not want her, not because she is a woman and not because she is a stranger, but because it is her job to disrobe, and I feel shame taking advantage of such a state. No small amount of guilt comes along with my wandering eyes, but as my pencil traces her contours, so does my hand in the secret recesses of my mind. I am not even certain how such a thing would happen, but the possibilities incense me to near madness.

One afternoon after class, I turn a hallway corner and she is there, the woman. Clothed, wrapped in a raincoat. Her gaze transfixes me, and this close I can see a band of gold around each of her pupils, as though her eyes are twin solar eclipses. She greets me, and I her.

We sit down together in a booth at a nearby diner, our knees occasionally brushing up against each other beneath the Formica. She drinks a cup of black coffee, which startles me, though I don't know why. I ask her if she has any children. She does, she says, a daughter, a beautiful little girl of eleven.

"Eleven is a terrifying age," she says. "I remember nothing before I was eleven, but then there it was, all color and horror. What a number," she says, "what a show." Then her face slips somewhere else for a moment, as if she has dipped beneath the surface of a lake, and when it comes back, she briefly speaks to her daughter's accomplishments in voice and music.

We do not discuss the specific fears of raising a girl-child. Truthfully, I am afraid even to ask. I also do not ask her if she's married, and she does not volunteer the information, though she does not wear a ring. We talk about my son, about the art class. I desperately want to know what state of need has sent her to disrobe before us, but perhaps I do not ask, because the answer would be, like adolescence, too frightening to forget.

I am captivated by her, there is no other way to put it. There is something easy about her, but not easy the way I was—the way I am. She's like dough, how the give of it beneath kneading hands disguises its sturdiness, its potential. When I look away from her and then look back, she seems twice as large as before.

"Perhaps we can talk again sometime," I say to her. "This has been a very pleasant afternoon."

She nods to me. I pay for her coffee.

I do not want to tell my husband about her, but he can sense some untapped desire. One night, he asks what roils inside of me and I confess it to him. I even describe the details of her ribbon, releasing an extra flood of shame.

He is so glad of this development that he begins to mutter a long and exhaustive fantasy as he removes his pants and enters me, and I cannot even hear all of it, though I imagine that within its parameters she and I are together, or perhaps both of us are with him.

I feel as if I have betrayed her somehow, and I never return to the class. I find other amusements to occupy my days.

(If you are reading this story out loud, force a listener to reveal a devastating secret, then open the nearest window to the street and scream it as loudly as you are able.)

One of my favorite stories is about an old woman and her husband—a man mean as Mondays, who scared her with the violence of his temper and the shifting nature of his whims. She was only able to keep him satisfied with her cooking, to which he was a complete captive. One day, he bought her a fat liver to cook for him, and she did, using herbs and broth. But the smell of her own artistry overtook her, and a few nibbles became a few bites, and soon the liver was gone. She had no money with which to purchase a second one, and she was terrified of her husband's reaction should he discover that his meal was gone. So she crept to the church next door, where a woman had been recently laid to rest. She approached the shrouded figure, then cut into it with a pair of kitchen shears and stole the liver from her corpse.

That night, the woman's husband dabbed his lips with a napkin and declared the meal the finest he'd ever eaten. When they went to sleep, the old woman heard the front door open, and a thin wail wafted through the rooms. *Who has my liver? Whooooo has my liver?*

The old woman could hear the voice coming closer and closer to the bedroom. There was a hush as the door swung open. The dead woman posed her query again.

The old woman flung the blanket off her husband.

"*He* has it!" she declared triumphantly.

Then she saw the face of the dead woman, and recognized her own mouth and eyes. She looked down at her abdomen, remembering, now, how she carved into her belly. She bled freely there in the bed, whispering something over and over as she died, something you and I will never be privy to. Next to her, as the blood seeped into the very heart of the mattress, her husband slumbered on.

That may not be the version of the story you're familiar with. But I assure you, it's the one you need to know.

My husband is strangely excited for Halloween. I took one of his old tweed coats and fashioned one for our son, so that he might be a tiny professor, or some other stuffy academic. I even give him a pipe on which to gnaw. Our son clicks it between his teeth in a way I find unsettlingly adult.

"Mama," my son says, "what are you?"

I am not in costume, so I tell him I am his mother.

The pipe falls from his little mouth onto the floor, and he screams so loudly I am unable to move. My husband swoops in and picks him up, talking to him in a low voice, repeating his name between his sobs.

It is only as his breathing returns to normal that I am able to identify my mistake. He is not old enough to know the story of the naughty girls who wanted the toy drum and were wicked toward their mother until she went away and was replaced with a new mother—one with glass eyes and thumping wooden tail. He is too young for the stories and their trueness, but I have inadvertently told him anyway—the story of the little boy who only discovered on Halloween that his mother was not his mother, except on the day when everyone wore a mask. Regret sluices hot up my throat. I try to hold him and kiss him, but he only wishes to go out onto the street, where the sun has dipped below the horizon and a hazy chill is bruising the shadows.

I have little use for this holiday. I do not wish to walk my son to strangers' houses or to assemble popcorn balls and wait for trick-or-treat callers to show up at the door demanding ransom. Still, I wait inside with a whole tray of the sticky confections, answering the door to tiny queens and ghosts. I think of my son. When they leave, I put down the tray and rest my head in my hands.

Our son comes home laughing, gnawing on a piece of candy that has turned his mouth the color of a plum. I am angry at my husband. I wish he had waited to come home before permitting the consumption of the cache. Has he never heard the stories? The pins pressed into the chocolates, the razor blades sunk into the apples? It is like him to not understand what there is to be afraid of in this world, but I am still furious. I examine my son's mouth, but there is no sharp metal plunged into his palate. He laughs and spins around the house, dizzy and electrified from the treats and excitement. He wraps his arms around my legs, the earlier incident forgotten. The forgiveness tastes sweeter than any candy that can be given at any door. When he climbs into my lap, I sing to him until he falls asleep.

Our son grows and grows. He is eight, ten. First, I tell him fairy tales—the very oldest ones, with the pain and death and forced marriage pared away like dead foliage. Mermaids grow feet and it feels like laughter. Naughty pigs trot away from grand feasts, reformed and uneaten. Evil witches leave the castle and move into small cottages and live out their days painting portraits of woodland creatures.

As he grows, though, he asks too many questions. Why would they not eat the pig, hungry as they were and wicked as he had been? Why was the witch permitted to go free after her terrible deeds? And the sensation of fins to feet being anything less than agonizing he rejects outright after cutting his hand with a pair of scissors.

"It would hoight," he says, for he is struggling with his *r*'s.

I agree with him as I bandage the cut. It would. So then I tell him stories closer to true: children who go missing along a particular stretch of railroad track, lured by the sound of a phantom train to parts unknown; a black dog that appears at a person's doorstep three days before her passing; a trio of frogs that corner you in the marshlands and tell your fortune for a price. My husband, I think, would forbid these stories, but my son listens to them with solemnity and keeps them to himself.

The school puts on a performance of *Little Buckle-Boy*, and he is the lead, the buckle-boy, and I join a committee of mothers making costumes for the children. I am chief costume maker in a room full of women, all of us sewing together little silk petals for the flower-children and making tiny white pantaloons for the pirates. One of the mothers has a pale yellow ribbon on her finger, and it constantly tangles in her thread. She swears and cries. One day I even have to use the sewing shears to pick at the offending threads. I try to be delicate. She shakes her head as I free her from the peony.

"It's such a bother, isn't it?" she says. I nod. Outside the window, the children play—knocking each other off the playground equipment, popping the heads off dandelions. The play goes beautifully. Opening night, our son blazes through his monologue. Perfect pitch and cadence. No one has ever done better.

Our son is twelve. He asks me about the ribbon, point-blank. I tell him that we are all different, and sometimes you should not ask questions. I assure him that he'll understand when he is grown. I distract him with stories that have no ribbons: angels who desire to be human and ghosts who don't realize they're dead and children who turn to ash. He stops smelling like a child—milky-sweetness replaced with something sharp and burning, like a hair sizzling on the stove.

Our son is thirteen, fourteen. His hair is a little too long but I can't bear to cut it short. My husband scrambles the locks with his hand on his way to work, and kisses me on the side of the mouth. On his way to school, our son waits for the neighbor boy, who walks with a brace. He exhibits the subtlest compassion, my son. No instinct for cruelty, like some. "The world has enough bullies," I've told him over and over. This is the year he stops asking for my stories

Our son is fifteen, sixteen, seventeen. He is a brilliant boy. He has his father's knack for people, my air of mystery. He begins to court a beautiful girl from his high school who has a bright smile and a warm presence. I am happy to meet her, but never insist that we should wait up for their return, remembering my own youth.

When he tells us that he has been accepted at a university to study engineering, I am overjoyed. We march through the house, singing songs and laughing. When my husband comes home, he joins in the jubilee, and we drive to a local seafood restaurant. His father tells him, over halibut, "We are so proud of you." Our son laughs and says that he also wishes to marry his girl. We clasp hands and are even happier. Such a good boy. Such a wonderful life to look forward to.

Even the luckiest woman alive has not seen joy like this.

There's a classic, a real classic, that I haven't told you yet.[5]

A girlfriend and a boyfriend went parking. Some people say that means kissing in a car, but I know the story. I was there. They were parked on the edge of a lake. They were turning around in the backseat as if the world were moments from ending. Maybe it was. She offered herself and he took her, and after it was over, they turned on the radio.

---

5. This story appears as "The Hook" in *Scary Stories to Tell in the Dark* by Alvin Schwartz, where Machado clearly derived much of her inspiration.

The voice on the radio announced that a mad, hook-handed murderer had escaped from a local asylum. The boyfriend chuckled as he flipped to a music station. As the song ended, the girlfriend heard a thin scratching sound, like a paper clip over glass. She looked at her boyfriend and then pulled her cardigan over her bare shoulders, wrapping one arm around her breasts.

"We should go," she said.

"Nah," the boyfriend said. "Let's do that again. I've got all night."

"What if the killer comes here?" the girl asked. "The asylum is very close."

"We'll be fine, baby," the boyfriend said. "Don't you trust me?"

The girlfriend nodded reluctantly.

"Well, then—" he said, his voice trailing off in that way she would come to know so well. He took her hand off her chest and placed it onto himself. She finally looked away from the lakeside. Outside, the moonlight glinted off the shiny steel hook. The killer waved at her, grinning.

I'm sorry. I've forgotten the rest of the story.

The house is so silent without our son. I walk through it, touching all the surfaces. I am happy but something inside of me is shifting into a strange new place.

That night, my husband asks if I wish to christen the newly empty rooms. We have not coupled so fiercely since before our son was born. Bent over the kitchen table, something old is lit within me, and I remember the way we had desired before, how we had left love streaked on all of the surfaces, how he relished in my darkest spaces. I scream with ferocity, not caring if the neighbors hear, not caring if anyone looks through the window with its undrawn curtains and sees my husband buried in my mouth. I would go out on the lawn if he asked me, let him take me from behind in sight of the whole neighborhood. I could have met anyone at that party when I was seventeen—stupid boys or prudish boys or violent boys. Religious boys who would have made me move to some distant country to convert its denizens, or some such nonsense. I could have experienced untold numbers of sorrows or dissatisfactions. But as I straddle him on the floor, riding him and crying out, I know that I made the right choice.

We fall asleep exhausted, sprawled naked in our bed. When I wake up, my husband is kissing the back of my neck, probing the ribbon with his tongue. My body rebels wildly, still throbbing with the memories of pleasure but bucking hard against betrayal. I say his name, and he does not respond. I say it again, and he holds me against him and continues. I wedge my elbows in his side, and when he loosens from me in surprise, I sit up and face him. He looks confused and hurt, like my son the day I shook the can of pennies.

Resolve runs out of me. I touch the ribbon. I look at the face of my husband, the beginning and end of his desires all etched there. He is not a bad man, and that, I realize suddenly, is the root of my hurt. He is not a bad man at all. To describe him as evil or wicked or corrupted would do a deep disservice to him. And yet—

"Do you want to untie the ribbon?" I ask him. "After these many years, is that what you want of me?"

His face flashes gaily, and then greedily, and he runs his hand up my bare breast and to my bow. "Yes," he says. "Yes."

I do not have to touch him to know that he grows at the thought.

I close my eyes. I remember the boy of the party, the one who kissed me and broke me open by that lakeside, who did with me what I wanted. Who gave me a son and helped him grow into a man himself.

"Then," I say, "do what you want."

With trembling fingers, he takes one of the ends. The bow undoes, slowly, the long-bound ends crimped with habit. My husband groans, but I do not think he realizes it. He loops his finger through the final twist and pulls. The ribbon falls away. It floats down and curls on the bed, or so I imagine, because I cannot look down to follow its descent.

My husband frowns, and then his face begins to open with some other expression—sorrow, or maybe preemptive loss. My hand flies up in front of me—an involuntary motion, for balance or some other futility—and beyond it his image is gone.

"I love you," I assure him, "more than you can possibly know."

"No," he says, but I don't know to what he's responding.

If you are reading this story out loud, you may be wondering if that place my ribbon protected was wet with blood and openings, or smooth and neutered like the nexus between the legs of a doll. I'm afraid I can't tell you, because I don't know. For these questions and others, and their lack of resolution, I am sorry.

My weight shifts, and with it, gravity seizes me. My husband's face falls away, and then I see the ceiling, and the wall behind me. As my lopped head tips backward off my neck and rolls off the bed, I feel as lonely as I have ever been.

■

Author Biography

Carmen Maria Machado is the author of the bestselling memoir *In the Dream House*, the graphic novel *The Low, Low Woods*, and the award-winning short story collection *Her Body and Other Parties*. She has been a finalist for the National Book Award and winner of numerous prestigious awards including the Bard Fiction Prize, Lambda Literary Awards, and the National Book Critics Circle's John Leonard Prize. In 2018, the *New York Times* listed *Her Body and Other Parties* as one of "15 remarkable books by women that are shaping the way we read and write fiction in the 21st century." Her work has appeared in major publications and received fellowships from the Guggenheim Foundation, among others.

Discuss

1. How do the story's direct addresses to readers ("If you are reading this story out loud...") affect your experience as a reader? What is the significance of transforming readers into active participants in the telling?
2. How does becoming a mother change the narrator's relationship to her own body and autonomy?
3. How does this story exemplify weird literature's capacity to make social critique through fantastical elements? What makes the "weird" approach more effective than straightforward realism for addressing these themes?

Write

Control and Marriage Analysis: Examine how the husband's obsession with the green ribbon represents broader patterns of emotional and psychological control throughout the narrator's marriage, using direct quotations from the story to support your observations. Trace how his persistent attempts to access the ribbon despite her clear refusal reflects larger control mechanisms in their relationship, including his behavior during intimacy, pregnancy, and daily married life. Conclude by analyzing what the story suggests about traditional marriage roles and whether the narrator ever truly possesses power in the relationship, focusing exclusively on evidence only from this story.

Ms. Bovary Goes House Hunting in 2014

Chrys Tobey

The following poem uses a persona, in which the poet Chrys Tobey adopts the voice of a character rather than speaking in her own voice. This poetic device allows the exploration of different perspectives and experiences beyond the poet's. Through it, the poet can investigate themes of identity, power, and social issues by channeling voices that offer unique insights or emotional truths. In this case, the poem allows the dead women to brazenly speak about, and for, themselves—finally.

"She was the lover in every novel, the heroine in every play,
the vague *she* in every volume of poetry."
–Gustave Flaubert, from *Madame Bovary*[1]

I don't want to live in the sprawl, somewhere in the stifling
heat of the wide streets; I want to live in this tiny two-bedroom
with the pulse of the city beneath my feet; I want
a sink that works and space for a desk. But a woman should
want bay windows and velvet drapes and material things!
A woman should want a house big enough for little feet.

1. Gustave Flaubert shocked Victorian society in 1856 when he published *Madame Bovary*, portraying a doctor's wife who wants to escape from a tedious marriage.

A woman should honor her mother's words—*We're here to have babies!*
A woman should marry a doctor. A woman should
be a muse. Oh, silly me. But place your finger over
the *m* in *muse* and see what's left, and trace the lineage
of women held hostage by a man's pen, the lineage
of women whose hearts were stilled by booze. No, there will
be no pitter-patter in this room. The backyard is big enough for my dog.
This house may be big enough for my thoughts.

▪

My Alter Egos Ran Off With This Poem

Chrys Tobey

In this persona poem published in 2017, Chrys Tobey speaks through the voices of historical figures. This approach creates a weird, unsettling effect by collapsing time. Ancient rulers like Cleopatra and Catherine the Great suddenly exist in the same textual space, speaking back to centuries of lies, myths, and reductions of powerful women to sexual objects. The poet demonstrates again how women's legacies have been distorted, simplified, and overshadowed by patriarchal narratives often obsessed with their bodies rather than their minds.

1. Catherine The Great[1]

I did not roll out of a carpet
like Cleopatra or wait for this crown
like a fatherless child waits by the window.
I accepted my fate the same way
I knew not to get up from breakfast
until I finished my milk. The same way
my mother accepted a legacy

---

1. Catherine the Great (1729–1796) was a German princess who usurped the Russian throne, expanded the empire to the Black Sea, and compulsively collected art, while cheerfully ignoring the fact that an "enlightened despot" is still a despot. Check out the TV series *The Great* for a fabulous reimagining.

of biting her tongue, her silence the cloak
of silver weighing me down on my wedding day.
This crown was a screaming newborn—
Here, take it, they said, and I did—
its diamonds and pearls still crushing my head.

2. Cleopatra[2]

So I rolled out of a carpet. I know history
loves a good slut, but let me be clear:
it was not to suck Caesar off.
I jumped through a hoop to build
a city of gold, a library as full as a fat man's belly.
I fed mouths, and I knew the world was not flat.
But still, all you can think about is who I gave head.
How I wore too much gold. I was growing old.
Even Catherine The Great had feathers
flying from her bed. But a woman knows
what will bring her power: it's not a night of grunts
and sweat, but a mind sharp enough
to slice through his neck.

3. Marie Antoinette[3]

I wanted my head to be their kickball.
I wanted them to get some use out of it,
like a native people paying homage

---

2. Cleopatra (69–30 BCE) was a queen of Egypt who spoke nine languages and ruled for nearly two decades, yet history remembers her mainly for being hot.

3. Marie Antoinette (1755–1793) was guillotined on October 16, after losing her husband and son and being separated from her remaining children. Her reported last words—an apology to her executioner for stepping on his foot—capture a woman who had lost everything but her manners.

to the buffalo they're about to eat.
What a waste—years of learning languages,
words and numbers, little planets in my mind.
How I'd imagine my skirt was a hot air balloon
that would sail me to Saint Petersburg, set me
next to Empress Catherine. How we'd drink
champagne and speak of Voltaire. How we'd
laugh about the first time we tried to have sex
in a place as foreign as the moon
with boys available as the night sky.
How I envy her—a woman who never
had to smell the executioner's sour breath,
never had to watch his trembling hand.

▪

Author Biography

Chrys Tobey is a poet and writer whose work has appeared in *The Sun*, *Ploughshares*, *Rattle*, *New Ohio Review*, *The Minnesota Review*, *The Cincinnati Review*, and elsewhere. Her poetry has been nominated for the Pushcart, Best of the Net, and featured in Verse Daily. Her first book of poetry, *A Woman is a Woman is a Woman is a Woman*, was published in 2017 from Steel Toe Books. She lives in Portland, Oregon, with her rockstar lady-love, stepcats, and dog of ten years.

Discuss

1. In "Ms. Bovary Goes House Hunting in 2014," what is your interpretation of this section: "A woman should / be a muse. Oh, silly me. But place your finger over / the *m* in *muse* and see what's left..."?
2. Why do you think the poet chose to write from the perspectives of these three historical women instead of speaking in her own voice?
3. Each woman in these poems addresses misconceptions about their legacy. How are they remembered compared to how they wish to be remembered? Be specific for each woman.

Write

Historical Voice Swap: Choose a famous historical figure and write a short poem or paragraph from their perspective, focusing on which common misconception about their life they would most want to correct. Consider using dialogue and make sure to describe the person and the scene so the reader can "see" what is happening.

A Wife Manufactured to Order

Alice W. Fuller

Weird literature thrives on the uncanny, with stories that blur the boundaries between human and machine, between natural and artificial. Alice W. Fuller's manufactured bride perfectly inhabits this strange territory, using a fantastical premise to expose sometimes very real anxieties about marriage, gender, and autonomy. Written in 1895, this weird short story that features a manufactured woman delivering a satire on marriage was way ahead of its time (and still relevant today)!

As I was going down G Street in the city of W——[1] a strange sign attracted my attention. I stopped, looked, fairly rubbed my eyes to see if they were rightly focused; yes, there it was plainly lettered in gilt: "Wives made to order! Satisfaction guaranteed or money refunded."

Well! well! does some lunatic live here, I wonder? By Jove! I will investigate. I had inherited (I suppose from my mother) a bit of curiosity, and the truth of the matter was this: now nearing the age of forty, I thought it might be advisable to settle down in a home of my own; but alas! to settle down to a life of strife and turmoil, that would not be pleasant; and that I should have to do, I knew very well, if I should marry any of my numerous

---

1. The dash convention (W——) was common in 19th-century fiction to suggest a real but unnamed location, creating a lofty air of authenticity while maintaining ambiguity.

lady acquaintances—especially Florence Ward, the one I most admired. She unfortunately had strong-minded ways, and inclinations to be investigating woman's rights, politics, theosophy,[2] and all that sort of thing. Bah! I could never endure it. I should be miserable, and the outcome would be a separation; I knew it. To be dictated to, perhaps found fault with—no, no, it would never do; better be a bachelor and at least live in peace. But—what does this sign mean? I'll find out for myself.

A ring of the bell brought a little white-haired, wiry sort of a man to the door. "Walk in, walk in, sir," he said.

I asked for an explanation of the strange sign over the door.

"Just step right in here and be seated, sir. My master is engaged at present, sir, with a great politician who had to separate from his wife; was so fractious, sir, got so many strange notions in her head; in fact, she wanted to hold the reins herself. You may have seen it—the papers have been full of it. Why, law bless you, sir, the poor man couldn't say his soul was his own, and he is here now making arrangements with master to make him a quieter sort of wife, some one to do the honors of the home without feelin' neglected if he happens to be a little courteous to some of his young lady friends. You see, master makes 'em to order, makes 'em to think just as you do, just as you want 'em to; then you've got a happy home, something to live for. Beautiful—golly! I've seen some of the beautifulest women turned out, 'most make your mouth water to look at." And so the old man rattled on until I was quite bewildered.

I interrupted him by asking if I could see his master.

"Oh, certainly, sir; you just make yourself comfortable and I will let you know when he is through."

---

2. Theosophy, a spiritual and philosophical movement founded in 1875, combined elements of Eastern religions, Western esotericism, and occultism. It appealed to educated, progressive women in the late 19th century as an alternative to Christianity—you can imagine how well *that* went over.

I sat for some time like one in a dream, wondering if this could be so, and with many wonderful modern inventions in mind I began to think it possible. And then there was a vision of a happy home, a wife beautiful as a dream, gentle and loving, without a thought for anyone but me; one who would never reproach me if I didn't happen to get home just at what she thought was the proper time; one who would not ask me to go to church when she knew it was against my wishes; one who would never find fault with me if I wished to go to a baseball game on Sunday, or bother me to take her to the theatre or opera. A man, you know, can't give much time to such things without interfering greatly with his comfort. Oh! could all this be realized? But just then my reverie was broken by the old man, who was saying: "Just step this way. Master, let me introduce you to Mr. Charles Fitzsimmons."

Short, thick-set, florid complexion, pale blue eyes with a sinister twinkle, was the description of Mr. Sharper, whom I confronted. Reaching out his hand, which was cold and clammy and reminded me very much of a piece of cold boiled pork, he said:

"Now, young man, what can I do for you? Want a life-companion, a pleasant one? Man of means, no doubt, and can enjoy yourself; a little fun now and then with the boys and no harm at all—none in the least. When a man comes home tired, doesn't like to be dictated to; want someone always to meet you with a smile, someone that doesn't expect you to be fondlin' and pettin' 'em all the time. I understand it—I know just how it is. Law bless my soul, I'e made more'n one man happy, and I've only been in the business a short time, too. Now, sir, I can get you up any style you want—*wax*, but can't be detected."

"Do you mean to say you manufacture a woman out of wax, who will talk?"

"That's just what I do; you give me the subjects you most enjoy talking upon, and tell me what kind of a looking wife you want, and leave the rest to me, and you will never regret it. I will furnish as many 'phones' as you wish; most men don't care for such a variety for a wife—too much talk, you know;" and he chuckled and laughed like a big baby.

"What are your prices, may I ask?"

"Well, it's owing a good deal to how they are got up—from five hundred to a thousand dollars."

"Well," I said, "I think that rather high."

"Dear man alive, a pleasant companion for life for a few hundred dollars! Most men don't grumble at all for the sake of having their own way and a pleasant home, and you see she ain't always asking for money." (Sure enough, I hadn't thought of that.)

"Very well, I will decide upon the matter and let you know"

"All right, young man; you'll come back. They all do, them as knows about it."

I went to my room at the hotel and thought it all out, thought of the pleasant evenings I could have with some one whose thoughts were like my own, some one who would not vex me by differing in opinion. I wondered what Florence would say. I really believed she cared for me, but she knew how I disliked so many of the topics she persisted in talking upon. What mattered it to me what Emerson said, or Edward Bellamy wrote, or Henry George, or Pentecost?[3] What did I care about Hume or Huxley or Stuart Mill? any of those sciences, Christian Science or Divine Science or mind cure?—bah! it was all nonsense.[4] The topics of the day

---

3. Charles lists prominent 19th-century intellectuals and reformers, dismissing them as irrelevant to his life. Ralph Waldo Emerson (transcendentalist philosopher), Edward Bellamy (utopian socialist), Henry George (economic reformer advocating land reform), and Hugh O. Pentecost (social reformer and free thought advocate) all represented progressive thinking about society, economics, and justice.

4. More intellectual and spiritual movements Charles dismisses: David Hume (philosopher), Thomas Huxley (biologist), and John Stuart Mill (advocate for women's equality). Christian Science and Divine Science were spiritual movements emphasizing mental and spiritual healing, popular then among women. Fuller piles up these references to show Florence's wide-ranging interests *and* Charles's aggressive ignorance.

were enough, and if I attended closely to my business I needed recreation, not such things as she would prescribe. Still Florence was interesting to talk to, and I rather liked her at times when she talked everyday talk; but I could not marry her, and it was her own fault. She knew my sentiments, and if she would persist in going on as she did I couldn't help it.

Yes, I decided I would have a home of my own, and a wife made to order at once. Before leaving the city I made all necessary arrangements, hurried home, rented a house, and went to see old Susan Tyler, whom I engaged as housekeeper; she was deaf and had an impediment in her speech, but she was a fine housekeeper. All my preparations made the ideal home! Oh! how my heart beat as I looked around!—what happiness to do as I liked, a beautiful, uncomplaining wife ready to grant every wish and meet me with a smile! What would the boys say when, out a little late at night, I should be so perfectly at ease? I could just see jealousy on their faces, and I laughed outright for joy. Tomorrow I was going for my bride. Side looks and innuendos were thrust at me from all quarters, but I was too happy to demur or explain. When I reached the city I could scarcely wait for the appointed time.

Alighting from the carriage, the door was opened, and I was ushered into the presence of the most beautiful creature I had ever beheld. The hands extended towards mine, the lips opened, and a low, sweet voice said, "Dear Charles, how glad I am you have come!" I stood spellbound, and only a chuckle from Mr. Sharper brought me to my senses.

"Kiss your affianced, why don't you?" he said, and chuckled again.

I felt as though I wanted to knock him down for speaking so in that beautiful creature's presence. And then a little soft rippling laugh, and she moved towards me. Oh, could I get that beast to leave the room! Why did he stand there chuckling in that manner?

"Sir," I said, "you will oblige me by leaving the room for a few moments."

With that he chuckled still louder and muttered, "Bless me, I really believe he thinks her alive." Then to me: "To be sure, to be sure, but you only have a short time before going to the minister's, and I must show you how to adjust her. When you get home"—and he chuckled again—"you can be just as sentimental as you please, but just now we will attend to business. Here are a box of tubes made to talk as you wished them. They are adjusted so. Place the one you wish in your sleeve. You can carelessly touch her right here if there is anyone around. Here is a spring in each hand and the tips of her fingers. I will give you a book of instructions, and you will soon learn to arrange her with very little effort, just to suit yourself, and I am sure you will be very happy. Now, sir, the time is up; you can go to the minister's."

As I put her wraps around her and drew her arm through mine she murmured so sweetly, "Thank you, dear." How glad I was to get out of the presence of that vile man who was constantly pulling or pushing her; I could scarcely keep my hands off from him, and my serene Margurette—for I decided to call her that—would only smile and say, "Thank you!" "Oh, how lovely!" "Ah, indeed!" I was almost vexed with her to think she did not resent it. I wanted her all to myself where I could have the smiles, and thought I should be thankful when we were in our own home.

During our journey I could not help noticing the admiring glances from my fellow travellers, but my beautiful wife did not return any of their looks. In fact, I overheard a couple of young dudes say, "Just wait till that old codger's back is turned, and we shall see whether she will have no smiles for any but him." I had half a notion to adjust her to give them some cutting reply and then go into the smoker awhile, for I was sure they would try to get into conversation with her; but pshaw! I hadn't ordered any tubes of that kind. I believed I'd send and get one in case of an emergency. No, I wouldn't have such in the house; I wanted an amiable wife, and when we were once at home it would not be necessary. I wouldn't *have to* go with her anywhere unless I wanted to. Only think of that!—never feel that my wife would ask me to go with her and I have to refuse, then ten to one have her cry and make a fuss about it. I knew how it was, for I had seen too much of that sort of thing in the homes of my friends.

Business ran smoothly; everything was perfect harmony; my home was heaven on earth. I smoked when I wished to. I went to my baseball games. I stayed out as long as I pleased, played cards when I wished, drank champagne or whatever I fancied, in fact had as good a time as I did before marriage. My male friends congratulated me upon my good fortune, and I was considered the luckiest man anywhere around. No one knew how I had made the good luck for myself.

There are some things in life I could never understand. One of them is that, when everything seems so prosperous, calamity is so often in the wake. And that was the case with me. After so many prosperous years a financial crash came. I tried to ward it off; I was up early and late. Margurette never complained, but was always sweet and smiling, with the same endearing words. Sometimes as the years went by I felt as though I would not object to her differing with me a little, for variety's sake; still it was best. When I would say, "Margurette, do you really think so?" and I would speak so cross to her often—I don't know but that I did so more than was necessary; still a man must have some place where he can be himself, and if he can't have that privilege at home, what's the use of having a home?—but she was never out of patience, and my wife would only say, "Yes, darling," so low and sweet. I remember once I said, when I was worried more than usual, "I am damned tired of this sort of thing," and she laughed so sweetly and called me her "own precious boy."

But the crash came, and there was no use trying to stay it any longer. I came home sick and tired. It was nine o'clock at night, with a cold, drizzling rain falling. Susan had gone to bed sick, and forgotten to light a fire in the grate. I went into the library, where Margurette always waited for me. No lights; I stumbled over a chair. I accidentally touched Margurette. She put up her lips to kiss me and laughingly said, "Precious darling, tired tonight?" Great God! I came very near striking her.

"Margurette, don't call me darling, talk to me; talk to me about something—anything sensible. Don't you know I am a ruined man? Everything I have got has been swept away from me."

"There, precious, I love you," and she laughed again.

"Did you not hear what I said?" I screamed.

But she only laughed the more and said, "Oh, how lovely!"

I rushed from the house. I could not endure it longer; I was like one mad. My first thought was, Where can I go, to whom can I go for sympathy? I cannot stand this strain much longer, and to show weakness to men, I could never do that. I will go to Florence, I said. I will see what she says. Strange I should think of her just then!

I asked the servant who admitted me for Miss Florence.

"She is indisposed and cannot see anyone tonight."

"But," I said, writing on a card hastily, "take this to her."

Only a few moments elapsed and she came in, holding out her hand in an assuring and friendly way. "I am surprised to see you tonight, Mr. Fitzsimmons."

"O Florence!" I cried, "I am in trouble. I believe I shall lose my mind if I cannot have someone to go to; and you, dear Florence, you will know my needs; you can counsel, you can understand me."

"Sir!" Florence said, "are you mad, that you come here to insult me?"

"But I love you. I know it. I love the traits that I once thought I despised."

"Stop where you are! I did not receive you to hear such language. You forget yourself and me; you forget that you are a married man—shame upon you for humiliating me so!"

"Florence, Florence, I am not married; it is all a lie, a deception."

"Have you lost your reason, Mr. Fitzsimmons? Sit down, pray, and let me call my father. You are ill."

"Stop," I cried, "I do not need your father. I need you. Listen to me. I imagined I could never be happy with a wife who differed in opinion from me. In fact, I had almost decided to remain single all the rest of my days, until I came across a man who manufactured wives to order. Wait, Florence, until I have finished—do not look at me so. I am indeed sane. My wife was manufactured to my own ideas, a perfect human being as I supposed."

"Mr. Fitzsimmons, let me call my father." And Florence started towards the door. She was so pale that she frightened me, but I clutched her frantically.

"Listen," I said, "will you go with me? I will prove that all I have told you is true."

My earnestness seemed to reassure her. She stopped as if carefully thinking, then asked me to repeat what I had already told her. Finally she said yes, she would go.

We were soon in the presence of my beautiful Margurette, whom I literally hated—I could not endure her face. "Now, Florence, see," I cried; and I had my wife talk the namby-pamby lingo I once thought so sweet. "Oh! how I hate her!" and I glared at her like a madman. "Florence, save me. I am a ruined man. Everything has been swept away—the last today. I am a pauper, an egotist, a bigot, a selfish—"

"Stop!" cried Florence. "You wrong yourself; you are a man in your prime. What if your money has gone, you have your health and your faculties, I guess." (and there was a merry twinkle in her eyes); "The whole world is before you, and best of all, no one to interfere with you or argue on disagreeable topics."

"O Florence! I am punished enough for my selfishness. O God!" and I threw myself on the couch, "were I not a pauper, too, there might be some hope for happiness yet."

"You are not a pauper," said Florence. "You are the master of your fate, and if you are not happy it is your own fault."

"Florence, I can never be happy without you. I know now it is too late."

"Too late—never say that. But could you be happy with me, 'a woman wedded to an idea,' 'strongminded'? Why, Charles, I am liable to investigate all sorts of scientific subjects and reforms. And then supposing I should talk about it sometimes; if it was not for that I might think of the matter. As far as money is concerned, that would have little to do with my actions. Still, Charles, upon the whole I should be afraid to marry the 'divorced' husband of so amiable a wife as your present one is. I, with my faults and imperfections!—the contrast would be too great."

"Florence, Florence," I said, "say no more. All I ask is, can you overlook my folly and take me for better, for worse? I have learned my lesson. I see now it is only a petty and narrow type of man who would wish to live only with his own personal echo. I want a woman, one who retains her individuality, a thinking woman. Will you be mine?"

"I will consider the matter favorably," said Florence, "but we shall have to wait a year, for opinion's sake, as I suppose there are not many who know how you had your late wife manufactured to order."

And we both laughed.

▪

Author Biography

Very little biographical information is known about Alice W. Fuller. We do know that "A Wife Manufactured to Order" was published in 1895 during a period of intense debate about women's rights, marriage reform, and the "New Woman" movement. We know she married, had four children, and died in 1956 at 83 years old.

Discuss

1. How does this 1890s story relate to contemporary phenomena like AI and virtual companions or the idea that people can "program" perfect partners?
2. When Charles loses his fortune and needs sympathy, he "literally hates" Margurette and "could not endure her face." Why? What has changed?
3. What do you think Fuller is saying about men who oppose women's rights, education, and independence?

Write

Either-Or: In this story, Fuller presents two models or versions of womanhood: Margurette (manufactured to be perfectly agreeable) and Florence (the "strong-minded" woman interested in "woman's rights, politics, theosophy"). Write an essay arguing how Fuller uses this contrast to critique the limited options available to women—and the men who choose them.

Overtones: A One-Act Play

Alice Gerstenberg

This groundbreaking 1915 play by Alice Gerstenberg splits two women into their "cultured" and "primitive" selves, allowing audiences to see both the civilized tea party happening on the surface and the psychological warfare underneath. As you read, notice how the stage directions about costumes, veils, and movement help create this double reality—and consider what your own "primitive self" might be whispering during your next polite conversation.

CHARACTERS

HARRIET, a cultured woman
HETTY, her primitive self
MARGARET, a cultured woman
MAGGIE, her primitive self

TIME: *The present.*

SCENE: HARRIET'S *fashionable living room. The door at the back leads to the hall. In the center a tea table with a chair either side. At the back a cabinet.*

HARRIET'S *gown is a light, "jealous" green. Her counterpart,* HETTY, *wears a gown of the same design but in a darker shade.* MARGARET *wears a gown of lavender chiffon while her counterpart,* MAGGIE, *wears a gown of the same design in purple, a purple scarf veiling her face. Chiffon is used to give a sheer effect, suggesting a possibility of primitive and cultured selves merging into one woman. The primitive and cultured selves never come into actual physical contact but try to sustain the impression of mental conflict.* HARRIET *never sees* HETTY, *never talks to her but rather thinks aloud looking into space.* HETTY, *however, looks at* HARRIET, *talks intently and shadows her continually. The same is true of* MARGARET *and* MAGGIE. *The voices of the cultured women are affected and lingering, the voices of the primitive impulsive and more or less staccato.*

When the curtain rises HARRIET *is seated right of tea table, busying herself with the tea things.*

HETTY. Harriet. [*There is no answer.*] Harriet, my other self. [*There is no answer.*] My trained self.

HARRIET [*listens intently*]. Yes?

[*From behind* HARRIET'S *chair* HETTY *rises slowly.*]

HETTY. I want to talk to you.

HARRIET. Well?

HETTY [*looking at* HARRIET *admiringly*]. Oh, Harriet, you are beautiful today.

HARRIET. Am I presentable, Hetty?

HETTY. Suits me.

HARRIET. I've tried to make the best of the good points.

HETTY. My passions are deeper than yours. I can't keep on the mask as you do. I'm crude and real, you are my appearance in the world.

HARRIET. I am what you wish the world to believe you are.

HETTY. You are the part of me that has been trained.

HARRIET. I am your educated self.

HETTY. I am the rushing river; you are the ice over the current.

HARRIET. I am your subtle overtones.

HETTY. But together we are one woman, the wife of Charles Goodrich.

HARRIET. There I disagree with you, Hetty, I alone am his wife.

HETTY [*indignantly*]. Harriet, how can you say such a thing!

HARRIET. Certainly. I am the one who flatters him. I have to be the one who talks to him. If I gave you a chance you would tell him at once that you dislike him.

HETTY [*moving away*], I don't love him, that's certain.

HARRIET. You leave all the fibbing to me. He doesn't suspect that my calm, suave manner hides your hatred. Considering the amount of scheming it causes me it can safely be said that he is my husband.

HETTY. Oh, if you love him—

HARRIET. I? I haven't any feelings. It isn't my business to love anybody.

HETTY. Then why need you object to calling him my husband?

HARRIET. I resent your appropriation of a man who is managed only through the cleverness of my artifice.

HETTY. You may be clever enough to deceive him, Harriet, but I am still the one who suffers. I can't forget he is my husband. I can't forget that I might have married John Caldwell.

HARRIET. How foolish of you to remember John, just because we met his wife by chance.

HETTY. That's what I want to talk to you about. She may be here at any moment. I want to advise you about what to say to her this afternoon.

HARRIET. By all means tell me now and don't interrupt while she is here. You have a most annoying habit of talking to me when people are present. Sometimes it is all I can do to keep my poise and appear not to be listening to you.

HETTY. Impress her.

HARRIET. Hetty, dear, is it not my custom to impress people?

HETTY. I hate her.

HARRIET. I can't let her see that.

HETTY. I hate her because she married John.

HARRIET. Only after you had refused him.

HETTY [*turning on* HARRIET]. Was it my fault that I refused him?

HARRIET. That's right, blame me.

HETTY. It was your fault. You told me he was too poor and never would be able to do anything in painting. Look at him now, known in Europe, just returned from eight years in Paris, famous.

HARRIET. It was too poor a gamble at the time. It was much safer to accept Charles's money and position.

HETTY. And then John married Margaret within the year.

HARRIET. Out of spite.

HETTY. Freckled, gawky-looking thing she was, too.

HARRIET [*a little sadly*]. Europe improved her. She was stunning the other morning.

HETTY. Make her jealous today.

HARRIET. Shall I be haughty or cordial or caustic or—

HETTY. Above all else you must let her know that we are rich.

HARRIET. Oh, yes, I do that quite easily now.

HETTY. You must put it on a bit.

HARRIET. Never fear.

HETTY. Tell her I love my husband.

HARRIET. My husband—

HETTY. Are you going to quarrel with me?

HARRIET [*moves away*]. No, I have no desire to quarrel with you. It is quite too uncomfortable. I couldn't get away from you if I tried.

HETTY [*stamping her foot and following* HARRIET]. You were a stupid fool to make me refuse John, I'll never forgive you—never—

HARRIET [*stopping and holding up her hand*]. Don't get me

all excited. I'll be in no condition to meet her properly this afternoon.

HETTY [*passionately*]. I could choke you for robbing me of John.

HARRIET [*retreating*]. Don't muss me!

HETTY. You don't know how you have made me suffer.

HARRIET [*beginning to feel the strength of* HETTY'S *emotion surge through her and trying to conquer it*]. It is not my business to have heartaches.

HETTY. You're bloodless. Nothing but sham—sham—while I—

HARRIET [*emotionally*]. Be quiet! I can't let her see that I have been fighting with my inner self.

HETTY. And now after all my suffering you say it has cost you more than it has cost me to be married to Charles. But it's the pain here in my heart—I've paid the price—I've paid—Charles is not your husband!

HARRIET [*trying to conquer emotion*]. He is.

HETTY [*follows* HARRIET]. He isn't.

HARRIET [*weakly*]. He is.

HETTY [*towering over* HARRIET]. He isn't! I'll kill you!

HARRIET [*overpowered, sinks into a chair*]. Don't—don't—you're stronger than I—you're—

HETTY. Say he's mine.

HARRIET. He's ours.

HETTY [*the telephone rings*]. There she is now.

[HETTY *hurries to 'phone but* HARRIET *regains her supremacy*.]

HARRIET [*authoritatively*]. Wait! I can't let the telephone girl down there hear my real self. It isn't proper. [*At 'phone.*] Show Mrs. Caldwell up.

HETTY. I'm so excited, my heart's in my mouth.

HARRIET [*at the mirror*]. A nice state you've put my nerves into.

HETTY. Don't let her see you're nervous.

HARRIET.[1] Quick, put the veil on, or she'll see *you* shining through me.

[HARRIET *takes a scarf of chiffon that has been lying over the back of a chair and drapes it on* HETTY, *covering her face. The chiffon is the same color of their gowns but paler in shade so that it pales* HETTY'S *darker gown to match* HARRIET'S *lighter one. As* HETTY *moves in the following scene the chiffon falls away revealing now and then the gown of deeper dye underneath.*]

HETTY. Tell her Charles is rich and fascinating—boast of our friends, make her feel she needs us.

HARRIET. I'll make her ask John to paint us.

HETTY. That's just my thought—if John paints our portrait—

HARRIET. We can wear an exquisite gown—

HETTY. And make him fall in love again and—

HARRIET [*schemingly*]. Yes.

[MARGARET *parts the portieres*[2] *back center and extends her hand.* MARGARET *is followed by her counterpart* MAGGIE.]

Oh, Margaret, I'm so glad to see you!

HETTY [*to* MAGGIE]. That's a lie.

MARGARET [*in superficial voice throughout*]. It's enchanting to see you, Harriet.

MAGGIE [*in emotional voice throughout*]. I'd bite you, if I dared.

HARRIET [*to* MARGARET]. Wasn't our meeting a stroke of luck?

MARGARET [*coming down left of table*]. I've thought of you so often, Harriet; and to come back and find you living in New York.

HARRIET [*coming down right of table*]. Mr. Goodrich has many interests here.

---

1. [Original note] The vaudeville production did not use HARRIET'S line about the veil because at the rise of the curtain Hetty is already veiled in chiffon the same dark green shade as her gown.

2. Portieres are curtains hung over a doorway.

MAGGIE [*to* MARGARET]. Flatter her.

MARGARET. I know, Mr. Goodrich is so successful.

HETTY [*to* HARRIET]. Tell her we're rich.

HARRIET [*to* MARGARET]. Won't you sit down?

MARGARET [*takes a chair*]. What a beautiful cabinet![3]

HARRIET. Do you like it? I'm afraid Charles paid an extravagant price.

MAGGIE [*to* HETTY]. I don't believe it.

MARGARET [*sitting down. To* HARRIET]. I am sure he must have.

HARRIET [*sitting down*]. How well you are looking, Margaret.

HETTY. Yes, you are not. There are circles under your eyes.

MAGGIE [*to* HETTY]. I haven't eaten since breakfast and I'm hungry.

MARGARET [*to* HARRIET]. How well you are looking, too.

MAGGIE [*to* HETTY]. You have hard lines about your lips, are you happy?

HETTY [*to* HARRIET]. Don't let her know that I'm unhappy.

HARRIET [*to* MARGARET]. Why shouldn't I look well? My life is full, happy, complete—

MAGGIE. I wonder.

HETTY [*in* HARRIET'S *ear*]. Tell her we have an automobile.[4]

MARGARET [*to* HARRIET]. My life is complete, too.

MAGGIE. My heart is torn with sorrow; my husband cannot make a living. He will kill himself if he does not get an order for a painting.

MARGARET [*laughs*]. You must come and see us in our studio. John has been doing some excellent portraits. He cannot begin to fill his orders.

HETTY [*to* HARRIET]. Tell her we have an automobile.

---

3. [Original note] What beautiful lamps! (In vaudeville production)

4. In 1915, there were only 15 cars for every 1,000 people, making having one quite a coup.

HARRIET [*to* MARGARET]. Do you take lemon in your tea?

MAGGIE. Take cream. It's more filling.

MARGARET [*looking nonchalantly at tea things*]. No, cream, if you please. How cozy!

MAGGIE [*glaring at tea things*]. Only cakes! I could eat them all!

HARRIET [*to* MARGARET]. How many lumps?

MAGGIE [*to* MARGARET]. Sugar is nourishing.

MARGARET [*to* HARRIET], Three, please. I used to drink very sweet coffee in Turkey and ever since I've—

HETTY. I don't believe you were ever in Turkey.

MAGGIE. I wasn't, but it is none of your business.

HARRIET [*pouring tea*]. Have you been in Turkey, do tell me about it.

MAGGIE [*to* MARGARET]. Change the subject.

MARGARET [*to* HARRIET]. You must go there. You have so much taste in dress you would enjoy seeing their costumes.

MAGGIE. Isn't she going to pass the cake?

MARGARET [*to* HARRIET]. John painted several portraits there.

HETTY [*to* HARRIET]. Why don't you stop her bragging and tell her we have an automobile?

HARRIET [*offers cake across the table to* MARGARET]. Cake?

MAGGIE [*stands back of* MARGARET, *shadowing her as* HETTY *shadows* HARRIET. MAGGIE *reaches claws out for the cake and groans with joy*]. At last! [*But her claws do not touch the cake.*]

MARGARET [*with a graceful, nonchalant hand places cake upon her plate and bites at it slowly and delicately*]. Thank you.

HETTY [*to* HARRIET]. Automobile!

MAGGIE [*to* MARGARET]. Follow up the costumes with the suggestion that she would make a good model for John. It isn't too early to begin getting what you came for.

MARGARET [*ignoring* MAGGIE]. What delicious cake.

HETTY [*excitedly to* HARRIET]. There's your chance for the auto.

HARRIET [*nonchalantly to* MARGARET]. Yes, it is good cake, isn't it? There are always a great many people buying it at Harper's. I sat in my automobile fifteen minutes this morning waiting for my chauffeur to get it.

MAGGIE [*to* MARGARET]. Make her order a portrait.

MARGARET [*to* HARRIET]. If you stopped at Harper's you must have noticed the new gowns at Henderson's. Aren't the shop windows alluring these days?

HARRIET. Even my chauffeur notices them.

MAGGIE. I know you have an automobile, I heard you the first time.

MARGARET. I notice gowns now with an artist's eye as John does. The one you have on, my dear, is very paintable.

HETTY. Don't let her see you're anxious to be painted.

HARRIET [*nonchalantly*]. Oh, it's just a little model.

MAGGIE [*to* MARGARET]. Don't seem anxious to get the order.

MARGARET [*nonchalantly*]. Perhaps it isn't the gown itself but the way you wear it that pleases the eye. Some people can wear anything with grace.

HETTY. Yes, I'm very graceful.

HARRIET [*to* MARGARET]. You flatter me, my dear.

MARGARET. On the contrary, Harriet, I have an intense admiration for you. I remember how beautiful you were—as a girl. In fact, I was quite jealous when John was paying you so much attention.

HETTY. She is gloating because I lost him.

HARRIET. Those were childhood days in a country town.

MAGGIE [*to* MARGARET]. She's trying to make you feel that John was only a country boy.

MARGARET. Most great men have come from the country. There is a fair chance that John will be added to the list.

HETTY. I know it and I am bitterly jealous of you.

HARRIET. Undoubtedly he owes much of his success to you, Margaret, your experience in economy and your ability to endure hardship. Those first few years in Paris must have been a struggle.

MAGGIE. She is sneering at your poverty.

MARGARET. Yes, we did find life difficult at first, not the luxurious start a girl has who marries wealth.

HETTY [*to* HARRIET]. Deny that you married Charles for his money.

[HARRIET *deems it wise to ignore* HETTY'S *advice.*]

MARGARET. But John and I are so congenial in our tastes, that we were impervious to hardship or unhappiness.

HETTY [*in anguish*]. Do you love each other? Is it really true?

HARRIET [*sweetly*]. Did you have all the romance of starving for his art?

MAGGIE [*to* MARGARET]. She's taunting you. Get even with her.

MARGARET. Not for long. Prince Rier soon discovered John's genius, and introduced him royally to wealthy Parisians who gave him many orders.

HETTY [*to* MAGGIE]. Are you telling the truth or are you lying?

HARRIET. If he had so many opportunities there, you must have had great inducements to come back to the States.

MAGGIE [*to* HETTY]. We did, but not the kind you think.

MARGARET. John became the rage among Americans travelling in France, too, and they simply insisted upon his coming here.

HARRIET. Whom is he going to paint here?

MAGGIE [*frightened*]. What names dare I make up?

MARGARET [*calmly*]. Just at present Miss Dorothy Ainsworth of Oregon is posing. You may not know the name, but she is the daughter of a wealthy miner who found gold in Alaska.

HARRIET. I dare say there are many Western people we have never heard of.

MARGARET. You must have found social life in New York very interesting, Harriet, after the simplicity of our home town.

HETTY [*to* MAGGIE]. There's no need to remind us that our beginnings were the same.

HARRIET. Of course Charles's family made everything delightful for me. They are so well connected.

MAGGIE [*to* MARGARET]. Flatter her.

MARGARET. I heard it mentioned yesterday that you had made yourself very popular. Someone said you were very clever!

HARRIET [*pleased*]. Who told you that?

MAGGIE. Nobody!

MARGARET [*pleasantly*]. Oh, confidences should be suspected—respected, I mean. They said, too, that you are gaining some reputation as a critic of art.

HARRIET. I make no pretenses.

MARGARET. Are you and Mr. Goodrich interested in the same things, too?

HETTY. No!

HARRIET. Yes, indeed, Charles and I are inseparable.

MAGGIE. I wonder.

HARRIET. Do have another cake.

MAGGIE [*in relief*]. Oh, yes.

[*Again her claws extend but do not touch the cake.*]

MARGARET [*takes cake delicately*]. I really shouldn't—after my big luncheon. John took me to the Ritz and we are invited to the Bedfords' for dinner—they have such a magnificent house near the drive—I really shouldn't, but the cakes are so good.

MAGGIE. Starving!

HARRIET [*to* MARGARET]. More tea?

MAGGIE. Yes!

MARGARET. No, thank you. How wonderfully life has arranged itself for you. Wealth, position, a happy marriage, every opportunity to enjoy all pleasures; beauty, art—how happy you must be.

HETTY [*in anguish*]. Don't call me happy. I've never been happy since I gave up John. All these years without him—a future without him—no—no—I shall win him back—away from you—away from you——

HARRIET [*does not see* MAGGIE *pointing to cream and* MARGARET *stealing some*]. I sometimes think it is unfair for anyone to be as happy as I am. Charles and I are just as much in love now as when we married. To me he is just the dearest man in the world.

MAGGIE [*passionately*]. My John is. I love him so much I could die for him. I'm going through hunger and want to make him great and he loves me. He worships me!

MARGARET [*leisurely to* HARRIET]. I should like to meet Mr. Goodrich. Bring him to our studio. John has some sketches to show. Not many, because all the portraits have been purchased by the subjects. He gets as much as four thousand dollars now.

HETTY [*to* HARRIET]. Don't pay that much.

HARRIET [*to* MARGARET]. As much as that?

MARGARET. It is not really too much when one considers that John is in the foremost rank of artists today. A picture painted by him now will double and treble in value.

MAGGIE. It's all a lie. He is growing weak with despair.

HARRIET. Does he paint all day long?

MAGGIE. No, he draws advertisements for our bread.

MARGARET [*to* HARRIET]. When you and your husband come to see us, telephone first—

MAGGIE. Yes, so he can get the advertisements out of the way.

MARGARET. Otherwise you might arrive while he has a sitter, and John refuses to let me disturb him then.

HETTY. Make her ask for an order.

HARRIET [*to* MARGARET]. Le Grange offered to paint me for a thousand.

MARGARET. Louis Le Grange's reputation isn't worth more than that.

HARRIET. Well, I've heard his work well mentioned.

MAGGIE. Yes, he is doing splendid work.

MARGARET. Oh, dear me, no. He is only praised by the masses. He is accepted not at all by artists themselves.

HETTY [*anxiously*]. Must I really pay the full price?

HARRIET. Le Grange thought I would make a good subject.

MAGGIE [*to* MARGARET]. Let her fish for it.

MARGARET. Of course you would. Why don't you let Le Grange paint you, if you *trust* him?

HETTY. She doesn't seem anxious to have John do it.

HARRIET. But if Le Grange isn't accepted by artists, it would be a waste of time to pose for him, wouldn't it?

MARGARET. Yes, I think it would.

MAGGIE [*passionately to* HETTY *across back of table*]. Give us the order. John is so despondent he can't endure much longer. Help us! Help me! Save us!

HETTY [*to* HARRIET]. Don't seem too eager.

HARRIET. And yet if he charges only a thousand one might consider it.

MARGARET. If you really wish to be painted, why don't you give a little more and have a portrait really worth while? John might be induced to do you for a little below his usual price considering that you used to be such good friends.

HETTY [*in glee*]. Hurrah!

HARRIET [*quietly to* MARGARET]. That's very nice of you to suggest—of course I don't know—

MAGGIE [*in fear*]. For God's sake, say yes.

MARGARET [*quietly to* HARRIET]. Of course, I don't know whether John would. He is very peculiar in these matters. He sets his value on his work and thinks it beneath him to discuss price.

HETTY [*to* MAGGIE]. You needn't try to make us feel small.

MARGARET. Still, I might quite delicately mention to him that inasmuch as you have many influential friends you would be very glad to—to—

MAGGIE [*to* HETTY]. Finish what I don't want to say.

HETTY [*to* HARRIET]. Help her out.

HARRIET. Oh, yes, introductions will follow the exhibition of my portrait. No doubt I—

HETTY [*to* HARRIET]. Be patronizing.

HARRIET. No doubt I shall be able to introduce your husband to his advantage.

MAGGIE [*relieved*]. Saved.

MARGARET. If I find John in a propitious mood I shall take pleasure, for your sake, in telling him about your beauty. Just as you are sitting now would be a lovely pose.

MAGGIE [*to* MARGARET]. We can go now.

HETTY [*to* HARRIET]. Don't let her think she is doing us a favor.

HARRIET. It will give me pleasure to add my name to your husband's list of patronesses.

MAGGIE [*excitedly to* MARGARET]. Run home and tell John the good news.

MARGARET [*leisurely to* HARRIET]. I little guessed when I came for a pleasant chat about old times that it would develop into business arrangements. I had no idea, Harriet, that you had any intention of being painted. By Le Grange, too. Well, I came just in time to rescue you.

MAGGIE [*to* MARGARET]. Run home and tell John. Hurry, hurry!

HETTY [*to* HARRIET]. You managed the order very neatly. She doesn't suspect that you wanted it.

HARRIET. Now if I am not satisfied with my portrait I shall blame you, Margaret, dear. I am relying upon your opinion of John's talent.

MAGGIE [*to* MARGARET]. She doesn't suspect what you came for. Run home and tell John!

HARRIET. You always had a brilliant mind, Margaret.

MARGARET. Ah, it is you who flatter, now.

MAGGIE [*to* MARGARET]. You don't have to stay so long. Hurry home!

HARRIET. Ah, one does not flatter when one tells the truth.

MARGARET [*smiles*]. I must be going or you will have me completely under your spell.

HETTY [*looks at clock*]. Yes, do go. I have to dress for dinner.

HARRIET [*to* MARGARET]. Oh, don't hurry.

MAGGIE [*to* HETTY]. I hate you!

MARGARET [*to* HARRIET]. No, really I must, but I hope we shall see each other often at the studio. I find you so stimulating.

HETTY [*to* MAGGIE]. I hate you!

HARRIET [*to* MARGARET]. It is indeed gratifying to find a kindred spirit.

MAGGIE [*to* HETTY]. I came for your gold.

MARGARET [*to* HARRIET]. How delightful it is to know you again.

HETTY [*to* MAGGIE]. I am going to make you and your husband suffer.

HARRIET. My kind regards to John.

MAGGIE [*to* HETTY]. He has forgotten all about you.

MARGARET [*rises*]. He will be so happy to receive them.

HETTY [*to* MAGGIE]. I can hardly wait to talk to him again.

HARRIET. I shall wait, then, until you send me word?

MARGARET [*offering her hand*]. I'll speak to John about it as soon as I can and tell you when to come.

[HARRIET *takes* MARGARET'S *hand affectionately.* HETTY *and* MAGGIE *rush at each other, throw back their veils, and fling their speeches fiercely at each other.*]

HETTY. I love him—I love him—

MAGGIE. He's starving—I'm starving—

HETTY. I'm going to take him away from you—

MAGGIE. I want your money—and your influence.

HETTY and MAGGIE. I'm going to rob you—rob you.

[*There is a cymbal crash, the lights go out and come up again slowly, leaving only* MARGARET *and* HARRIET *visible.*]

MARGARET [*quietly to* HARRIET]. I've had such a delightful afternoon.

HARRIET [*offering her hand*]. It has been a joy to see you.

MARGARET [*sweetly to* HARRIET]. Good-bye.

HARRIET [*sweetly to* MARGARET *as she kisses her*]. Good-bye, my dear.

Curtain.

▪

Author Biography

Alice Gerstenberg (1885–1972) was born to a wealthy Chicago family. She graduated from Bryn Mawr College in 1907 and became a pioneering force in Chicago's Little Theatre movement as a founder of multiple theater organizations, including The Playwrights' Theatre of Chicago. As a playwright, she wrote experimental one-act plays featuring women in lead roles that were popular in schools and small theaters nationwide, with her psychological drama "Overtones" (1915) being her most enduring work. She never married.

Discuss

1. What is the difference between how the "cultured" women (Harriet and Margaret) speak and act compared to their "primitive" selves (Hetty and Maggie)?
2. The "inside" selves can see and talk to each other, but the "cultured" selves cannot see their primitive sides. What does this suggest about self-awareness?
3. What do Hetty and Maggie really want from this visit? How are their goals different from what Harriet and Margaret pretend to want?

Write

A Visual Theatre Analysis: Analyze the use of costumes, veils, and staging to reinforce the play's themes. Focus on specific stage directions about colors, the chiffon veils, and how the characters move and interact. Argue how these visual elements help the audience understand the difference between public personas and private desires.

The Yellow Wallpaper

Charlotte Perkins Gilman

What happens when a woman's intelligence is dismissed as hysteria and her creativity is forbidden because it's considered harmful? Charlotte Perkins Gilman gives us one outcome as we follow a woman confined to a room with disturbing yellow wallpaper during her "rest cure" for postpartum depression. Published in 1892, this is a brilliantly weird example of gothic literature, a genre brimming with supernatural elements and grand psychological terror. As you read, pay attention to how the narrator's relationship with writing and the wallpaper changes until her final escape. While reading, think: *What would I have done in her situation*?

It is very seldom that mere ordinary people like John and myself secure ancestral halls for the summer.

A colonial mansion, a hereditary estate, I would say a haunted house, and reach the height of romantic felicity—but that would be asking too much of fate!

Still I will proudly declare that there is something queer about it.

Else, why should it be let so cheaply? And why have stood so long untenanted?

John laughs at me, of course, but one expects that in marriage.

John is practical in the extreme. He has no patience with faith, an intense horror of superstition, and he scoffs openly at any talk of things not to be felt and seen and put down in figures.

John is a physician, and *perhaps*—(I would not say it to a living soul, of course, but this is dead paper and a great relief to my mind)—*perhaps* that is one reason I do not get well faster.

You see, he does not believe I am sick!

And what can one do?

If a physician of high standing, and one's own husband, assures friends and relatives that there is really nothing the matter with one but temporary nervous depression—a slight hysterical tendency—what is one to do?

My brother is also a physician, and also of high standing, and he says the same thing.

So I take phosphates or phosphites—whichever it is, and tonics, and journeys, and air, and exercise, and am absolutely forbidden to "work" until I am well again.[1]

Personally, I disagree with their ideas.

Personally, I believe that congenial work, with excitement and change, would do me good.

But what is one to do?

I did write for a while in spite of them; but it *does* exhaust me a good deal—having to be so sly about it, or else meet with heavy opposition.

I sometimes fancy that in my condition if I had less opposition and more society and stimulus—but John says the very worst thing I can do is to think about my condition, and I confess it always makes me feel bad.

So I will let it alone and talk about the house.

The most beautiful place! It is quite alone, standing well back from the road, quite three miles from the village. It makes me think of English places that you read about, for there are hedges

---

1. Victorian doctors believed that intense mental work, especially in women, depleted phosphorus from the brain and nervous system. They theorized that replenishing phosphates would restore mental and physical vigor. They were wrong—on many counts.

and walls and gates that lock, and lots of separate little houses for the gardeners and people.

There is a *delicious* garden! I never saw such a garden—large and shady, full of box-bordered paths, and lined with long grape-covered arbors with seats under them.

There were greenhouses, too, but they are all broken now.

There was some legal trouble, I believe, something about the heirs and co-heirs; anyhow, the place has been empty for years.

That spoils my ghostliness, I am afraid; but I don't care—there is something strange about the house—I can feel it.

I even said so to John one moonlight evening, but he said what I felt was a *draught*, and shut the window.

I get unreasonably angry with John sometimes. I'm sure I never used to be so sensitive. I think it is due to this nervous condition.

But John says if I feel so I shall neglect proper self-control; so I take pains to control myself,—before him, at least,—and that makes me very tired.

I don't like our room a bit. I wanted one downstairs that opened on the piazza and had roses all over the window, and such pretty old-fashioned chintz[2] hangings! but John would not hear of it.

He said there was only one window and not room for two beds, and no near room for him if he took another.

He is very careful and loving, and hardly lets me stir without special direction.

I have a schedule prescription for each hour in the day; he takes all care from me, and so I feel basely ungrateful not to value it more.

He said we came here solely on my account, that I was to have

---

2. These multicolored cotton fabrics, named for the Hindu word for "spotted," became so popular in 17th-century Europe that France and England banned them to protect domestic textile industries, though the French court at Versailles openly ignored the ban and continued to use them. *Mais oui!*

perfect rest and all the air I could get. "Your exercise depends on your strength, my dear," said he, "and your food somewhat on your appetite; but air you can absorb all the time." So we took the nursery, at the top of the house.

It is a big, airy room, the whole floor nearly, with windows that look all ways, and air and sunshine galore. It was nursery first and then playground and gymnasium, I should judge; for the windows are barred for little children, and there are rings and things in the walls.

The paint and paper look as if a boys' school had used it. It is stripped off—the paper—in great patches all around the head of my bed, about as far as I can reach, and in a great place on the other side of the room low down. I never saw a worse paper in my life.

One of those sprawling flamboyant patterns committing every artistic sin.

It is dull enough to confuse the eye in following, pronounced enough to constantly irritate, and provoke study, and when you follow the lame, uncertain curves for a little distance they suddenly commit suicide—plunge off at outrageous angles, destroy themselves in unheard-of contradictions.

The color is repellant, almost revolting; a smouldering, unclean yellow, strangely faded by the slow-turning sunlight.[3]

It is a dull yet lurid orange in some places, a sickly sulphur tint in others.

No wonder the children hated it! I should hate it myself if I had to live in this room long.

There comes John, and I must put this away,—he hates to have me write a word.

---

3. Arsenic-based pigments produced vibrant, fashionable colors. These cheap yet toxic pigments were widely used in wallpaper, often poisoning household inhabitants—especially women, who spent more time in the home. Symptoms included headaches, confusion, hallucinations, and paranoia. You know, "hysteria."

⁂

We have been here two weeks, and I haven't felt like writing before, since that first day.

I am sitting by the window now, up in this atrocious nursery, and there is nothing to hinder my writing as much as I please, save lack of strength.

John is away all day, and even some nights when his cases are serious.

I am glad my case is not serious!

But these nervous troubles are dreadfully depressing.

John does not know how much I really suffer. He knows there is no *reason* to suffer, and that satisfies him.

Of course it is only nervousness. It does weigh on me so not to do my duty in any way!

I meant to be such a help to John, such a real rest and comfort, and here I am a comparative burden already!

Nobody would believe what an effort it is to do what little I am able—to dress and entertain, and order things.

It is fortunate Mary is so good with the baby. Such a dear baby!

And yet I *cannot* be with him, it makes me so nervous.

I suppose John never was nervous in his life. He laughs at me so about this wallpaper!

At first he meant to re-paper the room, but afterwards he said that I was letting it get the better of me, and that nothing was worse for a nervous patient than to give way to such fancies.

He said that after the wallpaper was changed it would be the heavy bedstead, and then the barred windows, and then that gate at the head of the stairs, and so on.

"You know the place is doing you good," he said, "and really, dear, I don't care to renovate the house just for a three months' rental."

"Then do let us go downstairs," I said, "there are such pretty rooms there."

Then he took me in his arms and called me a blessed little goose, and said he would go down cellar if I wished, and have it whitewashed into the bargain.

But he is right enough about the beds and windows and things.

It is as airy and comfortable a room as any one need wish, and, of course, I would not be so silly as to make him uncomfortable just for a whim.

I'm really getting quite fond of the big room, all but that horrid paper.

Out of one window I can see the garden, those mysterious deep-shaded arbors, the riotous old-fashioned flowers, and bushes and gnarly trees.

Out of another I get a lovely view of the bay and a little private wharf belonging to the estate. There is a beautiful shaded lane that runs down there from the house. I always fancy I see people walking in these numerous paths and arbors, but John has cautioned me not to give way to fancy in the least. He says that with my imaginative power and habit of story-making a nervous weakness like mine is sure to lead to all manner of excited fancies, and that I ought to use my will and good sense to check the tendency. So I try.

I think sometimes that if I were only well enough to write a little it would relieve the press of ideas and rest me.

But I find I get pretty tired when I try.

It is so discouraging not to have any advice and companionship about my work. When I get really well John says we will ask Cousin Henry and Julia down for a long visit; but he says he would as soon put fireworks in my pillowcase as to let me have those stimulating people about now.

I wish I could get well faster.

But I must not think about that. This paper looks to me as if it *knew* what a vicious influence it had!

There is a recurrent spot where the pattern lolls like a broken neck and two bulbous eyes stare at you upside-down.

I get positively angry with the impertinence of it and the everlastingness. Up and down and sideways they crawl, and those absurd, unblinking eyes are everywhere. There is one place where two breadths didn't match, and the eyes go all up and down the line, one a little higher than the other.

I never saw so much expression in an inanimate thing before, and we all know how much expression they have! I used to lie awake as a child and get more entertainment and terror out of blank walls and plain furniture than most children could find in a toy store.

I remember what a kindly wink the knobs of our big old bureau used to have, and there was one chair that always seemed like a strong friend.

I used to feel that if any of the other things looked too fierce I could always hop into that chair and be safe.

The furniture in this room is no worse than inharmonious, however, for we had to bring it all from downstairs. I suppose when this was used as a playroom they had to take the nursery things out, and no wonder! I never saw such ravages as the children have made here.

The wallpaper, as I said before, is torn off in spots, and it sticketh closer than a brother[4]—they must have had perseverance as well as hatred.

Then the floor is scratched and gouged and splintered, the plaster itself is dug out here and there, and this great heavy bed, which is all we found in the room, looks as if it had been through the wars.

But I don't mind it a bit—only the paper.

---

4. Proverbs 18:24 from the King James Version of the Bible: "A man that hath friends must shew himself friendly: and there is a friend that sticketh closer than a brother."

There comes John's sister. Such a dear girl as she is, and so careful of me! I must not let her find me writing.

She is a perfect, and enthusiastic housekeeper, and hopes for no better profession. I verily believe she thinks it is the writing which made me sick!

But I can write when she is out, and see her a long way off from these windows.

There is one that commands the road, a lovely, shaded, winding road, and one that just looks off over the country. A lovely country, too, full of great elms and velvet meadows.

This wallpaper has a kind of sub-pattern in a different shade, a particularly irritating one, for you can only see it in certain lights, and not clearly then.

But in the places where it isn't faded, and where the sun is just so, I can see a strange, provoking, formless sort of figure, that seems to sulk about behind that silly and conspicuous front design.

There's sister on the stairs!

⁂

Well, the Fourth of July is over! The people are gone and I am tired out. John thought it might do me good to see a little company, so we just had mother and Nellie and the children down for a week.

Of course I didn't do a thing. Jennie sees to everything now.

But it tired me all the same.

John says if I don't pick up faster he shall send me to Weir Mitchell in the fall.

But I don't want to go there at all. I had a friend who was in his hands once, and she says he is just like John and my brother, only more so!

Besides, it is such an undertaking to go so far.

I don't feel as if it was worthwhile to turn my hand over for anything, and I'm getting dreadfully fretful and querulous.

I cry at nothing, and cry most of the time.

Of course I don't when John is here, or anybody else, but when I am alone.

And I am alone a good deal just now. John is kept in town very often by serious cases, and Jennie is good and lets me alone when I want her to.

So I walk a little in the garden or down that lovely lane, sit on the porch under the roses, and lie down up here a good deal.

I'm getting really fond of the room in spite of the wallpaper. Perhaps *because* of the wallpaper.

It dwells in my mind so!

I lie here on this great immovable bed—it is nailed down, I believe—and follow that pattern about by the hour. It is as good as gymnastics, I assure you. I start, we'll say, at the bottom, down in the corner over there where it has not been touched, and I determine for the thousandth time that I *will* follow that pointless pattern to some sort of a conclusion.

I know a little of the principle of design, and I know this thing was not arranged on any laws of radiation, or alternation, or repetition, or symmetry, or anything else that I ever heard of.

It is repeated, of course, by the breadths, but not otherwise.

Looked at in one way each breadth stands alone, the bloated curves and flourishes—a kind of "debased Romanesque"[5] with *delirium tremens*—go waddling up and down in isolated columns of fatuity.

But, on the other hand, they connect diagonally, and the sprawling outlines run off in great slanting waves of optic horror, like a lot of wallowing seaweeds in full chase.

The whole thing goes horizontally, too, at least it seems so, and I exhaust myself in trying to distinguish the order of its going in that direction.

---

5. Here, Gilman is saying that the wallpaper mimics Romanesque architectural patterns but does so badly—it's a cheap, mass-produced Victorian imitation of a once-dignified medieval style.

They have used a horizontal breadth for a frieze, and that adds wonderfully to the confusion.

There is one end of the room where it is almost intact, and there, when the cross-lights fade and the low sun shines directly upon it, I can almost fancy radiation after all,—the interminable grotesques seem to form around a common center and rush off in headlong plunges of equal distraction.

It makes me tired to follow it. I will take a nap, I guess.

⁂

I don't know why I should write this.

I don't want to.

I don't feel able.

And I know John would think it absurd. But I *must* say what I feel and think in some way—it is such a relief!

But the effort is getting to be greater than the relief.

Half the time now I am awfully lazy, and lie down ever so much.

John says I mustn't lose my strength, and has me take cod-liver oil[6] and lots of tonics and things, to say nothing of ale and wine and rare meat.

Dear John! He loves me very dearly, and hates to have me sick. I tried to have a real earnest reasonable talk with him the other day, and tell him how I wish he would let me go and make a visit to Cousin Henry and Julia.

But he said I wasn't able to go, nor able to stand it after I got there; and I did not make out a very good case for myself, for I was crying before I had finished.

It is getting to be a great effort for me to think straight. Just this nervous weakness, I suppose.

And dear John gathered me up in his arms, and just carried me

6. Cod liver oil is a cure that has come in and out (and now in again) of fashion.

upstairs and laid me on the bed, and sat by me and read to me till it tired my head.

He said I was his darling and his comfort and all he had, and that I must take care of myself for his sake, and keep well.

He says no one but myself can help me out of it, that I must use my will and self-control and not let any silly fancies run away with me.

There's one comfort, the baby is well and happy, and does not have to occupy this nursery with the horrid wallpaper.

If we had not used it that blessed child would have! What a fortunate escape! Why, I wouldn't have a child of mine, an impressionable little thing, live in such a room for worlds.

I never thought of it before, but it is lucky that John kept me here after all. I can stand it so much easier than a baby, you see.

Of course I never mention it to them any more,—I am too wise,—but I keep watch of it all the same.

There are things in that paper that nobody knows but me, or ever will.

Behind that outside pattern the dim shapes get clearer every day.

It is always the same shape, only very numerous.

And it is like a woman stooping down and creeping about behind that pattern. I don't like it a bit. I wonder—I begin to think—I wish John would take me away from here!

It is so hard to talk with John about my case, because he is so wise, and because he loves me so.

But I tried it last night.

It was moonlight. The moon shines in all around, just as the sun does.

I hate to see it sometimes, it creeps so slowly, and always comes in by one window or another.

John was asleep and I hated to waken him, so I kept still and watched the moonlight on that undulating wallpaper till I felt creepy.

The faint figure behind seemed to shake the pattern, just as if she wanted to get out.

I got up softly and went to feel and see if the paper *did* move, and when I came back John was awake.

"What is it, little girl?" he said. "Don't go walking about like that—you'll get cold."

I thought it was a good time to talk, so I told him that I really was not gaining here, and that I wished he would take me away.

"Why darling!" said he, "our lease will be up in three weeks, and I can't see how to leave before.

"The repairs are not done at home, and I cannot possibly leave town just now. Of course if you were in any danger I could and would, but you really are better, dear, whether you can see it or not. I am a doctor, dear, and I know. You are gaining flesh and color, your appetite is better. I feel really much easier about you."

"I don't weigh a bit more," said I, "nor as much; and my appetite may be better in the evening, when you are here, but it is worse in the morning when you are away."

"Bless her little heart!" said he with a big hug; "she shall be as sick as she pleases! But now let's improve the shining hours by going to sleep, and talk about it in the morning!"

"And you won't go away?" I asked gloomily.

"Why, how can I, dear? It is only three weeks more and then we will take a nice little trip of a few days while Jennie is getting the house ready. Really, dear, you are better!"

"Better in body perhaps—" I began, and stopped short, for he sat up straight and looked at me with such a stern, reproachful look that I could not say another word.

"My darling," said he, "I beg of you, for my sake and for our child's sake, as well as for your own, that you will never for one instant let that idea enter your mind! There is nothing so dangerous, so fascinating, to a temperament like yours. It is a false and foolish fancy. Can you not trust me as a physician when I tell you so?"

So of course I said no more on that score, and we went to sleep before long. He thought I was asleep first, but I wasn't, and lay there for hours trying to decide whether that front pattern and the back pattern really did move together or separately.

⁂

On a pattern like this, by daylight, there is a lack of sequence, a defiance of law, that is a constant irritant to a normal mind.

The color is hideous enough, and unreliable enough, and infuriating enough, but the pattern is torturing.

You think you have mastered it, but just as you get well under way in following, it turns a back somersault and there you are. It slaps you in the face, knocks you down, and tramples upon you. It is like a bad dream.

The outside pattern is a florid arabesque, reminding one of a fungus. If you can imagine a toadstool in joints, an interminable string of toadstools, budding and sprouting in endless convolutions—why, that is something like it.

That is, sometimes!

There is one marked peculiarity about this paper, a thing nobody seems to notice but myself, and that is that it changes as the light changes.

When the sun shoots in through the east window—I always watch for that first long, straight ray—it changes so quickly that I never can quite believe it.

That is why I watch it always.

By moonlight—the moon shines in all night when there is a moon—I wouldn't know it was the same paper.

At night in any kind of light, in twilight, candlelight, lamplight, and worst of all by moonlight, it becomes bars! The outside pattern I mean, and the woman behind it is as plain as can be.

I didn't realize for a long time what the thing was that showed behind,—that dim sub-pattern,—but now I am quite sure it is a woman.

By daylight she is subdued, quiet. I fancy it is the pattern that keeps her so still. It is so puzzling. It keeps me quiet by the hour.

I lie down ever so much now. John says it is good for me, and to sleep all I can.

Indeed, he started the habit by making me lie down for an hour after each meal.

It is a very bad habit, I am convinced, for, you see, I don't sleep.

And that cultivates deceit, for I don't tell them I'm awake—O no!

The fact is, I am getting a little afraid of John.

He seems very queer sometimes, and even Jennie has an inexplicable look.

It strikes me occasionally, just as a scientific hypothesis,—that perhaps it is the paper!

I have watched John when he did not know I was looking, and come into the room suddenly on the most innocent excuses, and I've caught him several times *looking at the paper*! And Jennie too. I caught Jennie with her hand on it once.

She didn't know I was in the room, and when I asked her in a quiet, a very quiet voice, with the most restrained manner possible, what she was doing with the paper—she turned around as if she had been caught stealing, and looked quite angry—asked me why I should frighten her so!

Then she said that the paper stained everything it touched, that she had found yellow smooches on all my clothes and John's, and she wished we would be more careful!

Did not that sound innocent? But I know she was studying that pattern, and I am determined that nobody shall find it out but myself!

⁂

Life is very much more exciting now than it used to be. You see I have something more to expect, to look forward to, to watch. I really do eat better, and am more quiet than I was.

John is so pleased to see me improve! He laughed a little the other day, and said I seemed to be flourishing in spite of my wallpaper.

I turned it off with a laugh. I had no intention of telling him it was *because* of the wallpaper—he would make fun of me. He might even want to take me away.

I don't want to leave now until I have found it out. There is a week more, and I think that will be enough.

⁂

I'm feeling ever so much better! I don't sleep much at night, for it is so interesting to watch developments; but I sleep a good deal in the daytime.

In the daytime it is tiresome and perplexing.

There are always new shoots on the fungus, and new shades of yellow all over it. I cannot keep count of them, though I have tried conscientiously.

It is the strangest yellow, that wallpaper! It makes me think of all the yellow things I ever saw—not beautiful ones like buttercups, but old foul, bad yellow things.

But there is something else about that paper—the smell! I noticed it the moment we came into the room, but with so much air and sun it was not bad. Now we have had a week of fog and rain, and whether the windows are open or not, the smell is here.

It creeps all over the house.

I find it hovering in the dining-room, skulking in the parlor, hiding in the hall, lying in wait for me on the stairs.

It gets into my hair.

Even when I go to ride, if I turn my head suddenly and surprise it—there is that smell!

Such a peculiar odor, too! I have spent hours in trying to analyze it, to find what it smelled like.

It is not bad—at first, and very gentle, but quite the subtlest, most enduring odor I ever met.

In this damp weather it is awful. I wake up in the night and find it hanging over me.

It used to disturb me at first. I thought seriously of burning the house—to reach the smell.

But now I am used to it. The only thing I can think of that it is like is the *color* of the paper! A yellow smell.

There is a very funny mark on this wall, low down, near the mopboard. A streak that runs round the room. It goes behind every piece of furniture, except the bed, a long, straight, even *smooch*, as if it had been rubbed over and over.

I wonder how it was done and who did it, and what they did it for. Round and round and round—round and round and round—it makes me dizzy!

⁂

I really have discovered something at last.

Through watching so much at night, when it changes so, I have finally found out.

The front pattern *does* move—and no wonder! The woman behind shakes it!

Sometimes I think there are a great many women behind, and sometimes only one, and she crawls around fast, and her crawling shakes it all over.

Then in the very bright spots she keeps still, and in the very shady spots she just takes hold of the bars and shakes them hard.

And she is all the time trying to climb through. But nobody could climb through that pattern—it strangles so; I think that is why it has so many heads.

They get through, and then the pattern strangles them off and turns them upside down, and makes their eyes white!

If those heads were covered or taken off it would not be half so bad.

⁂

I think that woman gets out in the daytime!

And I'll tell you why—privately—I've seen her!

I can see her out of every one of my windows!

It is the same woman, I know, for she is always creeping, and most women do not creep by daylight.

I see her on that long-shaded lane, creeping up and down. I see her in those dark grape arbors, creeping all around the garden.

I see her on that long road under the trees, creeping along, and when a carriage comes she hides under the blackberry vines.

I don't blame her a bit. It must be very humiliating to be caught creeping by daylight!

I always lock the door when I creep by daylight. I can't do it at night, for I know John would suspect something at once.

And John is so queer now, that I don't want to irritate him. I wish he would take another room! Besides, I don't want anybody to get that woman out at night but myself.

I often wonder if I could see her out of all the windows at once.

But, turn as fast as I can, I can only see out of one at one time.

And though I always see her she *may* be able to creep faster than I can turn!

I have watched her sometimes away off in the open country, creeping as fast as a cloud shadow in a high wind.

⁂

If only that top pattern could be gotten off from the under one! I mean to try it, little by little.

I have found out another funny thing, but I shan't tell it this time! It does not do to trust people too much.

There are only two more days to get this paper off, and I believe John is beginning to notice. I don't like the look in his eyes.

And I heard him ask Jennie a lot of professional questions about me. She had a very good report to give.

She said I slept a good deal in the daytime.

John knows I don't sleep very well at night, for all I'm so quiet!

He asked me all sorts of questions, too, and pretended to be very loving and kind.

As if I couldn't see through him!

Still, I don't wonder he acts so, sleeping under this paper for three months.

It only interests me, but I feel sure John and Jennie are secretly affected by it.

⁂

Hurrah! This is the last day, but it is enough. John is to stay in town overnight, and won't be out until this evening.

Jennie wanted to sleep with me—the sly thing! but I told her I should undoubtedly rest better for a night all alone.

That was clever, for really I wasn't alone a bit! As soon as it was moonlight, and that poor thing began to crawl and shake the pattern, I got up and ran to help her.

I pulled and she shook, I shook and she pulled, and before morning we had peeled off yards of that paper.

A strip about as high as my head and half around the room.

And then when the sun came and that awful pattern began to laugh at me I declared I would finish it to-day!

We go away to-morrow, and they are moving all my furniture down again to leave things as they were before.

Jennie looked at the wall in amazement, but I told her merrily that I did it out of pure spite at the vicious thing.

She laughed and said she wouldn't mind doing it herself, but I must not get tired.

How she betrayed herself that time!

But I am here, and no person touches this paper but me—not *alive*!

She tried to get me out of the room—it was too patent! But I said it was so quiet and empty and clean now that I believed I would lie down again and sleep all I could; and not to wake me even for dinner—I would call when I woke.

So now she is gone, and the servants are gone, and the things are gone, and there is nothing left but that great bedstead nailed down, with the canvas mattress we found on it.

We shall sleep downstairs to-night, and take the boat home to-morrow.

I quite enjoy the room, now it is bare again.

How those children did tear about here!

This bedstead is fairly gnawed!

But I must get to work.

I have locked the door and thrown the key down into the front path.

I don't want to go out, and I don't want to have anybody come in, till John comes.

I want to astonish him.

I've got a rope up here that even Jennie did not find. If that woman does get out, and tries to get away, I can tie her!

But I forgot I could not reach far without anything to stand on!

This bed will *not* move!

I tried to lift and push it until I was lame, and then I got so angry I bit off a little piece at one corner—but it hurt my teeth.

Then I peeled off all the paper I could reach standing on the floor. It sticks horribly and the pattern just enjoys it! All those strangled heads and bulbous eyes and waddling fungus growths just shriek with derision!

I am getting angry enough to do something desperate. To jump out of the window would be admirable exercise, but the bars are too strong even to try.

Besides I wouldn't do it. Of course not. I know well enough that a step like that is improper and might be misconstrued.

I don't like to *look* out of the windows even—there are so many of those creeping women, and they creep so fast.

I wonder if they all come out of that wallpaper as I did?

But I am securely fastened now by my well-hidden rope—you don't get *me* out in the road there!

I suppose I shall have to get back behind the pattern when it comes night, and that is hard!

It is so pleasant to be out in this great room and creep around as I please!

I don't want to go outside. I won't, even if Jennie asks me to.

For outside you have to creep on the ground, and everything is green instead of yellow.

But here I can creep smoothly on the floor, and my shoulder just fits in that long smooch around the wall, so I cannot lose my way.

Why, there's John at the door!

It is no use, young man, you can't open it!

How he does call and pound!

Now he's crying for an axe.

It would be a shame to break down that beautiful door!

"John dear!" said I in the gentlest voice, "the key is down by the front steps, under a plantain leaf!"

That silenced him for a few moments.

Then he said—very quietly indeed, "Open the door, my darling!"

"I can't," said I. "The key is down by the front door under a plantain leaf!"

And then I said it again, several times, very gently and slowly, and said it so often that he had to go and see, and he got it, of course, and came in. He stopped short by the door.

"What is the matter?" he cried. "For God's sake, what are you doing!"

I kept on creeping just the same, but I looked at him over my shoulder.

"I've got out at last," said I, "in spite of you and Jane! And I've pulled off most of the paper, so you can't put me back!"

Now why should that man have fainted? But he did, and right across my path by the wall, so that I had to creep over him every time!

■

Why I Wrote "The Yellow Wallpaper"

Charlotte Perkins Gilman

Charlotte Perkins Gilman wrote this essay in 1913 to explain the real-life inspiration behind her famous story, revealing how her own experience with the "rest cure" nearly destroyed her mental health. Notice how Gilman positions herself not as a victim, but as a pragmatic reformer who used her writing as a tool for social change—she wanted to save other women from dangerous medical treatments, not necessarily to advance feminist ideology. While "The Yellow Wallpaper" is now celebrated as a cornerstone of feminist literature, Gilman's focus here is purely practical: she saw a medical problem that she experienced personally, and wrote a weird, gothic story to draw attention to it.

Many and many a reader has asked that. When the story first came out, in the *New England Magazine* about 1891, a Boston physician made protest in *The Transcript*. Such a story ought not to be written, he said; it was enough to drive anyone mad to read it.

Another physician, in Kansas I think, wrote to say that it was the best description of incipient insanity he had ever seen, and—begging my pardon—had I been there?

Now the story of the story is this:

For many years I suffered from a severe and continuous nervous breakdown tending to melancholia—and beyond. During about the third year of this trouble I went, in devout faith and some faint stir of hope, to a noted specialist in nervous diseases, the best known in the country. This wise man put me to bed and applied the rest cure, to which a still-good physique responded so promptly that he concluded there was nothing much the matter with me, and sent me home with solemn advice to "live as domestic a life as far as possible," to "have but two hours' intellectual life a day," and "never to touch pen, brush, or pencil again" as long as I lived. This was in 1887.

I went home and obeyed those directions for some three months, and came so near the borderline of utter mental ruin that I could see over.

Then, using the remnants of intelligence that remained, and helped by a wise friend, I cast the noted specialist's advice to the winds and went to work again—work, the normal life of every human being; work, in which is joy and growth and service, without which one is a pauper and a parasite—ultimately recovering some measure of power.

Being naturally moved to rejoicing by this narrow escape, I wrote *The Yellow Wallpaper*, with its embellishments and additions, to carry out the ideal (I never had hallucinations or objections to my mural decorations) and sent a copy to the physician who so nearly drove me mad. He never acknowledged it.

The little book is valued by alienists[1] and as a good specimen of one kind of literature. It has, to my knowledge, saved one woman from a similar fate—so terrifying her family that they let her out into normal activity and she recovered.

But the best result is this. Many years later I was told that the great specialist had admitted to friends of his that he had

---

1. A 19th-century term for doctors who specialized in mental illness, "alienist" comes from the French *aliéné*, meaning "insane" or "mentally estranged"—literally, someone alienated from their normal mental state.

altered his treatment of neurasthenia[2] since reading *The Yellow Wallpaper.*

It was not intended to drive people crazy, but to save people from being driven crazy, and it worked.

▪

Author Biography

Charlotte Perkins Gilman (1860–1935) was a writer and social reformer who fought for women's economic independence and suffrage in the early 1900s. When she was a child, her father abandoned the family, and her mother moved often with her children from relative to relative, living in poverty. After the birth of her child, the author suffered postpartum depression and underwent the now-controversial rest cure treatment that inspired "The Yellow Wallpaper." In 1888 Gilman separated from her husband to maintain her sanity—(they divorced in 1894)—and began her lifelong advocacy that women could never be truly free without economic independence.

---

2. Neurasthenia was a fashionable 19th-century diagnosis described as "nervous exhaustion" or "depleted nerve force."

Discuss

1. How does the narrator's husband John treat her, and what does his behavior reveal about attitudes toward women and mental health in this time period?
2. Track how the narrator's descriptions of the wallpaper change from the beginning to the end of the story. What do these changes reveal about her mental condition?
3. Why do you think Gilman sent a copy of the story to Dr. Mitchell, the physician who treated her? What does his lack of response tell us?
4. While "The Yellow Wallpaper" is now considered a feminist classic, Gilman frames it here as medical reform. Do you think a work can be feminist even if the author doesn't explicitly intend it to be? Why or why not?

Write

Writing to Change the World: Analyze how Gilman used creative writing as a tool for social change, examining both "The Yellow Wallpaper" and her essay. Consider her strategies for reaching different audiences (medical professionals, women patients, general readers) and evaluate the effectiveness of using fiction versus nonfiction to advocate for reform, acknowledging the power of her pathos.

Part 2

Weird Environmentalism

What We Fed to the Manticore

Talia Lakshmi Kolluri

Talia Lakshmi Kolluri's short story, published in 2022, transforms a mythical man-eating beast into a metaphor for environmental collapse—like you do. The story demonstrates how weird fiction can make the incomprehensible scale of climate change emotionally tangible. Perhaps our environmental crisis requires monsters to help us understand what we've unleashed upon ourselves.

They say that life in the Sundarbans revolves around two things: the tide and the tigers.

We are not the tide.

We are the tigers.

It was not what we ate that troubled the villagers, because we had been eating very little. It was what we fed to the Manticore.[1] He arrived hungry. And he could never be satisfied.

We were gathered in a grove of mangrove trees that I had come to think of as our own. They had been special to me. The villagers called them sundari trees, but I knew them as looking-glass mangroves. Their exposed roots stood perpendicular to the ground, like curved knife-edges, wandering in the shape of little rivers. Secretly, I had begun to name each of them. I named one for my mother, and one for the sky. I imagined that they had their

1. A manticore is a fearsome creature from Persian mythology that has a human head, a lion's body, and a scorpion's tail, complete with poisonous darts.

own name for me, but they never told me what it was. These mangroves offered a sanctuary I could hide in. I could curl behind the bend of a root blade and stay there for hours, unnoticed. They used to be within my territory, and I loved winding my way among their pale trunks, alone, scratching the bark and rubbing my face against them.

They were mine until they weren't anymore.

I don't remember when we came together. At first it happened little by little. Brother returned to me. Then Small One. And then all at once, there were five of us. The water had become saltier, and sometimes I couldn't drink it without retching. Some of the plants were wilting. All of us had been struggling to find prey. I had been looking for deer tracks, but everywhere I went, I was the first to press my feet into the smooth silt. And so we gathered, dry-tongued, listless, and hungry. Drawn together for comfort, or something like it.

We lay sprawled on a stretch of damp silt a few yards from the bank of a nearby tributary, leaving impressions of our bodies in the earth, so that a villager walking through might understand that a tiger had lain here, or here. The canopy of the trees filtered the sun and cast a moving pattern of dappled light everywhere I looked. If I narrowed my eyes and tilted my head, I could almost see a small deer or a flying fox. But shadows do nothing for hunger, and we were ravenous.

When he came to us, it was dusk, and he was a stranger.

The air was dense and we had not eaten in thirteen days. We were lying among a peculiar field of roots that reminded me that the trees will thrive even as we are wasting, that the mangroves are resourceful in ways we have never been. Some of the trees send pneumatophores,[2] traveling root branches, to collect air for them. They pierce the mud and reach straight up so the ground is stippled with breathing spears. This was the space where the stranger found us.

"Sister, who is that?" asked Small One.

"I don't know," I said, bringing myself up a little higher. "It looks like a tiger."

"Are you certain?" asked Notched Ear.

"Either it is a tiger or it is food," said Crooked Tail. Her tail had taken on a permanent bend after it had been broken during a fight with one of her litter mates when she was a cub. She licked her paw and then turned her head to lie on it.

Small One squinted, trying to make out the loping form that was growing in our field of vision. "It looks too large to be a tiger. What if it thinks that we are the food?" She moved closer to Crooked Tail and started chuffing, looking for comfort. Some of us still thought of her as a cub.

"Maybe it isn't a tiger," I said. I stood up and took a few steps toward the stranger to get a better look, but feeling exposed, I walked back to the others and tried to settle down.

"We can't take on another one," said Brother. "There is nothing to hunt and there's no room in the grove for anyone else."

"No," I said, looking again. Looking more carefully. "That is not a tiger." Its fur was almost familiar, but not quite. It was a glossy continuum of deep red. No stripes.

I raised my head when the stranger came close and saw a man's face nestled in his mane, also red. The fur was lush, and I had an urge to groom it for him. He looked down on me and smiled, baring three rows of neat, sharp teeth.

---

2. Pneumatophores are aerial roots, like snorkels, that grow up toward the sky from wetland plants to absorb oxygen from the air since the soil in the wetlands is so, well, wet.

"I am here," he said. The others looked at each other and then at me, their eyes saying things like "tiger" and "not tiger," refusing to commit to either one. Then they lowered their heads and flattened their ears before I had a chance to do the same. Small One slunk over to the curve of a nearby root blade. Her belly was low to the ground.

"We haven't been waiting for anyone," I said. I sniffed the air near him. It smelled strange, like plants I did not recognize—and, faintly, like blood. "Perhaps you are looking for somebody else."

"I came looking for you." He had a beautiful voice. Like a bird trumpeting over the forest. It made me feel ashamed of my own.

"For me?"

"For all of you. I am hungry." I was afraid to meet his eyes, so I focused instead on his strange mouth. His gums were clean and pink and glistened with saliva.

"We have nothing for you," I said. "We are hungrier than you are."

"Oh?"

"Yes," I said. The others remained still, using the rest of their energy to keep themselves flat on the earth. Brother was squeezing his eyes shut.

"Nothing to share, then?"

"Nothing." I tried to hold the stranger's gaze but his stare drilled through my own eyes into a corner of my mind. I imagined him slinking in there, looking for something that I wasn't willing to reveal. "We go for days without eating," I finally said. "There are hardly any chital deer in the forest these days."

"Perhaps I should eat all of you," said the stranger. "You're better than nothing."

I swallowed deliberately, understanding that I had made some sort of mistake. I heard quiet chuffing, and at first, I didn't realize that it was me. "Some of us," I said after a moment, and began to regret it even as I spoke, "some of us have gone into the villages."

"And why is that?" he asked. "What would a tiger need with a village?"

"There were cattle. We've eaten one or two of the cows. And when there were no cows, we've eaten the goats, and when there are no goats..." I looked down and realized I'd been digging a shallow space into the silt with my paw. I didn't want to say what could have come next. That now there were no goats. That the next step would be eating the villagers, but that we weren't willing to go that far. That we had chosen to go hungry. I knew he would never tolerate staying hungry himself. But he understood my silence, and I hated myself for letting him think that a village without cows or goats was still a thing that could be ravaged. When I glanced at Brother I saw that he had bitten off the top of a pneumatophore.

"I see," the stranger said. "The village." He stood for a while looking at things. I watched him cast his eyes to the riverbank. The water moving swiftly in a nearby tributary. The rustling mangrove leaves. Our grove. Us. Me. And then he turned and walked toward the thick of the forest.

"That is not a tiger," I said, to no one in particular. I felt that we had escaped something by a narrow margin.

"What is it then?" asked Small One. She peered at me over the edge of the root blade.

"That is the Manticore," I said as I watched his haunches sway. And I watched his scorpion-tipped tail start to whip. And I watched him shrink into the distance.

The Manticore told me he was in the mood for hunting. I was lying among the mangrove roots, watching him pace the border of our grove of trees. I had been gazing at the silver scales on the underside of the leaves and picturing the night sky. Earlier that day, I had marked the trunks of the outer trees, but the Manticore had come in anyway.

"Will you come with me?" he asked. He looked over the edge of the root blade where I had burrowed into its curve. From my hiding place, it felt as if he was towering over me. My tree had given me up.

"I'm not hungry." That was a lie. And he knew. He had been watching me for hours and had seen me lapping salt water. Rubbing my cheeks on the root spears. Curling into myself to sleep. Not eating.

"I can feed you."

"I don't want what you've been eating."

The night before, I had come upon him on my way back to the grove from a river crossing. He had a man in his mouth. The man's body was bloated and swollen—he must have drowned before the Manticore found him. His lips were unnaturally huge and his tongue poked out of his mouth. His eyes were open. The Manticore saw me and held my gaze, and then bit down firmly on the man.[3]

Now, as he paced, I tried to avert my eyes. I hoped he didn't have another corpse tucked in the brush behind him.

"I have to go," I said. I stood up and stretched, perhaps a little longer than I needed. I didn't want him to follow me.

"And where are you going?" he asked.

"Nowhere," I said.

"Hunting?"

"No." And then I thought better of it. "Maybe. I thought I saw a chital. Unless you've eaten it already."

"Eaten what?" The Manticore stared at me. "The deer. Have you eaten it?"

"No."

"Well, I'll hunt it then." I turned to go. I walked toward another

3. In mythology, manticores prefer humans over other meat, and the only animal they could not defeat or eat was the lion.

crossing on the riverbank. It was deeper water but I wanted some distance between us. The Manticore felt otherwise, and followed me. I felt him staring.

"Would you like to solve a riddle?" he asked.

"No," I said, still walking away.

"Not even one?" He had caught up to me without losing his breath. We walked together, with the Manticore leading the way. He kept whipping his tail back and forth. Its scorpion tip barely missed my face each time.

"I wouldn't know how to solve one."

"If you solve it, I will leave you alone."

"Go away."

"As you like," said the Manticore. He coiled himself low to the ground and sprang forth across the widest part of the river. I saw him land effortlessly on the other side and then disappear into a dense patch of mangroves.

"Watch this," the Manticore said. It was dawn and I hadn't eaten for sixteen days. "I'm going to eat that one." I followed his line of sight from the reeds to the center of the river. A dinghy was slipping along the water. Two men were in the boat, murmuring to each other, as though they were trying not to disturb the morning.

"Which one?" I asked.

"The one in the back." He stared at the man crouched near the stern, pushing a long pole into the river bottom in time with his partner at the prow. I knew him, the man in back with the pole, the man unknowingly tempting the Manticore.

"Don't eat him," I said.

"Why not?" the Manticore asked.

"I know him."

"I don't care." And the Manticore darted down the bank and within seconds had crept into the river. I watched him swim quietly behind the boat, his head barely above the water's surface.

I thought of how I had met the man. How once during an unquiet storm I had been separated from my mangroves and carried into the village by an overflowing tributary. The village was stripped of trees. I didn't know how to be a tiger without the forest. I had been swept into a shed near the man's home. I was soggy and confused and curled up against the wall farthest from the doorway. When he turned on the light and saw me illuminated in the harsh glow of a single naked bulb, he inhaled sharply and wiped rain from his face. I could hear the voices of other men calling to each other. Looking for tigers. Planning to kill the ones who had intruded upon the village after the storm. Hungry tigers. We stared at each other, this man and I. He held a rifle in one hand and it was pointed at a corner of the shed. It wobbled unsteadily. His other hand gripped the worn door frame. His breathing was labored, and I saw a throbbing vein in his neck. The shed smelled like ocean water and mud and waste from the man's livestock. I could smell his sweat through the other odors. I inhaled deeply and grimaced so that I could capture as many scents as possible, but I couldn't smell any other tigers. I felt profoundly alone. We stared at each other and then he quietly backed out of the building. He closed the door partway and called out to the others that there were no tigers in his shed. No tigers on his property.

"Leave him," I said to myself as the Manticore slunk up alongside the dinghy, undetected. The man's honey mask[4] was sitting askew, pushed back on his head. Its plastic, rigid face, with a painted beard, was a poor substitute for his own. He was clean shaven. He was old enough to have a child, but young enough that his face still held the echo of the boy he had once been. I closed my eyes.

"Not him," I pleaded as I watched a gentle breeze ripple the cotton fabric of the man's shirt. As I watched the sunrise glint off

---

4. A honey mask is worn to protect the face when retrieving honey.

the dinghy's metal hull. As I saw the man lean over and skim the surface of the river with his fingers. As I saw the reflection of the sunrise in the river break apart and scatter.

The Manticore flung one wet paw over the edge of the boat and I started pacing along the riverbank. The man turned too late, and the Manticore swiftly struck him with the other paw and dragged him into the river with his teeth.

I started chuffing quietly, comforting no one, when I saw the Manticore drag the man to the opposite bank of the river, leaving a trail of blood in the water. I watched the man's partner, who had been left behind at the prow of the boat, alone and weeping.

Shame when the man's honey mask drifted to my side of the shore. Shame when I picked it up gently in my mouth and took it back to my grove of trees. It smelled faintly of coconut. It tasted like plastic.

I wished the Manticore would leave us.

"Are you ready to hunt with me yet?" The Manticore stood over me. Sun filtered through the leaves of the mangrove canopy, scattering their silhouettes across the ground. I looked up at their silver undersides, but I couldn't imagine the night sky anymore. I hadn't eaten for nineteen days. I didn't know how long I'd been sleeping. I raised my head and looked over my shoulder to see my own form stretched along the sand. I was diminished. I was sinking into the landscape. My fur was fading. Orange dissolved into tawny. Tawny faded into beige. I was almost the color of the sand. Indistinguishable from the silt and roots. Ready to be washed away by the river.

"No," I said, resting my head on my paws again.

"Will you ever be ready?"

"No."

When I think of it now, I realize we couldn't have stopped him.

Even if we wanted to. No matter how often he is fed, a Manticore is always unsatisfied.

I was swimming through a river crossing when I felt the air become heavy. I struggled to draw it into my nose. By the time I found the Manticore winding his way among the roots of a strange mangrove, one I did not recognize, the wind was twisting its branches, bending them to the earth.

"What is happening?" I asked.

"You will not eat them," said the Manticore, "but that doesn't mean that they will never be eaten."

I walked alone to find our grove, but the paths had changed and I was afraid I would become lost. The plants were cowering from the strong wind, and the river surged in the wrong places. I tried to cross a tributary at three different points and backed away each time because the current looked too strong for me. I saw strange items traveling swiftly down the rushing waterways. A child's toy. A bowl. A tattered book. I was frightened, and I didn't feel like a tiger anymore, just a feeble attempt at what I believed a tiger to be. I was nearly worthless. I thought I should offer myself to the Manticore. He would eat all that was left of me—then no trace of my emptiness would remain.

When I came to our grove, only two of the others were there.

"We were thinking," said Notched Ear, "that perhaps the Manticore is right. Perhaps we should have eaten the villagers."

"He is wrong," I said.

"We are hungry," said Small One. "He will probably eat all of them. There won't be any left for us."

"I don't want us to become like him," I said.

"It doesn't matter," said Notched Ear. "The village thinks it's been us all along. I found two new traps today. And Small One was almost shot. They are looking for us." He turned away from me and made his way down a sodden path toward the river.

"Where are you going?" I asked.

"I'm going to eat," he said. "I'm going to snatch one of the villagers from a boat, like he did." As he walked away, he leaned into the wind, as though it was determined to push him back to me.

"It's too late," I said to myself. I lay down in the silt and felt its fine wet grains soak into my coat. I ignored Small One when she stole away to the bank of a different crossing. I lay alone among my mangrove roots, watching the sky weep. Watching the wind fell trees that had withstood all the other storms I had ever seen. Listening to the surge of the water as the entire web of the Sundarbans waterways swelled over the embankments that shielded the land. Knowing that this was much bigger than the last storm, bigger than all the storms I had seen since I was a cub. Imagining that the furious sea followed close behind, pushing salt water into the network of land and rivers so that all that would remain when the storm subsided would be the stripped earth, and the birds, and the sea.

The sky was dark and mottled when the Manticore found me. Broken branches enclosed me like a cage, and I was partially submerged in the seawater that had washed in. Little rivulets of muddy water ran from my coat. I saw his feet before I saw the rest of him. They were powerful and inexplicably clean. His red coat was still glossy and beautiful despite the dust and water and muck brought in by the growing storm.

"Are you ready for a riddle now?" he asked.

"No," I said. I was too defeated to think about anything.

"Are you sure, tiger? I'm still hungry, and I'm growing tired of the taste of the villagers."

"You're going to eat me anyway," I said.

"Maybe not. I'll give you a simple one. What flies higher than a kingfisher, swims deeper than a whale, and is master of the land and the trees?"

"I don't know."

"Try to answer." The Manticore looked as if he was smiling at me. Benevolently, almost, and with pity. I said nothing. "It's a cyclone, tiger," he went on. "You should know that." The storm was making it difficult for me to see. The rain cut the sky like claws shredding bark. The Manticore seemed as though he was speaking to me from a few steps away and from a great distance all at once. I blinked once or twice and only felt more confused.

"You failed my riddle," he said.

"And you're going to eat me now."

"Yes." He stared at me quietly and neither of us moved. I thought about my mangroves. How I would like to say good-bye to each of them. How I had already forgotten all their names.

"What will be left of me when you're finished?" I asked.

"Nothing," the Manticore said. "I will leave no bones." And he opened his mouth wide, baring three rows of neat sharp teeth.

There are so many stories to tell in this world. There is the sleeping girl, the old man with regrets, the captive princess. There is vengeance on parents; there are star-crossed lovers, adventurous youth, and all different kinds of lonely people. There are heroes, and villains, and quests. And then there are all the stories about the animals and magical creatures.

Or maybe there is only one story. A living thing is born, it moves through the world, and then it dies. For this story, it's less about the telling and more about the retelling.

Maybe, instead, it happened like this.

In the end, there was nothing left of the village, because everything was taken by the Manticore.

Life in the Sundarbans revolves around two things: the tide and the tigers.

He was the tide, and we were the tigers.

We were hungry, but would not eat. He was ravenous and would not stop eating.

First he ate all the deer. And then the monkeys. And then he ate the peacocks, and the fishing cats. He cracked open the shells of turtles and ate the meat inside, and afterward he licked the shells like they were bowls. He peeled back the skin of crocodiles and ate them while their bodies were still twisting and rolling in the water. He snatched flying foxes midair, and bit through all the pangolins,[5] one by one.

When he had eaten all the animals, he turned his hungry jaws on the villagers. He pulled them off boats and out of kitchens. He followed them to forest hives and ate everything but their honey masks. He left no clothes; he left no bones.

And when he tired of eating people, he tried to swallow the village whole. He opened his mouth wider and wider until he became the mist drifting everywhere. Until he became the heaviness of the air that pressed down on the remaining villagers. The Manticore became the sharp wind and the grit and the water that swept in to decimate everything.

And the Manticore became the storm that knocked children down and pushed grandfathers up against crumbling walls. And the Manticore leveled homes. And the Manticore felled trees. And the Manticore tore down power lines and sent them whipping to the earth, like crackling serpents. And he surged over embankments. And he came down on the villages in torrential, unending curtains of rain.

And the Manticore became walls of water rushing in to drown us, drowning us, drowning everyone.

---

5. Pangolins, also known as scaly anteaters, are the most trafficked mammals in the world. In Asia and Africa, pangolin meat and scales are used in traditional medicines. In the United States, their skins are used in leather goods.

And the Manticore became the sea.
And the Manticore consumed us all.

■

Author Biography

Talia Lakshmi Kolluri is a South Asian American writer and environmental attorney from Northern California. Her debut collection of short stories, *What We Fed to the Manticore* (Tin House, 2022), was a finalist for the 2023 Carol Shields Prize for Fiction and the 2023 Northern California Book Award for Fiction, was longlisted for the 2023 Andrew Carnegie Medal for Excellence in Fiction, the 2023 Aspen Words Literary Prize, and the 2023 Pen/Robert W. Bingham Prize for Debut Short Story Collection, and was selected as a 2023 ALA RUSA Notable Book. A lifelong Californian, Kolluri lives in the Central Valley with her husband and two cats.

Discuss

1. Analyze the Manticore as both literal creature and environmental metaphor. How do his characteristics—insatiable hunger, ability to become the storm, consumption without satisfaction—reflect aspects of climate change or human environmental impact?
2. Think about the narrator's final acceptance of being eaten by the Manticore. Is this resignation, sacrifice, or transformation?
3. Do you feel this story was successful in getting you to think about ecological issues? Why or why not?

Write

Exploring Climate Fiction: Research the genre of climate fiction (cli-fi) and analyze how "What We Fed to the Manticore" fits within or challenges typical cli-fi conventions. Evaluate the effectiveness of using mythological, weird creatures versus realistic scenarios for communicating environmental urgency.

Common Pigeon

Jane Hirshfield

What if the birds sometimes called "rats with wings" are actually unsung heroes with an impressive list of achievements? Jane Hirshfield's poem, published in 2025, takes an unusual look at the humble pigeon—a creature we often shoo away—and discovers that we have a lot in common with these urban survivors.

Called Rock Dove, *Columba livia*,
Paloma brava, "rats with wings"—
of all birds, surely the most ignored,
dishonored, despised.
No birder exults, adding you to their life list.

On the dinner plate: squab.

And yet:
Able to fly 93 miles per hour on your black-barred wings.

Your longest recorded flight: 7,200 miles,
France to Saigon, in twenty-four days.

One 1918 trench-taken messenger pigeon,
Kaiser, holds your record life-span: thirty-one years.
Also: America's longest-held POW.
First victory-paraded, then kept for breeding.

Another messenger,
shot down and battle-blinded on the Meuse-Argonne line,[1]
took wing again, delivered the capsuled note:
"*We are along the road parallel to 276.4.
Our own artillery is dropping a barrage directly
on us. For heaven's sake, stop it.*"

One hundred and ninety-four soldiers lived.
As did the bird, Cher Ami. Saved by an Army medic,
given the French *Croix de Guerre*,[2]
standing now in a Smithsonian display case, on one taxidermed leg.

Domesticable, a consorter with humans.
For this, your lives treated, too often, as ours are.

Subject—objects—of many studies and books.
For instance, *Making Pigeons Pay: A Manual of Practical
Information on the Management, Selection, Breeding,
Feeding, and Marketing of Pigeons*,
© 1946 by Wendell Mitchell Levi. Once a child who raised pigeons.

Some who keep you in rooftop pens and train you to race
have loved you,
waiting for months for one who didn't return.

City-falcons hunt you.
City-humans, sitting on benches, share with you their bread.

---

1. The Meuse-Argonne was the site of a major World War I offensive (September 26–November 11, 1918) in northeastern France, along the Meuse River and through the Argonne Forest.

2. "*Croix de Guerre*" means "War Cross" in French. It was awarded for feats of bravery by individuals or groups during the two World Wars.

Your ring-necked cousins
arrive each late June to eat my tree's ripening mulberries.
Crows larger, louder, less peaceful, come then to drive them away.

Your average weight, a large coffee mug's twelve ounces.
Your lives in the wild, 2.4 years.
Wing tip to wing tip, roughly twenty-three inches.

Your first-light conversations
held on an air conditioner's twelfth-story pigeon-sized ledge—
even the furious-at-being-wakened recognize this sound as true
affection.

We, who tell children they must not touch you,
gave you this habitat and story,

You are like us. You want to live.
You do what you must. You preen. You scavenge.
Are kept—like us—off places to rest on
only by spools of barbed wire. Are shooed. Are cursed.

Like ours, your newborn are helpless.

You live amidst and between us concealing your nests,
your dead, the first awkward flights
of your young.
You share the tending of eggs, the feeding of hatchlings.

Like us, you have learned the timing of stoplights.
Like us, you are adaptable, resilient, ingenious.
You return, when needed, to dwelling on riverside cliffs.

Meaning: you will be among the slower to vanish.
Meaning also, among the longer to suffer.

You will glean, like us,
this world for as long as you can.
Lift with your strong, slightly comical cere-topped beaks
its joy-scraps, grief-crusts, recalcitrant seeds.

In flocks crowding any corner and park,
you will hide amid flapping flusters and flushes of iridescence
your pigeonish judgments, jokes, meditations;

keep opaque from our knowing also the instruments—
magnetic? aural? optic-nerve sextant?—
of your solitary, almost spiritual, home-seeking navigation.

▪

Author Biography

Jane Hirshfield is the author of *The Asking: New & Selected Poems* (Knopf, 2023), as well as nine previous poetry collections, two books of essays, and four books collecting and co-translating world poets from the deep past. Hirshfield's honors include the Poetry Center Book Award, the California Book Award, and China's Zhongkun International Poetry Award, which she was the first American and the first woman to receive. A chancellor emerita of the Academy of American Poets and an elected member of the American Academy of Arts & Sciences, Hirshfield founded Poets for Science in 2017.

Discuss

1. Why do you think the poet chose to include specific facts and statistics about pigeons (flight speed, distances, weights) alongside more emotional observations?
2. What does the line "You are like us. You want to live. You do what you must" suggest about survival and dignity?
3. What does the poet mean by saying pigeons will be "among the slower to vanish" but also "among the longer to suffer"?

Write

In Defense of the Despised: Choose an animal that is commonly dismissed, feared, or considered a pest (like rats, spiders, mosquitoes, or crows). Research interesting facts about this animal and write an essay that challenges common perceptions about it. Use specific details and comparisons to humans, as the poet does with pigeons, to help readers see the animal in a new light. Be sure to include in-text citations and a Works Cited page, so all the facts can be checked.

Lost in a Pyramid, or the Mummy's Curse

Louisa May Alcott

"I like weird tales," a character in this short story says. We agree. And this one is weird indeed. Louisa May Alcott's gothic tale, published in 1869, follows a young woman who ignores warnings about an ancient Egyptian curse because surely a few "pretty seeds" couldn't possibly be *that* dangerous.

I

"And what are these, Paul?" asked Evelyn, opening a tarnished gold box and examining its contents curiously.

"Seeds of some unknown Egyptian plant," replied Forsyth, with a sudden shadow on his dark face, as he looked down at the three scarlet grains lying in the white hand lifted to him.

"Where did you get them?" asked the girl.

"That is a weird story, which will only haunt you if I tell it," said Forsyth, with an absent expression that strongly excited the girl's curiosity.

"Please tell it, I like weird tales, and they never trouble me. Ah, do tell it; your stories are always so interesting," she cried, looking up with such a pretty blending of entreaty and command in her charming face, that refusal was impossible.

"You'll be sorry for it, and so shall I, perhaps; I warn you beforehand, that harm is foretold to the possessor of those mysterious seeds," said Forsyth, smiling, even while he knit his black brows, and regarded the blooming creature before him with a fond yet foreboding glance.

"Tell on, I'm not afraid of these pretty atoms," she answered, with an imperious nod.

"To hear is to obey. Let me read the facts, and then I will begin," returned Forsyth, pacing to and fro with the far-off look of one who turns the pages of the past.

Evelyn watched him a moment, and then returned to her work, or play, rather, for the task seemed well suited to the vivacious little creature, half-child, half-woman.

"While in Egypt," commenced Forsyth, slowly, "I went one day with my guide and Professor Niles, to explore the Cheops.[1] Niles had a mania for antiquities of all sorts, and forgot time, danger and fatigue in the ardor of his pursuit. We rummaged up and down the narrow passages, half choked with dust and close air; reading inscriptions on the walls, stumbling over shattered mummy-cases, or coming face to face with some shriveled specimen perched like a hobgoblin on the little shelves where the dead used to be stowed away for ages. I was desperately tired after a few hours of it, and begged the professor to return. But he was bent on exploring certain places, and would not desist. We had but one guide, so I was forced to stay; but Jumal, my man, seeing how weary I was, proposed to us to rest in one of the larger passages, while he went to procure another guide for Niles. We consented, and assuring us that we were perfectly safe, if we did not quit the spot, Jumal left us, promising to return speedily. The professor sat down to take notes of his researches, and stretching myself on the soft sand, I fell asleep.

"I was roused by that indescribable thrill which instinctively warns us of danger, and springing up, I found myself alone. One

---

1. The Great Pyramid of Cheops was built on the plateau of Giza and is considered one of the Seven Wonders of the Ancient World.

torch burned faintly where Jumal had struck it, but Niles and the other light were gone. A dreadful sense of loneliness oppressed me for a moment; then I collected myself and looked well about me. A bit of paper was pinned to my hat, which lay near me, and on it, in the professor's writing were these words:

"'I've gone back a little to refresh my memory on certain points. Don't follow me till Jumal comes. I can find my way back to you, for I have a clue. Sleep well, and dream gloriously of the Pharaohs. N N.'

"I laughed at first over the old enthusiast, then felt anxious then restless, and finally resolved to follow him, for I discovered a strong cord fastened to a fallen stone, and knew that this was the clue he spoke of. Leaving a line for Jumal, I took my torch and retraced my steps, following the cord along the winding ways. I often shouted, but received no reply, and pressed on, hoping at each turn to see the old man poring over some musty relic of antiquity. Suddenly the cord ended, and lowering my torch, I saw that the footsteps had gone on.

"'Rash fellow, he'll lose himself, to a certainty,' I thought, really alarmed now.

"As I paused, a faint call reached me, and I answered it, waited, shouted again, and a still fainter echo replied.

"Niles was evidently going on, misled by the reverberations of the low passages. No time was to be lost, and, forgetting myself, I stuck my torch in the deep sand to guide me back to the clue, and ran down the straight path before me, whooping like a madman as I went. I did not mean to lose sight of the light, but in my eagerness to find Niles I turned from the main passage, and, guided by his voice, hastened on. His torch soon gladdened my eyes, and the clutch of his trembling hands told me what agony he had suffered.

"'Let us get out of this horrible place at once,' he said, wiping the great drops off his forehead.

"'Come, we're not far from the clue. I can soon reach it, and then we are safe'; but as I spoke, a chill passed over me, for a perfect labyrinth of narrow paths lay before us.

"Trying to guide myself by such landmarks as I had observed in my hasty passage, I followed the tracks in the sand till I fancied we must be near my light. No glimmer appeared, however, and kneeling down to examine the footprints nearer, I discovered, to my dismay, that I had been following the wrong ones, for among those marked by a deep boot-heel, were prints of bare feet; we had had no guide there, and Jumal wore sandals.

"Rising, I confronted Niles, with the one despairing word, 'Lost!' as I pointed from the treacherous sand to the fast-waning light.

"I thought the old man would be overwhelmed but, to my surprise, he grew quite calm and steady, thought a moment, and then went on, saying, quietly:

"'Other men have passed here before us; let us follow their steps, for, if I do not greatly err, they lead toward great passages, where one's way is easily found.'

"On we went, bravely, till a misstep threw the professor violently to the ground with a broken leg, and nearly extinguished the torch. It was a horrible predicament, and I gave up all hope as I sat beside the poor fellow, who lay exhausted with fatigue, remorse and pain, for I would not leave him.

"'Paul,' he said suddenly, 'if you will not go on, there is one more effort we can make. I remember hearing that a party lost as we are, saved themselves by building a fire. The smoke penetrated further than sound or light, and the guide's quick wit understood the unusual mist; he followed it, and rescued the party. Make a fire and trust to Jumal.'

"'A fire without wood?' I began; but he pointed to a shelf behind me, which had escaped me in the gloom; and on it I saw a slender mummy-case. I understood him, for these dry cases, which lie about in hundreds, are freely used as firewood. Reaching up, I pulled it down, believing it to be empty, but as it fell, it burst open, and out rolled a mummy. Accustomed as I was to such sights, it startled me a little, for danger had unstrung my nerves. Laying the little brown chrysalis aside, I smashed the case, lit the pile with my torch, and soon a light cloud of smoke drifted down the three passages which diverged from the cell-like place where we had paused.

"While busied with the fire, Niles, forgetful of pain and peril, had dragged the mummy nearer, and was examining it with the interest of a man whose ruling passion was strong even in death.

"'Come and help me unroll this. I have always longed to be the first to see and secure the curious treasures put away among the folds of these uncanny winding-sheets.[2] This is a woman, and we may find something rare and precious here,' he said, beginning to unfold the outer coverings, from which a strange aromatic odor came.

"Reluctantly I obeyed, for to me there was something sacred in the bones of this unknown woman. But to beguile the time and amuse the poor fellow, I lent a hand, wondering as I worked, if this dark, ugly thing had ever been a lovely, soft-eyed Egyptian girl.

"From the fibrous folds of the wrappings dropped precious gums and spices, which half intoxicated us with their potent breath, antique coins, and a curious jewel or two, which Niles eagerly examined.

"All the bandages but one were cut off at last, and a small head laid bare, round which still hung great plaits of what had once been luxuriant hair. The shriveled hands were folded on the breast, and clasped in them lay that gold box."

"Ah!" cried Evelyn, dropping it from her rosy palm with a shudder.

"Nay; don't reject the poor little mummy's treasure. I never have quite forgiven myself for stealing it, or for burning her," said

---

2. And you too could have borne witness, if you had been lucky enough to be invited to a mummy unwrapping in the 19th century, which were real events.

Forsyth, painting rapidly, as if the recollection of that experience lent energy to his hand.

"Burning her! Oh, Paul, what do you mean?" asked the girl, sitting up with a face full of excitement.

"I'll tell you. While busied with Madame la Momie, our fire had burned low, for the dry case went like tinder. A faint, far-off sound made our hearts leap, and Niles cried out: 'Pile on the wood; Jumal is tracking us; don't let the smoke fail now or we are lost!'

"'There is no more wood; the case was very small, and is all gone,' I answered, tearing off such of my garments as would burn readily, and piling them upon the embers.

"Niles did the same, but the light fabrics were quickly consumed, and made no smoke.

"'Burn that!' commanded the professor, pointing to the mummy.

"I hesitated a moment. Again came the faint echo of a horn. Life was dear to me. A few dry bones might save us, and I obeyed him in silence.

"A dull blaze sprung up, and a heavy smoke rose from the burning mummy, rolling in volumes through the low passages, and threatening to suffocate us with its fragrant mist. My brain grew dizzy, the light danced before my eyes, strange phantoms seemed to people the air, and, in the act of asking Niles why he gasped and looked so pale, I lost consciousness."

Evelyn drew a long breath, and put away the scented toys from her lap as if their odor oppressed her.

Forsyth's swarthy face was all aglow with the excitement of his story, and his black eyes glittered as he added, with a quick laugh:

"That's all; Jumal found and got us out, and we both forswore pyramids for the rest of our days."

"But the box: how came you to keep it?" asked Evelyn, eyeing it askance as it lay gleaming in a streak of sunshine.

"Oh, I brought it away as a souvenir, and Niles kept the other trinkets."

"But you said harm was foretold to the possessor of those scarlet seeds," persisted the girl, whose fancy was excited by the tale, and who fancied all was not told.

"Among his spoils, Niles found a bit of parchment, which he deciphered, and this inscription said that the mummy we had so ungallantly burned was that of a famous sorceress who bequeathed her curse to whoever should disturb her rest. Of course I don't believe that curse has anything to do with it, but it's a fact that Niles never prospered from that day. He says it's because he has never recovered from the fall and fright and I dare say it is so; but I sometimes wonder if I am to share the curse, for I've a vein of superstition in me, and that poor little mummy haunts my dreams still."

A long silence followed these words. Paul painted mechanically and Evelyn lay regarding him with a thoughtful face. But gloomy fancies were as foreign to her nature as shadows are to noonday, and presently she laughed a cheery laugh, saying as she took up the box again:

"Why don't you plant them, and see what wondrous flower they will bear?"

"I doubt if they would bear anything after lying in a mummy's hand for centuries," replied Forsyth, gravely.

"Let me plant them and try. You know wheat has sprouted and grown that was taken from a mummy's coffin; why should not these pretty seeds? I should so like to watch them grow; may I, Paul?"

"No, I'd rather leave that experiment untried. I have a queer feeling about the matter, and don't want to meddle myself or let anyone I love meddle with these seeds. They may be some horrible poison, or possess some evil power, for the sorceress evidently valued them, since she clutched them fast even in her tomb."

"Now, you are foolishly superstitious, and I laugh at you. Be generous; give me one seed, just to learn if it will grow. See I'll pay for it," and Evelyn, who now stood beside him, dropped a kiss on his forehead as she made her request, with the most engaging air.

But Forsyth would not yield. He smiled and returned the embrace with lover-like warmth, then flung the seeds into the fire, and gave her back the golden box, saying, tenderly:

"My darling, I'll fill it with diamonds or bonbons, if you please, but I will not let you play with that witch's spells. You've enough of your own, so forget the 'pretty seeds' and see what a Light of the Harem I've made of you."

Evelyn frowned, and smiled, and presently the lovers were out in the spring sunshine reveling in their own happy hopes, untroubled by one foreboding fear.

II

"I have a little surprise for you, love," said Forsyth, as he greeted his cousin three months later on the morning of his wedding day.

"And I have one for you," she answered, smiling faintly.

"How pale you are, and how thin you grow! All this bridal bustle is too much for you, Evelyn," he said, with fond anxiety, as he watched the strange pallor of her face, and pressed the wasted little hand in his.

"I am so tired," she said, and leaned her head wearily on her lover's breast. "Neither sleep, food, nor air gives me strength, and a curious mist seems to cloud my mind at times. Mamma says it is the heat, but I shiver even in the sun, while at night I burn with fever. Paul, dear, I'm glad you are going to take me away to lead a quiet, happy life with you, but I'm afraid it will be a very short one."

"My fanciful little wife! You are tired and nervous with all this worry, but a few weeks of rest in the country will give us back our blooming Eve again. Have you no curiosity to learn my surprise?" he asked, to change her thoughts.

The vacant look stealing over the girl's face gave place to one of interest, but as she listened it seemed to require an effort to fix her mind on her lover's words.

"You remember the day we rummaged in the old cabinet?"

"Yes," and a smile touched her lips for a moment.

"And how you wanted to plant those queer red seeds I stole from the mummy?"

"I remember," and her eyes kindled with sudden fire.

"Well, I tossed them into the fire, as I thought, and gave you the box. But when I went back to cover up my picture, and found one of those seeds on the rug, a sudden fancy to gratify your whim led me to send it to Niles and ask him to plant and report on its progress. Today I hear from him for the first time, and he reports that the seed has grown marvelously, has budded, and that he intends to take the first flower, if it blooms in time, to a meeting of famous scientific men, after which he will send me its true name and the plant itself. From his description, it must be very curious, and I'm impatient to see it."

"You need not wait; I can show you the flower in its bloom," and Evelyn beckoned with the mechante[3] smile so long a stranger to her lips.

Much amazed, Forsyth followed her to her own little boudoir, and there, standing in the sunshine, was the unknown plant. Almost rank in their luxuriance were the vivid green leaves on the slender purple stems, and rising from the midst, one ghostly-white flower, shaped like the head of a hooded snake, with scarlet stamens like forked tongues, and on the petals glittered spots like dew.

---

3. "Mechante" means wicked.

"A strange, uncanny flower! Has it any odor?" asked Forsyth, bending to examine it, and forgetting, in his interest, to ask how it came there.

"None, and that disappoints me, I am so fond of perfumes," answered the girl, caressing the green leaves which trembled at her touch, while the purple stems deepened their tint.

"Now tell me about it," said Forsyth, after standing silent for several minutes.

"I had been before you, and secured one of the seeds, for two fell on the rug. I planted it under a glass in the richest soil I could find, watered it faithfully, and was amazed at the rapidity with which it grew when once it appeared above the earth. I told no one, for I meant to surprise you with it; but this bud has been so long in blooming, I have had to wait. It is a good omen that it blossoms today, and as it is nearly white, I mean to wear it, for I've learned to love it, having been my pet for so long."

"I would not wear it, for, in spite of its innocent color, it is an evil-looking plant, with its adder's tongue and unnatural dew. Wait till Niles tells us what it is, then pet it if it is harmless."

"Perhaps my sorceress cherished it for some symbolic beauty—those old Egyptians were full of fancies. It was very sly of you to turn the tables on me in this way. But I forgive you, since in a few hours, I shall chain this mysterious hand forever. How cold it is! Come out into the garden and get some warmth and color for tonight, my love."

But when night came, no one could reproach the girl with her pallor, for she glowed like a pomegranate-flower, her eyes were full of fire, her lips scarlet, and all her old vivacity seemed to have returned. A more brilliant bride never blushed under a misty veil, and when her lover saw her, he was absolutely startled by the almost unearthly beauty which transformed the pale, languid creature of the morning into this radiant woman.

They were married, and if love, many blessings, and all good gifts lavishly showered upon them could make them happy, then this young pair were truly blest. But even in the rapture of the moment that made her his, Forsyth observed how icy cold was the little hand he held, how feverish the deep color on the soft cheek he kissed, and what a strange fire burned in the tender eyes that looked so wistfully at him.

Blithe and beautiful as a spirit, the smiling bride played her part in all the festivities of that long evening, and when at last light, life and color began to fade, the loving eyes that watched her thought it but the natural weariness of the hour. As the last guest departed, Forsyth was met by a servant, who gave him a letter marked "Haste." Tearing it open, he read these lines, from a friend of the professor's:

"DEAR SIR—Poor Niles died suddenly two days ago, while at the Scientific Club, and his last words were: 'Tell Paul Forsyth to beware of the Mummy's Curse, for this fatal flower has killed me.' The circumstances of his death were so peculiar, that I add them as a sequel to this message. For several months, as he told us, he had been watching an unknown plant, and that evening he brought us the flower to examine. Other matters of interest absorbed us till a late hour, and the plant was forgotten. The professor wore it in his buttonhole—a strange white, serpent-headed blossom, with pale glittering spots, which slowly changed to a glittering scarlet, till the leaves looked as if sprinkled with blood. It was observed that instead of the pallor and feebleness which had recently come over him, that the professor was unusually animated, and seemed in an almost unnatural state of high spirits. Near the close of the meeting, in the midst of a lively discussion, he suddenly dropped, as if smitten with apoplexy. He was conveyed home insensible, and after one lucid interval, in which he gave me the message I have recorded above, he died in great agony, raving of mummies, pyramids, serpents, and some fatal curse which had fallen upon him.

"After his death, livid scarlet spots, like those on the flower, appeared upon his skin, and he shriveled like a withered leaf. At my desire, the mysterious plant was examined, and pronounced by the best authority one of the most deadly poisons known to the Egyptian sorceresses. The plant slowly absorbs the vitality of whoever cultivates it, and the blossom, worn for two or three hours, produces either madness or death."

Down dropped the paper from Forsyth's hand; he read no further, but hurried back into the room where he had left his young wife. As if worn out with fatigue, she had thrown herself upon a couch, and lay there motionless, her face half-hidden by the light folds of the veil, which had blown over it.

"Evelyn, my dearest! Wake up and answer me. Did you wear that strange flower today?" whispered Forsyth, putting the misty screen away.

There was no need for her to answer, for there, gleaming spectrally on her bosom, was the evil blossom, its white petals spotted now with flecks of scarlet, vivid as drops of newly spilt blood.

But the unhappy bridegroom scarcely saw it, for the face above it appalled him by its utter vacancy. Drawn and pallid, as if with some wasting malady, the young face, so lovely an hour ago, lay before him aged and blighted by the baleful influence of the plant which had drunk up her life. No recognition in the eyes, no word upon the lips, no motion of the hand—only the faint breath, the fluttering pulse, and wide-opened eyes, betrayed that she was alive.

Alas for the young wife! The superstitious fear at which she had smiled had proved true: the curse that had bided its time for ages was fulfilled at last, and her own hand wrecked her happiness forever. Death in life was her doom, and for years Forsyth secluded himself to tend with pathetic devotion the pale ghost, who never, by word or look, could thank him for the love that outlived even such a fate as this.

▪

Author Biography

Louisa May Alcott was an American author who grew up in a transcendentalist family, which shaped her writing about strong, educated female characters. After working various jobs to support her family and serving as a Civil War nurse, she achieved lasting fame with her novel *Little Women* in 1868, based on her childhood with three sisters that became an instant success. Alcott was also a women's rights advocate who became the first woman to register to vote in Concord and wrote gothic thrillers under pseudonyms. Alcott never married but when her sister died, she adopted her niece. She died in Boston in 1888 at the age of 56.

Discuss

1. The story features an ancient plant from Egypt being cultivated in a completely different climate and ecosystem. What does this suggest about the consequences of removing species from their natural habitats?
2. What does the mummy represent in this story beyond just a source of ancient seeds? Consider themes of disturbing the dead and consequences of theft and defying the past.
3. Examine the story's ending. Is this purely a supernatural tale, or could there be a rational explanation for the events? What evidence supports each interpretation?

Write

Through the Lens of Environmentalism: Write an essay analyzing how the deadly plant represents nature fighting back against human interference. Examine how characters exploit the natural world—burning the mummy as fuel, stealing seeds, removing plants from their native environment—and how these actions lead to consequences. Focus on how the plant behaves like a predator, draining life from its caretakers, and argue whether Alcott suggests that nature punishes those who exploit it.

The City in the Sea

Edgar Allan Poe

Instead of offering comfort and meaning, this poem about death presents us with an impossible, dreamlike vision: a magnificent city ruled by Death, slowly sinking into Hell—a place where the familiar rules of our world don't apply. The poem, which came out in 1895, makes us uncomfortable not through jump scares or gore, but through its eerie stillness and its suggestion that all human achievement—no matter how grand—ultimately belongs to Death. By making the familiar strange, Edgar Allan Poe helps us see a truth we normally avoid: our own mortality and the futility of pretending our accomplishments will outlast us. Basically, we are all going down, my friends.

Lo! Death has reared himself a throne
In a strange city lying alone
Far down within the dim West,
Where the good and the bad and the worst and the best
Have gone to their eternal rest.
There shrines and palaces and towers
(Time-eaten towers that tremble not!)
Resemble nothing that is ours.
Around, by lifting winds forgot,
Resignedly beneath the sky
The melancholy waters lie.

No rays from the holy heaven come down
On the long night-time of that town;
But light from out the lurid sea
Streams up the turrets silently—
Gleams up the pinnacles far and free—
Up domes—up spires—up kingly halls—
Up fanes[1]—up Babylon-like walls[2]—
Up shadowy long-forgotten bowers
Of scultured[3] ivy and stone flowers—
Up many and many a marvelous shrine
Whose wreathed friezes intertwine
The viol, the violet, and the vine.[4]

Resignedly beneath the sky
The melancholy waters lie.
So blend the turrets and shadows there
That all seem pendulous in air,
While from a proud tower in the town
Death looks gigantically down.
There open fanes and gaping graves
Yawn level with the luminous waves;
But not the riches there that lie

---

1. "Fanes" is an archaic word for places of worship.

2. Babylon was an ancient Mesopotamian city famous for its wealth and eventual destruction. In the Bible, Babylon symbolizes human pride, moral corruption, and the inevitable fall.

3. "Scultured" is another spelling of "sculptured."

4. This line combines three symbols: the viol (a stringed musical instrument representing art and culture), the violet (a flower representing beauty and fragility), and the vine (a plant that both decorates and slowly destroys structures as it grows).

In each idol's diamond eye[5]—
Not the gaily-jeweled dead
Tempt the waters from their bed;
For no ripples curl, alas!
Along that wilderness of glass—
No swellings tell that winds may be
Upon some far-off happier sea—
No heavings hint that winds have been
On seas less hideously serene.

But lo, a stir is in the air!
The wave—there is a movement there!
As if the towers had thrown aside,
In slightly sinking, the dull tide—
As if their tops had feebly given
A void within the filmy Heaven.
The waves have now a redder glow—
The hours are breathing faint and low—
And when, amid no earthly moans,
Down, down that town shall settle hence,
Hell, rising from a thousand thrones,
Shall do it reverence.

▪

5. The submerged city contains pagan idols with jeweled eyes—symbols of both religious devotion and material wealth, suggesting that what humans value most means absolutely nothing to natural forces.

Author Biography

Edgar Allan Poe was an American writer who helped pioneer the modern horror story, detective fiction, and psychological thriller. Orphaned at age three, Poe struggled with poverty, alcoholism, and personal tragedy throughout his short life, including losing his young wife Virginia to tuberculosis in 1847. Despite his troubles—or perhaps inspired by them—he produced some of American literature's most remembered works, often about death, decay, and madness. Adding to the weirdness, he died at 40 after being found delirious on a Baltimore street. The cause of his death remains a mystery.

Discuss

1. How does the poem's dreamlike, surreal quality help convey its message about death differently than a straightforward, realistic poem might?
2. Why do you think Poe describes light coming "up" from the sea rather than down from heaven? What does this reversal suggest about the nature of this city?
3. Does the "weird" atmosphere make the subject more or less frightening?

Write

Weird Re-Imagining: Write a description of a familiar place (your bedroom, a campus building, a coffee shop) but make it "weird" by changing one fundamental rule of how that space works—perhaps gravity works differently, time moves strangely, or light behaves in an unnatural way. Like Poe, use specific sensory details and maintain a consistent eerie atmosphere. Your goal is to make the familiar feel unsettling without using gore or obvious horror elements.

The Colour Out of Space

H. P. Lovecraft

H. P. Lovecraft's 1927 short story—written in British English although he was American—stands as a pioneering work of ecological horror, anticipating our modern anxieties about environmental contamination and irreversible damage to ecosystems. The alien presence functions as a kind of cosmic pollutant, transforming fertile farmland into a sterile "blasted heath" through processes that defy scientific understanding. Through the systematic corruption of soil, water, vegetation, and all living creatures, Lovecraft dramatizes the terrifying fragility of the pastoral world and humanity's utter dependence on a stable, life-sustaining environment.

West of Arkham[1] the hills rise wild, and there are valleys with deep woods that no axe has ever cut. There are dark narrow glens where the trees slope fantastically, and where thin brooklets trickle without ever having caught the glint of sunlight. On the gentler slopes there are farms, ancient and rocky, with squat, moss-coated cottages brooding eternally over old New England secrets in the lee of great ledges; but these are all vacant now, the wide chimneys crumbling and the shingled sides bulging perilously beneath low gambrel roofs.

---

1. Arkham is a fictional city in Massachusetts that is featured in several of Lovecraft's stories.

The old folk have gone away, and foreigners do not like to live there. French-Canadians have tried it, Italians have tried it, and the Poles have come and departed. It is not because of anything that can be seen or heard or handled, but because of something that is imagined. The place is not good for the imagination and does not bring restful dreams at night. It must be this which keeps the foreigners away, for old Ammi Pierce has never told them of anything he recalls from the strange days. Ammi, whose head has been a little queer for years, is the only one who still remains, or whoever talks of the strange days; and he dares to do this because his house is so near the open fields and the travelled roads around Arkham.

There was once a road over the hills and through the valleys that ran straight where the blasted heath is now, but people ceased to use it and a new road was laid curving far toward the south. Traces of the old one can still be found amidst the weeds of a returning wilderness, and some of them will doubtless linger even when half the hollows are flooded for the new reservoir. Then the dark woods will be cut down and the blasted heath will slumber far below blue waters whose surface will mirror the sky and ripple in the sun. And the secrets of the strange days will be one with the deep's secrets; one with the hidden lore of old ocean, and all the mystery of primal earth.

When I went into the hills and vales to survey for the new reservoir they told me the place was evil. They told me this in Arkham, and because that is a very old town full of witch legends, I thought the evil must be something which grandams had whispered to children through centuries. The name "blasted heath" seemed to me very odd and theatrical, and I wondered how it had come into the folklore of a Puritan people. Then I saw that dark westward tangle of glens and slopes for myself and ceased to wonder at anything besides its own elder mystery. It was morning when I saw it, but shadow lurked always there. The trees grew too thickly, and their trunks were too big for any healthy New England wood.[2] There was too much silence in the dim alleys between them, and the floor was too soft with the dank moss and mattings of infinite years of decay.

In the open spaces, mostly along the line of the old road, there were little hillside farms; sometimes with all the buildings standing, sometimes with only one or two, and sometimes with only a lone chimney or fast-filling cellar. Weeds and briers reigned, and furtive wild things rustled in the undergrowth. Upon everything was a haze of restlessness and oppression; a touch of the unreal and the grotesque, as if some vital element of perspective or chiaroscuro[3] were awry. I did not wonder that the foreigners would not stay, for this was no region to sleep in. It was too much like a landscape of Salvator Rosa;[4] too much like some forbidden woodcut in a tale of terror.

But even all this was not so bad as the blasted heath. I knew it the moment I came upon it at the bottom of a spacious valley; for no other name could fit such a thing, or any other thing fit such a name. It was as if the poet had coined the phrase from having seen this one particular region. It must, I thought as I viewed it, be the outcome of a fire; but why had nothing new ever grown over those five acres of grey desolation that sprawled open to the sky like a great spot eaten by acid in the woods and fields? It lay largely to the north of the ancient road line, but encroached a little on the other side. I felt an odd reluctance about approaching, and did so at last only because my business took me through and past it. There was no vegetation of any kind on that broad

---

2. When the trees grow unnaturally thick, they don't allow light to reach the floor of the forest and support life there.

3. Chiaroscuro is the treatment of light in a painting.

4. Salvator Rosa (1615–1673) was an Italian painter known for creating landscapes of dark, untamed wilderness.

expanse, but only a fine grey dust or ash which no wind seemed ever to blow about. The trees near it were sickly and stunted, and many dead trunks stood or lay rotting at the rim.

As I walked hurriedly by I saw the tumbled bricks and stones of an old chimney and cellar on my right, and the yawning black maw of an abandoned well whose stagnant vapours played strange tricks with the hues of the sunlight. Even the long, dark woodland climb beyond seemed welcome in contrast, and I marvelled no more at the frightened whispers of Arkham people. There had been no house or ruin near; even in the old days the place must have been lonely and remote. And at twilight, dreading to repass that ominous spot, I walked circuitously back to the town by the curving road on the south. I vaguely wished some clouds would gather, for an odd timidity about the deep skyey[5] voids above had crept into my soul.

In the evening I asked old people in Arkham about the blasted heath, and what was meant by that phrase "strange days" which so many evasively muttered. I could not, however, get any good answers, except that all the mystery was much more recent than I had dreamed. It was not a matter of old legendry at all, but something within the lifetime of those who spoke. It had happened in the 'eighties, and a family had disappeared or was killed. Speakers would not be exact; and because they all told me to pay no attention to old Ammi Pierce's crazy tales, I sought him out the next morning, having heard that he lived alone in the ancient tottering cottage where the trees first begin to get very thick. It was a fearsomely archaic place, and had begun to exude the faint miasmal odour which clings about houses that have stood too long. Only with persistent knocking could I rouse the aged man, and when he shuffled timidly to the door I could tell he was not glad to see me. He was not so feeble as I had expected; but his

---

5. "Skyey" means of or related to the sky.

eyes drooped in a curious way, and his unkempt clothing and white beard made him seem very worn and dismal.

Not knowing just how he could best be launched on his tales, I feigned a matter of business; told him of my surveying, and asked vague questions about the district. He was far brighter and more educated than I had been led to think, and before I knew it had grasped quite as much of the subject as any man I had talked with in Arkham. He was not like other rustics I had known in the sections where reservoirs were to be. From him there were no protests at the miles of old wood and farmland to be blotted out, though perhaps there would have been had not his home lain outside the bounds of the future lake. Relief was all that he shewed; relief at the doom of the dark ancient valleys through which he had roamed all his life. They were better under water now—better under water since the strange days. And with this opening his husky voice sank low, while his body leaned forward and his right forefinger began to point shakily and impressively.

It was then that I heard the story, and as the rambling voice scraped and whispered on I shivered again and again despite the summer day. Often I had to recall the speaker from ramblings, piece out scientific points which he knew only by a fading parrot memory of professors' talk, or bridge over gaps where his sense of logic and continuity broke down. When he was done I did not wonder that his mind had snapped a trifle, or that the folk of Arkham would not speak much of the blasted heath. I hurried back before sunset to my hotel, unwilling to have the stars come out above me in the open; and the next day returned to Boston to give up my position. I could not go into that dim chaos of old forest and slope again, or face another time that grey blasted heath where the black well yawned deep beside the tumbled bricks and stones. The reservoir will soon be built now, and all those elder secrets will be safe forever under watery fathoms. But even then I do not believe I would like to visit that country by night—at least, not when the sinister stars are out; and nothing could bribe me to drink the new city water of Arkham.

It all began, old Ammi said, with the meteorite. Before that time there had been no wild legends at all since the witch trials, and even then these western woods were not feared half so much as the small island in the Miskatonic[6] where the devil held court beside a curious stone altar older than the Indians. These were not haunted woods, and their fantastic dusk was never terrible till the strange days. Then there had come that white noontide cloud, that string of explosions in the air, and that pillar of smoke from the valley far in the wood. And by night all Arkham had heard of the great rock that fell out of the sky and bedded itself in the ground beside the well at the Nahum Gardner place. That was the house which had stood where the blasted heath was to come—the trim white Nahum Gardner house amidst its fertile gardens and orchards.

Nahum had come to town to tell people about the stone, and had dropped in at Ammi Pierce's on the way. Ammi was forty then, and all the queer things were fixed very strongly in his mind. He and his wife had gone with the three professors from Miskatonic University who hastened out the next morning to see the weird visitor from unknown stellar space, and had wondered why Nahum had called it so large the day before. It had shrunk, Nahum said as he pointed out the big brownish mound above the ripped earth and charred grass near the archaic well-sweep in his front yard; but the wise men answered that stones do not shrink. Its heat lingered persistently, and Nahum declared it had glowed faintly in the night. The professors tried it with a geologist's hammer and found it was oddly soft. It was, in truth, so soft as to be almost plastic; and they gouged rather than chipped a specimen

6. "Miskatonic" is a made-up word referring to the imaginary river that runs through Lovecraft's Arkham. Also, perhaps a great name for your next cat.

to take back to the college for testing. They took it in an old pail borrowed from Nahum's kitchen, for even the small piece refused to grow cool. On the trip back they stopped at Ammi's to rest, and seemed thoughtful when Mrs. Pierce remarked that the fragment was growing smaller and burning the bottom of the pail. Truly, it was not large, but perhaps they had taken less than they thought.

The day after that—all this was in June of '82—the professors had trooped out again in a great excitement. As they passed Ammi's they told him what queer things the specimen had done, and how it had faded wholly away when they put it in a glass beaker. The beaker had gone, too, and the wise men talked of the strange stone's affinity for silicon. It had acted quite unbelievably in that well-ordered laboratory; doing nothing at all and shewing no occluded gases when heated on charcoal, being wholly negative in the borax bead, and soon proving itself absolutely non-volatile at any producible temperature, including that of the oxy-hydrogen blowpipe. On an anvil it appeared highly malleable, and in the dark its luminosity was very marked. Stubbornly refusing to grow cool, it soon had the college in a state of real excitement; and when upon heating before the spectroscope it displayed shining bands unlike any known colours of the normal spectrum there was much breathless talk of new elements, bizarre optical properties, and other things which puzzled men of science are wont to say when faced by the unknown.

Hot as it was, they tested it in a crucible with all the proper reagents. Water did nothing. Hydrochloric acid was the same. Nitric acid and even aqua regia merely hissed and spattered against its torrid invulnerability. Ammi had difficulty in recalling all these things, but recognised some solvents as I mentioned them in the usual order of use. There were ammonia and caustic soda, alcohol and ether, nauseous carbon disulphide and a dozen others; but although the weight grew steadily less as time passed, and the fragment seemed to be slightly cooling, there was no change in the solvents to shew that they had attacked the substance at all. It was a metal, though, beyond a doubt. It was magnetic, for one thing; and after its immersion in the acid solvents there seemed to be faint traces of the Widmannstätten figures[7] found on meteoric iron. When the cooling had grown very considerable, the testing was carried on in glass; and it was in a glass beaker that they left all the chips made of the original fragment during the work. The next morning both chips and beaker were gone without trace, and only a charred spot marked the place on the wooden shelf where they had been.

All this the professors told Ammi as they paused at his door, and once more he went with them to see the stony messenger from the stars, though this time his wife did not accompany him. It had now most certainly shrunk, and even the sober professors could not doubt the truth of what they saw. All around the dwindling brown lump near the well was a vacant space, except where the earth had caved in; and whereas it had been a good seven feet across the day before, it was now scarcely five. It was still hot, and the sages studied its surface curiously as they detached another and larger piece with hammer and chisel. They gouged deeply this time, and as they pried away the smaller mass they saw that the core of the thing was not quite homogeneous.

They had uncovered what seemed to be the side of a large coloured globule imbedded in the substance. The colour, which resembled some of the bands in the meteor's strange spectrum, was almost impossible to describe; and it was only by analogy that they called it colour at all. Its texture was glossy, and upon tapping it appeared to promise both brittleness and hollowness. One of the professors gave it a smart blow with a hammer, and

---

7. Named after the scientist who discovered them in 1808, Widmannstätten patterns can be found on some meteorites and are the result of interlocking metallic crystals, a design that has no earthly equivalent. Yes, read that again.

it burst with a nervous little pop. Nothing was emitted, and all trace of the thing vanished with the puncturing. It left behind a hollow spherical space about three inches across, and all thought it probable that others would be discovered as the enclosing substance wasted away.

Conjecture was vain; so after a futile attempt to find additional globules by drilling, the seekers left again with their new specimen—which proved, however, as baffling in the laboratory as its predecessor had been. Aside from being almost plastic, having heat, magnetism, and slight luminosity, cooling slightly in powerful acids, possessing an unknown spectrum, wasting away in air, and attacking silicon compounds with mutual destruction as a result, it presented no identifying features whatsoever; and at the end of the tests the college scientists were forced to own that they could not place it. It was nothing of this earth, but a piece of the great outside; and as such dowered[8] with outside properties and obedient to outside laws.

That night there was a thunderstorm, and when the professors went out to Nahum's the next day they met with a bitter disappointment. The stone, magnetic as it had been, must have had some peculiar electrical property; for it had "drawn the lightning," as Nahum said, with a singular persistence. Six times within an hour the farmer saw the lightning strike the furrow in the front yard, and when the storm was over nothing remained but a ragged pit by the ancient well-sweep, half-choked with caved-in earth. Digging had borne no fruit, and the scientists verified the fact of the utter vanishment. The failure was total; so that nothing was left to do but go back to the laboratory and test again the disappearing fragment left carefully cased in lead. That fragment lasted a week, at the end of which nothing of value

8. "Dowered" means to endow or to supply as part of a dowry (the traditional gift of money or other valuables paid from a woman's family to the man she's marrying).

had been learned of it. When it had gone, no residue was left behind, and in time the professors felt scarcely sure they had indeed seen with waking eyes that cryptic vestige of the fathomless gulfs outside; that lone, weird message from other universes and other realms of matter, force, and entity.

As was natural, the Arkham papers made much of the incident with its collegiate sponsoring, and sent reporters to talk with Nahum Gardner and his family. At least one Boston daily also sent a scribe, and Nahum quickly became a kind of local celebrity. He was a lean, genial person of about fifty, living with his wife and three sons on the pleasant farmstead in the valley. He and Ammi exchanged visits frequently, as did their wives; and Ammi had nothing but praise for him after all these years. He seemed slightly proud of the notice his place had attracted, and talked often of the meteorite in the succeeding weeks. That July and August were hot, and Nahum worked hard at his haying in the ten-acre pasture across Chapman's Brook; his rattling wain[9] wearing deep ruts in the shadowy lanes between. The labour tired him more than it had in other years, and he felt that age was beginning to tell on him.

Then fell the time of fruit and harvest. The pears and apples slowly ripened, and Nahum vowed that his orchards were prospering as never before. The fruit was growing to phenomenal size and unwonted gloss, and in such abundance that extra barrels were ordered to handle the future crop. But with the ripening came sore disappointment; for of all that gorgeous array of specious lusciousness not one single jot was fit to eat. Into the fine flavour of the pears and apples had crept a stealthy bitterness and sickishness, so that even the smallest of bites induced a lasting disgust. It was the same with the melons and tomatoes, and Nahum sadly saw that his entire crop was lost. Quick to connect

9. A wain is a horse-drawn cart.

events, he declared that the meteorite had poisoned the soil, and thanked heaven that most of the other crops were in the upland lot along the road.

Winter came early, and was very cold. Ammi saw Nahum less often than usual, and observed that he had begun to look worried. The rest of his family, too, seemed to have grown taciturn; and were far from steady in their churchgoing or their attendance at the various social events of the countryside. For this reserve or melancholy no cause could be found, though all the household confessed now and then to poorer health and a feeling of vague disquiet. Nahum himself gave the most definite statement of anyone when he said he was disturbed about certain footprints in the snow. They were the usual winter prints of red squirrels, white rabbits, and foxes, but the brooding farmer professed to see something not quite right about their nature and arrangement. He was never specific, but appeared to think that they were not as characteristic of the anatomy and habits of squirrels and rabbits and foxes as they ought to be. Ammi listened without interest to this talk until one night when he drove past Nahum's house in his sleigh on the way back from Clark's Corners. There had been a moon, and a rabbit had run across the road, and the leaps of that rabbit were longer than either Ammi or his horse liked. The latter, indeed, had almost run away when brought up by a firm rein. Thereafter Ammi gave Nahum's tales more respect, and wondered why the Gardner dogs seemed so cowed and quivering every morning. They had, it developed, nearly lost the spirit to bark.

In February, the McGregor boys from Meadow Hill were out shooting woodchucks, and not far from the Gardner place bagged a very peculiar specimen. The proportions of its body seemed slightly altered in a queer way impossible to describe, while its face had taken on an expression which no one ever saw in a woodchuck before. The boys were genuinely frightened, and threw the thing away at once, so that only their grotesque tales of it ever reached the people of the countryside. But the shying of the horses near Nahum's house had now become an acknowledged thing, and all the basis for a cycle of whispered legend was fast taking form.

People vowed that the snow melted faster around Nahum's than it did anywhere else, and early in March there was an awed discussion in Potter's general store at Clark's Corners. Stephen Rice had driven past Gardner's in the morning, and had noticed the skunk-cabbages coming up through the mud by the woods across the road. Never were things of such size seen before, and they held strange colours that could not be put into any words. Their shapes were monstrous, and the horse had snorted at an odour which struck Stephen as wholly unprecedented. That afternoon several persons drove past to see the abnormal growth, and all agreed that plants of that kind ought never to sprout in a healthy world. The bad fruit of the fall before was freely mentioned, and it went from mouth to mouth that there was poison in Nahum's ground. Of course it was the meteorite; and remembering how strange the men from the college had found that stone to be, several farmers spoke about the matter to them.

One day they paid Nahum a visit; but having no love of wild tales and folklore were very conservative in what they inferred. The plants were certainly odd, but all skunk-cabbages are more or less odd in shape and odour and hue. Perhaps some mineral element from the stone had entered the soil, but it would soon be washed away. And as for the footprints and frightened horses—of course this was mere country talk which such a phenomenon as the aërolite[10] would be certain to start. There was really nothing

10. "Aërolite" is another way to say stony meteorite. The term literally means "a stone from the air."

for serious men to do in cases of wild gossip, for superstitious rustics will say and believe anything. And so all through the strange days the professors stayed away in contempt. Only one of them, when given two phials of dust for analysis in a police job over a year and a half later, recalled that the queer colour of that skunk-cabbage had been very like one of the anomalous bands of light shewn by the meteor fragment in the college spectroscope, and like the brittle globule found imbedded in the stone from the abyss. The samples in this analysis case gave the same odd bands at first, though later they lost the property.

The trees budded prematurely around Nahum's, and at night they swayed ominously in the wind. Nahum's second son Thaddeus, a lad of fifteen, swore that they swayed also when there was no wind; but even the gossips would not credit this. Certainly, however, restlessness was in the air. The entire Gardner family developed the habit of stealthy listening, though not for any sound which they could consciously name. The listening was, indeed, rather a product of moments when consciousness seemed half to slip away. Unfortunately such moments increased week by week, till it became common speech that "something was wrong with all Nahum's folks." When the early saxifrage[11] came out it had another strange colour; not quite like that of the skunk-cabbage, but plainly related and equally unknown to anyone who saw it. Nahum took some blossoms to Arkham and shewed them to the editor of the Gazette, but that dignitary did no more than write a humorous article about them, in which the dark fears of rustics were held up to polite ridicule. It was a mistake of Nahum's to tell a stolid city man about the way the great, overgrown mourning-cloak butterflies behaved in connexion with these saxifrages.

---

11. A small flowering plant, "saxifrage" comes from the Latin word meaning "stone breaker."

April brought a kind of madness to the country folk, and began that disuse of the road past Nahum's which led to its ultimate abandonment. It was the vegetation. All the orchard trees blossomed forth in strange colours, and through the stony soil of the yard and adjacent pasturage there sprang up a bizarre growth which only a botanist could connect with the proper flora of the region. No sane wholesome colours were anywhere to be seen except in the green grass and leafage; but everywhere those hectic and prismatic variants of some diseased, underlying primary tone without a place among the known tints of earth. The Dutchman's breeches became a thing of sinister menace, and the bloodroots grew insolent in their chromatic perversion. Ammi and the Gardners thought that most of the colours had a sort of haunting familiarity, and decided that they reminded one of the brittle globule in the meteor.

Nahum ploughed and sowed the ten-acre pasture and the upland lot, but did nothing with the land around the house. He knew it would be of no use, and hoped that the summer's strange growths would draw all the poison from the soil. He was prepared for almost anything now, and had grown used to the sense of something near him waiting to be heard. The shunning of his house by neighbours told on him, of course; but it told on his wife more. The boys were better off, being at school each day; but they could not help being frightened by the gossip. Thaddeus, an especially sensitive youth, suffered the most.

In May the insects came, and Nahum's place became a nightmare of buzzing and crawling. Most of the creatures seemed not quite usual in their aspects and motions, and their nocturnal habits contradicted all former experience. The Gardners took to watching at night—watching in all directions at random for something ... they could not tell what. It was then that they all owned that Thaddeus had been right about the trees. Mrs. Gardner was the next to see it from the window as she watched the swollen boughs of a maple against a moonlit sky. The boughs surely moved, and there was no wind. It must be the sap. Strangeness had come into everything growing now. Yet it was none of Nahum's family at all who made the next discovery. Familiarity had dulled them, and what they could not see was glimpsed by a timid windmill salesman from Bolton who drove by one night in ignorance of the country legends. What he told in Arkham was given a short paragraph in the *Gazette*; and it was there that all the farmers, Nahum included, saw it first. The night had been dark and the buggy-lamps faint, but around a farm in the valley which everyone knew from the account must be Nahum's the darkness had been less thick. A dim though distinct luminosity seemed to inhere in all the vegetation, grass, leaves, and blossoms alike, while at one moment a detached piece of the phosphorescence appeared to stir furtively in the yard near the barn.

The grass had so far seemed untouched, and the cows were freely pastured in the lot near the house, but toward the end of May the milk began to be bad. Then Nahum had the cows driven to the uplands, after which the trouble ceased. Not long after this the change in grass and leaves became apparent to the eye. All the verdure was going grey, and was developing a highly singular quality of brittleness. Ammi was now the only person who ever visited the place, and his visits were becoming fewer and fewer. When school closed the Gardners were virtually cut off from the world, and sometimes let Ammi do their errands in town. They were failing curiously both physically and mentally, and no one was surprised when the news of Mrs. Gardner's madness stole around.

It happened in June, about the anniversary of the meteor's fall, and the poor woman screamed about things in the air which she could not describe. In her raving there was not a single specific noun, but only verbs and pronouns. Things moved and changed and fluttered, and ears tingled to impulses which were not wholly sounds. Something was taken away—she was being drained of something—something was fastening itself on her that ought not to be—someone must make it keep off—nothing was ever still in the night—the walls and windows shifted. Nahum did not send her to the county asylum, but let her wander about the house as long as she was harmless to herself and others. Even when her expression changed he did nothing. But when the boys grew afraid of her, and Thaddeus nearly fainted at the way she made faces at him, he decided to keep her locked in the attic. By July she had ceased to speak and crawled on all fours, and before that month was over Nahum got the mad notion that she was slightly luminous in the dark, as he now clearly saw was the case with the nearby vegetation.

It was a little before this that the horses had stampeded. Something had aroused them in the night, and their neighing and kicking in their stalls had been terrible. There seemed virtually nothing to do to calm them, and when Nahum opened the stable door they all bolted out like frightened woodland deer. It took a week to track all four, and when found they were seen to be quite useless and unmanageable. Something had snapped in their brains, and each one had to be shot for its own good. Nahum borrowed a horse from Ammi for his haying, but found it would not approach the barn. It shied, balked, and whinnied, and in the end he could do nothing but drive it into the yard while the men used their own strength to get the heavy wagon near enough the hayloft for convenient pitching. And all the while the vegetation was turning grey and brittle. Even the flowers whose hues had been so strange were greying now, and the fruit was coming out grey and dwarfed and tasteless. The asters and goldenrod bloomed grey and distorted, and the roses and zinneas and hollyhocks in the front yard were such blasphemous-looking things that Nahum's oldest boy Zenas cut them down. The strangely puffed insects died about that time, even the bees that had left their hives and taken to the woods.

By September all the vegetation was fast crumbling to a greyish powder, and Nahum feared that the trees would die before the poison was out of the soil. His wife now had spells of terrific screaming, and he and the boys were in a constant state of nervous tension. They shunned people now, and when school opened the boys did not go. But it was Ammi, on one of his rare visits, who first realised that the well water was no longer good. It had an evil taste that was not exactly foetid[12] nor exactly salty, and Ammi advised his friend to dig another well on higher ground to use till the soil was good again. Nahum, however, ignored the warning, for he had by that time become calloused to strange and unpleasant things. He and the boys continued to use the tainted supply, drinking it as listlessly and mechanically as they ate their meagre and ill-cooked meals and did their thankless and monotonous chores through the aimless days. There was something of stolid resignation about them all, as if they walked half in another world between lines of nameless guards to a certain and familiar doom.

Thaddeus went mad in September after a visit to the well. He had gone with a pail and had come back empty-handed, shrieking and waving his arms, and sometimes lapsing into an inane titter or a whisper about "the moving colours down there." Two in one family was pretty bad, but Nahum was very brave about it. He let the boy run about for a week until he began stumbling and hurting himself, and then he shut him in an attic room across the hall from his mother's. The way they screamed at each other from behind their locked doors was very terrible, especially to little Merwin, who fancied they talked in some terrible language that was not of earth. Merwin was getting frightfully imaginative, and his restlessness was worse after the shutting away of the brother who had been his greatest playmate.

---

12. "Foetid" is the British spelling of "fetid," a disgusting smell.

Almost at the same time the mortality among the livestock commenced. Poultry turned greyish and died very quickly, their meat being found dry and noisome upon cutting. Hogs grew inordinately fat, then suddenly began to undergo loathsome changes which no one could explain. Their meat was of course useless, and Nahum was at his wit's end. No rural veterinary would approach his place, and the city veterinary from Arkham was openly baffled. The swine began growing grey and brittle and falling to pieces before they died, and their eyes and muzzles developed singular alterations. It was very inexplicable, for they had never been fed from the tainted vegetation. Then something struck the cows. Certain areas or sometimes the whole body would be uncannily shrivelled or compressed, and atrocious collapses or disintegrations were common. In the last stages—and death was always the result—there would be a greying and turning brittle like that which beset the hogs. There could be no question of poison, for all the cases occurred in a locked and undisturbed barn. No bites of prowling things could have brought the virus, for what live beast of earth can pass through solid obstacles? It must be only natural disease—yet what disease could wreak such results was beyond any mind's guessing. When the harvest came there was not an animal surviving on the place, for the stock and poultry were dead and the dogs had run away. These dogs, three in number, had all vanished one night and were never heard of again. The five cats had left some time before, but their going was scarcely noticed since there now seemed to be no mice, and only Mrs. Gardner had made pets of the graceful felines.

On the nineteenth of October, Nahum staggered into Ammi's house with hideous news. The death had come to poor Thaddeus in his attic room, and it had come in a way which could not be told. Nahum had dug a grave in the railed family plot behind the farm, and had put therein what he found. There could have been nothing from outside, for the small barred window and locked door were intact; but it was much as it had been in the barn. Ammi and his wife consoled the stricken man as best they could, but shuddered as they did so. Stark terror seemed to cling round the Gardners and all they touched, and the very presence of one in the house was a breath from regions unnamed and unnamable. Ammi accompanied Nahum home with the greatest reluctance, and did what he might to calm the hysterical sobbing of little Merwin. Zenas needed no calming. He had come of late to do nothing but stare into space and obey what his father told him; and Ammi thought that his fate was very merciful. Now and then Merwin's screams were answered faintly from the attic, and in response to an inquiring look Nahum said that his wife was getting very feeble.

When night approached, Ammi managed to get away; for not even friendship could make him stay in that spot when the faint glow of the vegetation began and the trees may or may not have swayed without wind. It was really lucky for Ammi that he was not more imaginative. Even as things were, his mind was bent ever so slightly; but had he been able to connect and reflect upon all the portents around him he must inevitably have turned a total maniac. In the twilight he hastened home, the screams of the mad woman and the nervous child ringing horribly in his ears.

Three days later, Nahum lurched into Ammi's kitchen in the early morning, and in the absence of his host stammered out a desperate tale once more, while Mrs. Pierce listened in a clutching fright. It was little Merwin this time. He was gone. He had gone out late at night with a lantern and pail for water, and had never come back. He'd been going to pieces for days, and hardly knew what he was about. Screamed at everything. There had been a frantic shriek from the yard then, but before the father could get to the door, the boy was gone. There was no glow from the lantern he had taken, and of the child himself no trace. At the time Nahum thought the lantern and pail were gone too; but when dawn came, and the man had plodded back from his all-night search of the woods and fields, he had found some very curious things near the well. There was a crushed and apparently somewhat melted mass of iron which had certainly been the lantern; while a bent bail and twisted iron hoops beside it, both half-fused, seemed to hint at the remnants of the pail. That was all.

Nahum was past imagining, Mrs. Pierce was blank, and Ammi, when he had reached home and heard the tale, could give no guess. Merwin was gone, and there would be no use in telling the people around, who shunned all Gardners now. No use, either, in telling the city people at Arkham who laughed at everything. Thad was gone, and now Merwin was gone. Something was creeping and creeping and waiting to be seen and felt and heard. Nahum would go soon, and he wanted Ammi to look after his wife and Zenas if they survived him. It must all be a judgment of some sort; though he could not fancy what for, since he had always walked uprightly in the Lord's ways so far as he knew.

For over two weeks Ammi saw nothing of Nahum; and then, worried about what might have happened, he overcame his fears and paid the Gardner place a visit. There was no smoke from the great chimney, and for a moment the visitor was apprehensive of the worst. The aspect of the whole farm was shocking—greyish withered grass and leaves on the ground, vines falling in brittle wreckage from archaic walls and gables, and great bare trees clawing up at the grey November sky with a studied malevolence which Ammi could not but feel had come from some subtle change in the tilt of the branches. But Nahum was alive, after all. He was weak, and lying on a couch in the low-ceiled kitchen, but perfectly conscious and able to give simple orders to Zenas. The room was deadly cold; and as Ammi visibly shivered, the host shouted huskily to Zenas for more wood. Wood, indeed, was sorely needed; since the cavernous fireplace was unlit and empty, with a cloud of soot blowing about in the chill wind that came down the chimney. Presently Nahum asked him if the extra wood had made him any more comfortable, and then Ammi saw what had happened. The stoutest cord had broken at last, and the hapless farmer's mind was proof against more sorrow.

Questioning tactfully, Ammi could get no clear data at all about the missing Zenas. "In the well—he lives in the well—" was all that the clouded father would say. Then there flashed across the visitor's mind a sudden thought of the mad wife, and he changed his line of inquiry. "Nabby? Why, here she is!" was the surprised response of poor Nahum, and Ammi soon saw that he must search for himself. Leaving the harmless babbler on the couch, he took the keys from their nail beside the door and climbed the creaking stairs to the attic. It was very close and noisome up there, and no sound could be heard from any direction. Of the four doors in sight, only one was locked, and on this he tried various keys on the ring he had taken. The third key proved the right one, and after some fumbling Ammi threw open the low white door.

It was quite dark inside, for the window was small and half-obscured by the crude wooden bars; and Ammi could see nothing at all on the wide-planked floor. The stench was beyond enduring, and before proceeding further he had to retreat to another room and return with his lungs filled with breathable air. When he did enter he saw something dark in the corner, and upon seeing it more clearly he screamed outright. While he screamed he thought a momentary cloud eclipsed the window, and a second later he felt himself brushed as if by some hateful current of vapour. Strange colours danced before his eyes; and had not a present horror numbed him he would have thought of the globule in the meteor that the geologist's hammer had shattered, and of the morbid vegetation that had sprouted in the spring. As it was he thought only of the blasphemous monstrosity which confronted him, and which all too clearly had shared the nameless fate of young Thaddeus and the livestock. But the terrible thing about this horror was that it very slowly and perceptibly moved as it continued to crumble.

Ammi would give me no added particulars to this scene, but the shape in the corner does not reappear in his tale as a moving object. There are things which cannot be mentioned, and what is done in common humanity is sometimes cruelly judged by the law. I gathered that no moving thing was left in that attic room, and that to leave anything capable of motion there would have been a deed so monstrous as to damn any accountable being to eternal torment. Anyone but a stolid farmer would have fainted or gone mad, but Ammi walked conscious through that low doorway and locked the accursed secret behind him. There would be Nahum to deal with now; he must be fed and tended, and removed to some place where he could be cared for.

Commencing his descent of the dark stairs, Ammi heard a thud below him. He even thought a scream had been suddenly choked off, and recalled nervously the clammy vapour which had brushed by him in that frightful room above. What presence had his cry and entry started up? Halted by some vague fear, he heard still further sounds below. Indubitably there was a sort of heavy dragging, and a most detestably sticky noise as of some fiendish and unclean species of suction. With an associative sense goaded to feverish heights, he thought unaccountably of what he had seen upstairs. Good God! What eldritch[13] dream-world was this into which he had blundered? He dared move neither backward nor forward, but stood there trembling at the black curve of the boxed-in staircase. Every trifle of the scene burned itself into his brain. The sounds, the sense of dread expectancy, the darkness, the steepness of the narrow steps—and merciful heaven! ... the

---

13. "Eldritch" is an adjective describing things that are eerie or weird in a supernatural way. It implies a fearful, unnatural quality, and originates from early Scottish.

faint but unmistakable luminosity of all the woodwork in sight; steps, sides, exposed laths, and beams alike!

Then there burst forth a frantic whinny from Ammi's horse outside, followed at once by a clatter which told of a frenzied runaway. In another moment horse and buggy had gone beyond earshot, leaving the frightened man on the dark stairs to guess what had sent them. But that was not all. There had been another sound out there. A sort of liquid splash—water—it must have been the well. He had left Hero untied near it, and a buggy-wheel must have brushed the coping and knocked in a stone. And still the pale phosphorescence glowed in that detestably ancient woodwork. God! how old the house was! Most of it built before 1670, and the gambrel roof not later than 1730.

A feeble scratching on the floor downstairs now sounded distinctly, and Ammi's grip tightened on a heavy stick he had picked up in the attic for some purpose. Slowly nerving himself, he finished his descent and walked boldly toward the kitchen. But he did not complete the walk, because what he sought was no longer there. It had come to meet him, and it was still alive after a fashion. Whether it had crawled or whether it had been dragged by any external force, Ammi could not say; but the death had been at it. Everything had happened in the last half-hour, but collapse, greying, and disintegration were already far advanced. There was a horrible brittleness, and dry fragments were scaling off. Ammi could not touch it, but looked horrifiedly into the distorted parody that had been a face. "What was it, Nahum—what was it?" he whispered, and the cleft, bulging lips were just able to crackle out a final answer.

"Nothin' ... nothin' ... the colour ... it burns ... cold an' wet ... but it burns ... it lived in the well ... I seen it ... a kind o' smoke ... jest like the flowers last spring ... the well shone at night ... Thad an' Mernie an' Zenas ... everything alive ... suckin' the life out of everything ... in that stone ... it must a' come in that stone ... pizened the whole place ... dun't know what it wants ... that round thing them men from the college dug outen the stone ... they smashed it ... it was that same colour ... jest the same, like the flowers an' plants ... must a' ben more of 'e m ... seeds ... seeds ... they growed ... I seen it the fust time this week ... must a' got strong on Zenas ... he was a big boy, full o' life ... it beats down your mind an' then gits ye ... burns ye up ... in the well water ... you was right about that ... evil water ... Zenas never come back from the well ... can't git away ... draws ye ... ye know summ'at's comin', but 'tain't no use ... I seen it time an' agin senct Zenas was took ... whar's Nabby, Ammi? ... my head's no good ... dun't know how long senct I fed her ... it'll git her ef we ain't keerful ... jest a colour ... her face is gettin' to hev that colour sometimes towards night ... an' it burns an' sucks ... it come from some place whar things ain't as they is here ... one o' them professors said so ... he was right ... look out, Ammi, it'll do suthin' more ... sucks the life out ...."

But that was all. That which spoke could speak no more because it had completely caved in. Ammi laid a red checked tablecloth over what was left and reeled out the back door into the fields. He climbed the slope to the ten-acre pasture and stumbled home by the north road and the woods. He could not pass that well from which his horse had run away. He had looked at it through the window, and had seen that no stone was missing from the rim. Then the lurching buggy had not dislodged anything after all—the splash had been something else—something which went into the well after it had done with poor Nahum ....

When Ammi reached his house the horse and buggy had arrived before him and thrown his wife into fits of anxiety. Reassuring her without explanations, he set out at once for Arkham and notified the authorities that the Gardner family was no more. He indulged in no details, but merely told of the deaths of Nahum and Nabby, that of Thaddeus being already known, and mentioned that the cause seemed to be the same strange ailment which had killed the livestock. He also stated that Merwin and Zenas had disappeared. There was considerable questioning at the police station, and in the end Ammi was compelled to take three officers to the Gardner farm, together with the coroner, the medical examiner, and the veterinary who had treated the diseased animals. He went much against his will, for the afternoon was advancing and he feared the fall of night over that accursed place, but it was some comfort to have so many people with him.

The six men drove out in a democrat-wagon,[14] following Ammi's buggy, and arrived at the pest-ridden farmhouse about four o'clock. Used as the officers were to gruesome experiences, not one remained unmoved at what was found in the attic and under the red checked tablecloth on the floor below. The whole aspect of the farm with its grey desolation was terrible enough, but those two crumbling objects were beyond all bounds. No one could look long at them, and even the medical examiner admitted that there was very little to examine. Specimens could be analysed, of course, so he busied himself in obtaining them—and here it develops that a very puzzling aftermath occurred at the college laboratory where the two phials of dust were finally taken. Under the spectroscope both samples gave off an unknown spectrum, in which many of the baffling bands were precisely like those which the strange meteor had yielded in the previous year. The property of emitting this spectrum vanished in a month, the dust thereafter consisting mainly of alkaline phosphates and carbonates

Ammi would not have told the men about the well if he had thought they meant to do anything then and there. It was getting toward sunset, and he was anxious to be away. But he could not help glancing nervously at the stony curb by the great sweep, and

---

14. A democrat-wagon is a light weight, horse-drawn cart with two or more seats.

when a detective questioned him he admitted that Nahum had feared something down there—so much so that he had never even thought of searching it for Merwin or Zenas. After that nothing would do but that they empty and explore the well immediately, so Ammi had to wait trembling while pail after pail of rank water was hauled up and splashed on the soaking ground outside. The men sniffed in disgust at the fluid, and toward the last held their noses against the foetor[15] they were uncovering. It was not so long a job as they had feared it would be, since the water was phenomenally low. There is no need to speak too exactly of what they found. Merwin and Zenas were both there, in part, though the vestiges were mainly skeletal. There were also a small deer and a large dog in about the same state, and a number of bones of smaller animals. The ooze and slime at the bottom seemed inexplicably porous and bubbling, and a man who descended on handholds with a long pole found that he could sink the wooden shaft to any depth in the mud of the floor without meeting any solid obstruction.

Twilight had now fallen, and lanterns were brought from the house. Then, when it was seen that nothing further could be gained from the well, everyone went indoors and conferred in the ancient sitting room while the intermittent light of a spectral half-moon played wanly on the grey desolation outside. The men were frankly nonplussed by the entire case, and could find no convincing common element to link the strange vegetable conditions, the unknown disease of livestock and humans, and the unaccountable deaths of Merwin and Zenas in the tainted well. They had heard the common country talk, it is true; but could not believe that anything contrary to natural law had occurred. No doubt the meteor had poisoned the soil, but the illness of persons and

15. Like "foetid" earlier, "foetor" is the British spelling of "fetor," which means an unpleasant smell.

animals who had eaten nothing grown in that soil was another matter. Was it the well water? Very possibly. It might be a good idea to analyse it. But what peculiar madness could have made both boys jump into the well? Their deeds were so similar—and the fragments shewed that they had both suffered from the grey brittle death. Why was everything so grey and brittle?

It was the coroner, seated near a window overlooking the yard, who first noticed the glow about the well. Night had fully set in, and all the abhorrent grounds seemed faintly luminous with more than the fitful moonbeams; but this new glow was something definite and distinct, and appeared to shoot up from the black pit like a softened ray from a searchlight, giving dull reflections in the little ground pools where the water had been emptied. It had a very queer colour, and as all the men clustered round the window Ammi gave a violent start. For this strange beam of ghastly miasma was to him of no unfamiliar hue. He had seen that colour before, and feared to think what it might mean. He had seen it in the nasty brittle globule in that aërolite two summers ago, had seen it in the crazy vegetation of the springtime, and had thought he had seen it for an instant that very morning against the small barred window of that terrible attic room where nameless things had happened. It had flashed there a second, and a clammy and hateful current of vapour had brushed past him—and then poor Nahum had been taken by something of that colour. He had said so at the last—said it was the globule and the plants. After that had come the runaway in the yard and the splash in the well—and now that well was belching forth to the night a pale insidious beam of the same daemoniac[16] tint.

It does credit to the alertness of Ammi's mind that he puzzled even at that tense moment over a point which was essentially

16. "Daemoniac" is an older spelling of "demonic." And another great name for a cat.

scientific. He could not but wonder at his gleaning of the same impression from a vapour glimpsed in the daytime, against a window opening on the morning sky, and from a nocturnal exhalation seen as a phosphorescent mist against the black and blasted landscape. It wasn't right—it was against Nature—and he thought of those terrible last words of his stricken friend, "It come from some place whar things ain't as they is here... one o' them professors said so...."

All three horses outside, tied to a pair of shrivelled saplings by the road, were now neighing and pawing frantically. The wagon driver started for the door to do something, but Ammi laid a shaky hand on his shoulder. "Dun't go out thar," he whispered. "They's more to this nor what we know. Nahum said somethin' lived in the well that sucks your life out. He said it must be some'at growed from a round ball like one we all seen in the meteor stone that fell a year ago June. Sucks an' burns, he said, an' is jest a cloud of colour like that light out thar now, that ye can hardly see an' can't tell what it is. Nahum thought it feeds on everything livin' an' gits stronger all the time. He said he seen it this last week. It must be somethin' from away off in the sky like the men from the college last year says the meteor stone was. The way it's made an' the way it works ain't like no way o' God's world. It's some'at from beyond."

So the men paused indecisively as the light from the well grew stronger and the hitched horses pawed and whinnied in increasing frenzy. It was truly an awful moment; with terror in that ancient and accursed house itself, four monstrous sets of fragments—two from the house and two from the well—in the woodshed behind, and that shaft of unknown and unholy iridescence from the slimy depths in front. Ammi had restrained the driver on impulse, forgetting how uninjured he himself was after the clammy brushing of that coloured vapour in the attic room, but perhaps it is just as well that he acted as he did. No one will ever know what was abroad that night; and though the blasphemy from beyond had not so far hurt any human of unweakened mind, there is no telling what it might not have done at that last moment, and with its seemingly increased strength and the special signs of purpose it was soon to display beneath the half-clouded moonlit sky.

All at once one of the detectives at the window gave a short, sharp gasp. The others looked at him, and then quickly followed his own gaze upward to the point at which its idle straying had been suddenly arrested. There was no need for words. What had been disputed in country gossip was disputable no longer, and it is because of the thing which every man of that party agreed in whispering later on that the strange days are never talked about in Arkham. It is necessary to premise that there was no wind at that hour of the evening. One did arise not long afterward, but there was absolutely none then. Even the dry tips of the lingering hedge-mustard, grey and blighted, and the fringe on the roof of the standing democrat-wagon were unstirred. And yet amid that tense, godless calm the high bare boughs of all the trees in the yard were moving. They were twitching morbidly and spasmodically, clawing in convulsive and epileptic madness at the moonlit clouds; scratching impotently in the noxious air as if jerked by some alien and bodiless line of linkage with subterrene horrors writhing and struggling below the black roots.

Not a man breathed for several seconds. Then a cloud of darker depth passed over the moon, and the silhouette of clutching branches faded out momentarily. At this there was a general cry; muffled with awe, but husky and almost identical from every throat. For the terror had not faded with the silhouette, and in a fearsome instant of deeper darkness the watchers saw wriggling at that treetop height a thousand tiny points of faint and unhallowed radiance, tipping each bough like the fire of St. Elmo or the flames that came down on the apostles' heads at Pentecost.[17] It was a monstrous constellation of unnatural light, like a glutted swarm of corpse-fed fireflies dancing hellish sarabands over an accursed marsh; and its colour was that same nameless intrusion which Ammi had come to recognise and dread. All the while the shaft of phosphorescence from the well was getting brighter and brighter, bringing to the minds of the huddled men a sense of doom and abnormality which far outraced any image their conscious minds could form. It was no longer shining out, it was pouring out; and as the shapeless stream of unplaceable colour left the well it seemed to flow directly into the sky.

The veterinary shivered, and walked to the front door to drop the heavy extra bar across it. Ammi shook no less, and had to tug and point for lack of a controllable voice when he wished to draw notice to the growing luminosity of the trees. The neighing and stamping of the horses had become utterly frightful, but not a soul of that group in the old house would have ventured forth for any earthly reward. With the moments the shining of the trees increased, while their restless branches seemed to strain more and more toward verticality. The wood of the well-sweep was shining now, and presently a policeman dumbly pointed to some wooden sheds and bee-hives near the stone wall on the west. They were commencing to shine, too, though the tethered vehicles of the visitors seemed so far unaffected. Then there was a wild commotion and clopping in the road, and as Ammi quenched the lamp for better seeing they realised that the span of frantic greys had broke their sapling and run off with the democrat-wagon.

The shock served to loosen several tongues, and embarrassed whispers were exchanged. "It spreads on everything organic that's been around here," muttered the medical examiner.

---

17. St. Elmo's Fire is a natural electrical phenomenon. The flames of Pentecost refer to the biblical story of the Holy Spirit appearing as tongues of fire to signal the birth of the Christian church.

No one replied, but the man who had been in the well gave a hint that his long pole must have stirred up something intangible. "It was awful," he added. "There was no bottom at all. Just ooze and bubbles and the feeling of something lurking under there." Ammi's horse still pawed and screamed deafeningly in the road outside, and nearly drowned its owner's faint quaver as he mumbled his formless reflections. "It come from that stone... it growed down thar... it got everything livin'... it fed itself on 'em, mind and body... Thad an' Mernie, Zenas an' Nabby... Nahum was the last... they all drunk the water... it got strong on 'em... it come from beyond, whar things ain't like they be here... now it's goin' home...."

At this point, as the column of unknown colour flared suddenly stronger and began to weave itself into fantastic suggestions of shape which each spectator later described differently, there came from poor tethered Hero such a sound as no man before or since ever heard from a horse. Every person in that low-pitched sitting room stopped his ears, and Ammi turned away from the window in horror and nausea. Words could not convey it—when Ammi looked out again the hapless beast lay huddled inert on the moonlit ground between the splintered shafts of the buggy. That was the last of Hero till they buried him next day. But the present was no time to mourn, for almost at this instant a detective silently called attention to something terrible in the very room with them. In the absence of the lamplight it was clear that a faint phosphorescence had begun to pervade the entire apartment. It glowed on the broad-planked floor and the fragment of rag carpet, and shimmered over the sashes of the small-paned windows. It ran up and down the exposed corner-posts, coruscated about the shelf and mantel, and infected the very doors and furniture. Each minute saw it strengthen, and at last it was very plain that healthy living things must leave that house.

Ammi shewed them the back door and the path up through the fields to the ten-acre pasture. They walked and stumbled as in a dream, and did not dare look back till they were far away on the high ground. They were glad of the path, for they could not have gone the front way, by that well. It was bad enough passing the glowing barn and sheds, and those shining orchard trees with their gnarled, fiendish contours; but thank heaven the branches did their worst twisting high up. The moon went under some very black clouds as they crossed the rustic bridge over Chapman's Brook, and it was blind groping from there to the open meadows.

When they looked back toward the valley and the distant Gardner place at the bottom they saw a fearsome sight. All the farm was shining with the hideous unknown blend of colour; trees, buildings, and even such grass and herbage as had not been wholly changed to lethal grey brittleness. The boughs were all straining skyward, tipped with tongues of foul flame, and lambent tricklings of the same monstrous fire were creeping about the ridgepoles of the house, barn, and sheds. It was a scene from a vision of Fuseli,[18] and over all the rest reigned that riot of luminous amorphousness, that alien and undimensioned rainbow of cryptic poison from the well—seething, feeling, lapping, reaching, scintillating, straining, and malignly bubbling in its cosmic and unrecognisable chromaticism.

Then without warning the hideous thing shot vertically up toward the sky like a rocket or meteor, leaving behind no trail and disappearing through a round and curiously regular hole in the clouds before any man could gasp or cry out. No watcher can ever forget that sight, and Ammi stared blankly at the stars of Cygnus, Deneb twinkling above the others, where the unknown colour had melted into the Milky Way. But his gaze was the next moment called swiftly to earth by the crackling in the valley. It

18. Henry Fuseli (1741–1825) was a Swiss painter known for his gloomy, supernatural paintings.

was just that. Only a wooden ripping and crackling, and not an explosion, as so many others of the party vowed. Yet the outcome was the same, for in one feverish, kaleidoscopic instant there burst up from that doomed and accursed farm a gleamingly eruptive cataclysm of unnatural sparks and substance; blurring the glance of the few who saw it, and sending forth to the zenith a bombarding cloudburst of such coloured and fantastic fragments as our universe must needs disown.

Through quickly re-closing vapours they followed the great morbidity that had vanished, and in another second they had vanished too. Behind and below was only a darkness to which the men dared not return, and all about was a mounting wind which seemed to sweep down in black, frore[19] gusts from interstellar space. It shrieked and howled, and lashed the fields and distorted woods in a mad cosmic frenzy, till soon the trembling party realised it would be no use waiting for the moon to shew what was left down there at Nahum's.

Too awed even to hint theories, the seven shaking men trudged back toward Arkham by the north road. Ammi was worse than his fellows, and begged them to see him inside his own kitchen, instead of keeping straight on to town. He did not wish to cross the nighted, wind-whipped woods alone to his home on the main road. For he had had an added shock that the others were spared, and was crushed forever with a brooding fear he dared not even mention for many years to come. As the rest of the watchers on that tempestuous hill had stolidly set their faces toward the road, Ammi had looked back an instant at the shadowed valley of desolation so lately sheltering his ill-starred friend. And from that stricken, far-away spot he had seen something feebly rise, only to sink down again upon the place from which the great shapeless horror had shot into the sky. It was just a colour—but not any colour of our earth or heavens. And because Ammi recognised

19. "Frore" means frozen.

that colour, and knew that this last faint remnant must still lurk down there in the well, he has never been quite right since.

Ammi would never go near the place again. It is over half a century now since the horror happened, but he has never been there, and will be glad when the new reservoir blots it out. I shall be glad, too, for I do not like the way the sunlight changed colour around the mouth of that abandoned well I passed. I hope the water will always be very deep—but even so, I shall never drink it. I do not think I shall visit the Arkham country hereafter. Three of the men who had been with Ammi returned the next morning to see the ruins by daylight, but there were not any real ruins. Only the bricks of the chimney, the stones of the cellar, some mineral and metallic litter here and there, and the rim of that nefandous[20] well. Save for Ammi's dead horse, which they towed away and buried, and the buggy which they shortly returned to him, everything that had ever been living had gone. Five eldritch acres of dusty grey desert remained, nor has anything ever grown there since. To this day it sprawls open to the sky like a great spot eaten by acid in the woods and fields, and the few who have ever dared glimpse it in spite of the rural tales have named it "the blasted heath."

The rural tales are queer. They might be even queerer if city men and college chemists could be interested enough to analyse the water from that disused well, or the grey dust that no wind seems ever to disperse. Botanists, too, ought to study the stunted flora on the borders of that spot, for they might shed light on the country notion that the blight is spreading—little by little, perhaps an inch a year. People say the colour of the neighbouring herbage is not quite right in the spring, and that wild things leave queer prints in the light winter snow. Snow never seems quite so heavy on the blasted

---

20. "Nefandous" is an old way of saying that something is so horrible, it is unspeakable—and a final cat name suggestion, depending, of course, on the temperament of your feline.

heath as it is elsewhere. Horses—the few that are left in this motor age—grow skittish in the silent valley; and hunters cannot depend on their dogs too near the splotch of greyish dust.

They say the mental influences are very bad, too. Numbers went queer in the years after Nahum's taking, and always they lacked the power to get away. Then the stronger-minded folk all left the region, and only the foreigners tried to live in the crumbling old homesteads. They could not stay, though; and one sometimes wonders what insight beyond ours their wild, weird stores of whispered magic have given them. Their dreams at night, they protest, are very horrible in that grotesque country; and surely the very look of the dark realm is enough to stir a morbid fancy. No traveller has ever escaped a sense of strangeness in those deep ravines, and artists shiver as they paint thick woods whose mystery is as much of the spirit as of the eye. I myself am curious about the sensation I derived from my one lone walk before Ammi told me his tale. When twilight came I had vaguely wished some clouds would gather, for an odd timidity about the deep skyey voids above had crept into my soul.

Do not ask me for my opinion. I do not know—that is all. There was no one but Ammi to question; for Arkham people will not talk about the strange days, and all three professors who saw the aërolite and its coloured globule are dead. There were other globules—depend upon that. One must have fed itself and escaped, and probably there was another which was too late. No doubt it is still down the well—I know there was something wrong with the sunlight I saw above that miasmal brink. The rustics say the blight creeps an inch a year, so perhaps there is a kind of growth or nourishment even now. But whatever daemon hatchling is there, it must be tethered to something or else it would quickly spread. Is it fastened to the roots of those trees that claw the air? One of the current Arkham tales is about fat oaks that shine and move as they ought not to do at night.

What it is, only God knows. In terms of matter I suppose the thing Ammi described would be called a gas, but this gas obeyed laws that are not of our cosmos. This was no fruit of such worlds and suns as shine on the telescopes and photographic plates of our observatories. This was no breath from the skies whose motions and dimensions our astronomers measure or deem too vast to measure. It was just a colour out of space—a frightful messenger from unformed realms of infinity beyond all Nature as we know it; from realms whose mere existence stuns the brain and numbs us with the black extra-cosmic gulfs it throws open before our frenzied eyes.

I doubt very much if Ammi consciously lied to me, and I do not think his tale was all a freak of madness as the townfolk had forewarned. Something terrible came to the hills and valleys on that meteor, and something terrible—though I know not in what proportion—still remains. I shall be glad to see the water come. Meanwhile I hope nothing will happen to Ammi. He saw so much of the thing—and its influence was so insidious. Why has he never been able to move away? How clearly he recalled those dying words of Nahum's—"can't git away... draws ye... ye know summ'at's comin', but 'tain't no use...." Ammi is such a good old man—when the reservoir gang gets to work I must write the chief engineer to keep a sharp watch on him. I would hate to think of him as the grey, twisted, brittle monstrosity which persists more and more in troubling my sleep.

▪

Author Biography

H. P. Lovecraft is the "big papa" when it comes to weird literature and modern horror. Born in Providence, Rhode Island, Lovecraft lived a life marked by poverty, illness, and isolation. Despite publishing mostly in pulp magazines during his lifetime and dying in obscurity, his work gained immense recognition after his death. Lovecraft created an entire mythology—the Cthulhu Mythos—populated by ancient cosmic entities indifferent to humanity's existence. Though his racism and xenophobia are well-documented flaws that sometimes appear in his work, his literary innovations in weird fiction remain influential. He died of cancer very young, at 48.

Discuss

1. The story emphasizes that the colour/color is "not of our cosmos" and obeys alien laws. What makes this more frightening than a traditional monster or ghost? How does this relate to the concept of weird fiction?
2. The narrator notes that "the blight creeps an inch a year" and may still be spreading. What is the significance of this slow, ongoing contamination? How does it differ from sudden catastrophes, and what might it suggest about long-term environmental threats we cannot see or immediately perceive?
3. Discuss the progression from the first signs of trouble (strange fruit, unusual footprints) to total ecological collapse. What does this gradual escalation reveal about how environmental disasters unfold?

Write

Cascading Collapse: In an essay, trace the progression of the blight from the meteorite through soil, water, plants, animals, and finally humans. How does Lovecraft depict the interconnectedness of ecosystems and the way contamination moves through food chains and natural systems?

From "*exhibits from* The American Water Museum"

Natalie Diaz

Leveraging some of weird literature's signature moves—disjointed timelines, speaking landscapes, and the cheerful dissolution of boundaries between humans and nature—these sections from Natalie Diaz's longer poem, which came out in 2020, make ecological crisis feel more like a haunted house we're already living in, where the walls remember every injustice. Just like a good museum does.

0.
I can't tell you anything new about the river—
you can't tell a river to itself.

17.
A recording plays from somewhere high,
or low, floating up or down through the falling
dust-light.

It is a voice out of time, voice of quickness,
voice of glass—or wind. A melody, almost—of mud.
How it takes a deep blue to tumble wet stones
into a songline. The music any earth makes
when touched and shaped by the original green energy.
The song, if translated, might feel like this:

You have been made in my likeness.

I am inside you—I am you / or you are me.

Let us say to one another: *I am yours—*

and know finally that we will only ever be

as much as we are willing to save of one another.

4.
The guidebook's single entry:

There is no guide.
You built this museum.
You have always been
its Muse and Master.

5.
Admission is general and free
except for what the children pay—
and they pay in the kidneys.

99.
From an original rock painting in Topock, Arizona, now digitized on a wall-mounted monitor:

Before this city, the Creator pressed his staff
into the earth, and the earth opened—

it wasn't a wound, it was joy—joy!—!
Out of this opening leaped earth's most radical bloom: *our people*—

we blossoms from the original body: water,
flowering and flowing until it became itself, and we, us:
River. Body.

78.
The first violence against any body of water
is to forget the name its creator first called it.
Worse: forget the bodies who spoke that name.

An American way of forgetting Natives:
Discover them with City. Crumble them by City.
Erase them into Cities named for their bones, until

you are the new Natives of your new Cities.
Let the new faucets run in celebration, in excess.
Who lies beneath streets, universities, art museums?

My people!

I learn to love them from up here, through concrete.
La llorona[1] out on the avenues crying for everyone's
babies, for all the mothers, including River, grinded

to their knees and dust for the splendid City. Still,
we must sweep the dust, gather our own bodies like
messes of sand and memory. Who will excavate

---

1. La Llorona—the "Weeping Woman"—is a vengeful ghost in Latin American folklore who roams near bodies of water mourning the children she drowned in jealous rage after her husband's betrayal. Those who hear her wailing are said to suffer misfortune or death.

our clodded bodies from the banks, pick embedded
stones and sticks from the raw scrapes oozing
our backs and thighs? Who will call us back

to the water, wash the dirt from our eyes and hair?
Can anybody uncrush our hands, reshape them
from clay, let us touch one another's faces again?

Has anyone answered? We've been crying out
for 600 years—

Tengo sed.[2]

▪

Author Biography

Natalie Diaz was born on September 4, 1978, and raised in the Fort Mojave Indian Village in Needles, California, on the banks of the Colorado River. Mojave and an enrolled member of the Gila River Indian Tribe, she received her BA and MFA from Old Dominion University. Diaz is the author of *Postcolonial Love Poem* (Graywolf Press, 2020), winner of the Pulitzer Prize in Poetry and finalist for the National Book Award and the Forward Prize in Poetry, and *When My Brother Was an Aztec* (Copper Canyon Press, 2012), winner of an American Book Award.

2. "*Tengo sed*" is Spanish for "I'm thirsty."

Discuss

1. Who or what is speaking in these poems? How does the voice shift between fragments, and what does this suggest about the relationship between human, river, and land?
2. What role does the museum setting play in the sequence?
3. In Exhibit 78, Diaz invokes La Llorona, who drowned her children and now wails for them eternally. How does Diaz transform this ghost story into a collective mourning for Indigenous peoples, for River, for "all the mothers"?

Write

Museum Fragment Series: Create your own sequence of fragments that imagine a museum dedicated to something overlooked or forgotten in your community. Experiment with different voices—objects, spaces, memories—that might "speak" within this imagined institution.

From **Sift**

Alissa Hattman

This haunting, strange excerpt from Alissa Hattman's novel published in 2024 follows a narrator who ventures out from isolation with a mysterious Driver, traveling through a landscape devastated by environmental collapse—poisoned air, ash-covered fields, and dirty rivers. The story is told in small blocks of text intermixed with poetic elements. As you read, notice how the relationship between the two travelers evolves alongside their journey, and consider whether hope can survive even when everything familiar has been destroyed. This is a road trip story for the end times, where the biggest challenge isn't finding the best rest stops with shot glasses with city names, it's finding breathable air.

I

I thought that being inside would protect me, with its corners and its curtains, then a kindness took me by the throat and stretched me taut against the sky, beaming, and I found something more valuable than protection. If only you could have seen it, Mother. What light.

The Driver arrived with a crate and inside the crate were the last of the winter squashes—butternut, acorn, kabocha, sweet dumpling. It had been ages since I had eaten food from a vine, and I had so many questions, concerns. The Driver listened, then she said the best way to prepare kabocha was to cut out the insides and fill it with stars. I blushed and grew old with her, right there in the smoggy sunlight.

Long story short—I left with her, Mother. I went outside.

Here's another way to say it: I gathered up all that you gave me and bolted. Escaped into the toxic air with the only person I'd met who had learned how to keep living.

I remember blackened fields and a sky the color of cantaloupe. The air was full of smoke, but inside the vehicle—with its systems and its filters—we could breathe freely. I watched the flickering red skies turn into plumes of dark blue and the plumes of dark blue turn into rain and the rain turn into puddles and the puddles turn into ice and the ice turn back into puddles and the puddles into air. Certain cycles, flows. Observing is one way to go on.

The Driver and I shared the same road, the same vehicle, but we were both following the uneven edges inside our own minds. Hours dripped into the chasm between us.

Occasionally, I found courage enough to choke out a thought even though my throat was so thirsty. The Driver was kind. She taught me how to sift, to sip water from the air. *Stay very still*, she said. *Listen to everything thrumming. Inside too, you feel it?*

Sometimes I think about how far I am from my abandoned home, how this becoming has made me less animal and more vegetal, and when I think about this, I think of you, Mother, and wonder whether you would have lived this way too, had you known it was possible, and if you had known, whether we, as women, might have thrived like moss, parts and parcels. Now, as we've traveled through day and night and through dayless, nightless dark, I've grown hints of you up my back and have not always known if it is a comfort or a burden. Perhaps it is both.

It is no easy task. The trick is to keep the sips small. Teeny-tiny.

2

Remember when you said that the trauma of the old world was upon us? You were sitting on the kitchen floor, shoes kicked off, hair draped over your knees. You looked small, devastated. Remember how the days blurred—slow, slow and then quick? The fires, the raids. That moment when we thought we'd be safe. But then: heat, drought. Lockdown. Poisoned atmosphere. The new regime.

For years, we lived inside the house without you—the larder stocked with canned vegetables, old processed food. Cy taught me all the survival skills he could remember from Basic, but mostly we kept to ourselves. The shock of it all too hard to communicate. I'd sit for hours in what muted light broke through blackout curtains and try to understand. I'd call up memory like medicine—lying in the tall grass, the sun on my face before exposure was too dangerous.

The headaches were intense. My forehead felt as if it were splitting open, exposing me to something.

Many years passed. People died. You died. Then, one day, a knock at the door.

3

I write to you from the present, Mother. We sit together, you and I, here in this letter.

Why me? I ask The Driver about the crates.

You needed feeding, she says.

The Driver and I are passing through fields of ash. The day's drive has gone hot, ruddy and broke-open, spilling out.

I grew crop here, The Driver says, gesturing toward the burns. *Barley. Just last season.*

She says the word barley with such reverence. A loved one, now dead.

Where are we going? I ask.

To fertile soil, she says. *Soon there will be river. Then the land will get very dry before we reach trees, then mountain, then beyond mountain. That is my hope.*

And others?

Others? I can't say.

4

We drive and drive until we finally come to river. The Driver and I run barefoot down the revetment[1] and plunge our faces

1. A revetment is a structure built to protect an embankment, shoreline, or hillside from erosion.

into water. Here the air is clean, but the river is dirty. Even so, we drink until we are overfull. We sit on the edge of the concrete slope, thinking together now, trying to define this sudden expansion. The road, the river. We cannot touch the word for our condition. It is too vast.

The Driver becomes sick. She leans over and vomits water onto the pavement. The water is a small pond and in the pond are tadpoles and snails and black algae bottle caps slicked with half-memories and pain. I take up some of the water in my hands and watch The Driver's story swirl with my own.

Thank you, I say to the stories in the water that are not just our stories but also living creatures, the algae and the tadpoles, creatures with stories all their own.

Thank you, I say to The Driver, still ill. I am grateful that we are here together. I can see the acorn flush of her face peaking, sick with grief, and she sees me—sees my own story—sees the girl leaning against moss walls as spores grow up all around her.

Memory makes what it needs to make, The Artist once said at a talk. Remember when talks used to happen?

I remember looking at you in the mirror looking back at me looking at you. You were wearing cream-colored nylons. You prodded at your pinched skin and said that no matter what you try to suck in, something will always spill out. You showed me magazine images of women's bodies. This is the difference between real and airbrush, you said. I couldn't focus—I imagined some man doing the impossible, painting the air—but, or maybe because of that, it was a lesson that stuck in me and grew.

Here's what I want to tell you about travel. First, you have to find the right partner. That person should be resolute and know when (and when not) to talk. They should embrace change, because just when you think you understand the vehicle, it changes, and just when you understand your partner, they will change, and the river will change, and our insides will change and it will make us sick and then maybe we will be well, if just for a moment, before becoming unwell again and that is the whole process in a nut. The secret to travel is pacing. Sip slowly. Another lesson I have learned is that you should choose a person and put your trust not in that person but in how you move and how you sit still together. It won't feel as it felt before, but no matter. This is not any indicator of rightness or wrongness. Watch. Can you see it? How the gaze sits, leaps?

I will also say that traveling is not as easy as it used to be. Sometimes The Driver and I are traveling in a truck, sometimes a helicopter, sometimes something else entirely. The vehicle changes as we change. It does not run on gasoline or diesel or electricity; it is something we call truck or helicopter for lack of a better word. The important thing is that we are together, moving.

Let it go, says The Driver.

I let the pond drain back down into the river but lovingly. The tadpoles grow into frogs as they swim away. What remains of the story? Glints, traces.

Once the sun has faded, and our lungs have fully absorbed the clean air, we lace up our leather boots, and head to the car.

The Driver gets into the passenger seat.

There is no other option—I drive.

■

Author Biography

Alissa Hattman's debut novel *Sift* was shortlisted for the 2024 Ursula K. Le Guin Prize for Fiction. Her short stories have been nominated for the Pushcart Prize, longlisted for the Dzanc 2021 Prize for Fiction, and have appeared widely in *Carve*, *The Rumpus*, *The Gravity of the Thing*, *Mountain Bluebird Magazine*, *About Place Journal*, *Propeller*, *Big Other*, *Surely Magazine*, and elsewhere. She has taught writing classes and workshops for over 15 years and has worked as a fiction editor, book reviewer, zine librarian, writing group facilitator, and artist-in-residence at several arts centers, most recently Gullkistan Center for Creativity in Iceland. Originally from North Dakota, Hattman now lives between the Willamette and Molalla Rivers of Oregon with one human, two cats, and a massive backyard acacia covered in ivy and moss.

Discuss

1. The Driver teaches the narrator "how to sift, to sip water from the air." What does this skill suggest about survival in this post-apocalyptic environment?
2. What does the narrator mean by becoming "less animal and more vegetal"? How does this transformation relate to survival in their world?
3. The story suggests that "becoming unwell again" is part of "the whole process." How do you interpret that in terms of this story?

Write

"Dear Me": Write a letter to your past self from the future, set in a world recovering from environmental collapse, like this one. Consider how relationships, daily survival, and hope might function in such a world, and what advice you would give yourself twenty years earlier. Use the original story's techniques of blending realistic details with surreal elements to explore how humans might adapt—physically, emotionally, or spiritually—to a fundamentally changed planet.

The Last

Brittney Corrigan

In this short story from 2023, the main character, Fin, serves as the greeter at extinction's final checkpoint, performing water rituals for the last members of vanishing species as they pass through a mystical archway into whatever lies beyond. Brittney Corrigan's story functions as both elegy and indictment, mourning what's being lost while accusing those responsible. It transforms abstract biodiversity statistics into visceral, accelerating grief. Using this strange setting, we understand that we're witnessing not just individual deaths but the collapse of entire systems—yet we still feel the beauty.

When the northern white rhino shows up, Fin is ready for the rites. The animal's massive horn materializes first, followed by small, black eyes and then heavy, three-toed hooves. Fin had been watching the free-standing archway, waiting for the beast to step through the gnarled wooden aperture into the plain of light. Now, she stands before the arch, holding a tall stone pitcher of water. The gray armor of the rhino's shoulders emerges, then thick, wrinkled flanks, a curl of tail. The rhino is nervous, confused, its eyes wide and wary. But Fin is never afraid of what comes through the arch. She steps toward the rhino, carrying the stone vessel with practiced ease.

Fin can't remember ever being anywhere but here. She has always been the receiver, the celebrant, the caretaker of the beings that come through the arch. Fin is a fulcrum,[1] standing in the middle of the plain of light, the horizon gleaming beyond the arch. And beyond that horizon, the creatures she's already ushered through call to her, lonely in each other's company as they wait for her to return. Their voices tug at her, and she aches to go to them. A few decades back she could spend whole days among them, smoothing their feathers and stroking their fur. But new animals come through so often now that Fin can never leave the arch, can scarcely keep up with the rites.

The rhino takes a tentative step forward, lowers its head before Fin. She places a hand on its front horn, then tilts the pitcher over the rhino's forehead and pours slowly, so the water rivers between its ears and down its face. Fin walks along the length of the great ungulate,[2] pouring water over its back down to its tail, which relaxes as the last of the liquid drips down its leathery skin. The rhino shivers its hide, and its body begins to shimmer. The animal lifts its head toward the sounds coming from beyond the plain's edge. It looks back for a moment at Fin, who stands quietly, holding the empty pitcher. Then the rhino takes off in a run, charging across the plain of light.

The sorrow that inhabits Fin whenever an animal comes through the arch sometimes feels too heavy to hold. She remembers them all: the Pyrenean ibex with knobby, ringed horns whose back sagged with the ghost-weight of the fallen tree that killed it; the Tasmanian tiger still stinking of zoo as Fin washed its banded fur; the Xerces blue butterfly that landed on Fin's shoulder, allowed the anointing of its delicate wings. And many centuries before, the flightless dodo, stumbling through the archway,

---

1. A fulcrum is literally the pivot point on which a lever rests and moves. Here, it suggests that Fin is the central figure on whom everything depends—the person whose actions make the larger action possible.

2. An ungulate is a hoofed mammal.

unafraid. All of them burdened with their solitary passings.[3] All of them the last of their kind.

Fin walks a few paces to where a bright turquoise pool glistens on the plain of light. She dips her pitcher, fills it once again to the brim. For some time now, at least three creatures have come through the arch every hour. Insects with colorful bodies, birds with astonishing feathers or feathers muted as stone, frogs no bigger than Fin's thumbnail. Creatures from the oceans' depths, floating through the arch in search of the sea. Fin tends to all of them, sends them off across the plain of light.

Fin fills pitcher after pitcher of water as the pace of creatures entering the plain of light quickens. Sometimes animals from different continents come through the archway together, tangling with confusion and alarm. Fin cannot properly receive them; cannot give them the attention they deserve. She is coaxing a hawksbill turtle from the muscular arms of a mountain gorilla when a bird flies through the arch and continues right over Fin's head, toward the clamorous horizon. Fin cannot tell what species of bird it was, may never find it again. She worries what will happen when it crests the horizon, unanointed. Fin's pitcher is empty again. She lifts it with faltering hands.

A cheetah arrives at full sprint, streaking past her in a blur that becomes the plain of light itself. Fin rushes to refill the pitcher, but the turquoise pool is empty. Fin stands rooted, wrestling with the unfamiliar disquiet that rises through her. The air is crowded with insect noise, squawking, and howls. Her head rings with the

3. The dodo went extinct in the 17th century; the Tasmanian tiger in the 1930s; the Xerces butterfly in the 1940s; and the Pyrenean ibex in 2000. The last ibex, a female named Celia, was killed by a falling tree. Scientists preserved her tissue and cloned her in 2003, using a domestic goat as a surrogate. The clone was born alive but survived only seven minutes.

sounds of bats and dolphins trying to echolocate across the plain of light. Fin can feel the many species of whales calling to one another beyond the horizon, each in their own beautiful language. Then the plain shudders. Fin loses her balance, falls to the ground beside the arch.

A cascade of creatures streams through the opening, a mass of feathers and fur and scales. There are so many of them, the ground disappears. The sky becomes a riot of wings. Fin struggles to her feet just as an elephant lumbers through the arch, swinging its trunk sadly from side to side, regarding her with vast, liquid eyes. Fin runs her hands along its flanks, but it shies away from her, turns its head toward the horizon. No animal has ever refused Fin's comfort, her touch. She reaches for the pitcher, but it lies shattered at her feet. And for the first time in her existence on the plain of light, Fin is afraid.

For many moments, nothing else comes through the arch. All the creatures approach from beyond the horizon and fall silent, watching Fin. She turns her attention again to the archway, for now something else is approaching. Fin steps toward the arch to meet it, and relief washes over her like water. The creature before her is upright, skin smooth and barren except for long hairs sprouting from the slope of its skull. Its eyes are terrified, remorseful, and it hesitates before the creatures on the plain of light. As it passes through the arch, it flounders, and Fin reaches out. She takes its trembling fingers within her empty hands.

▪

Author Biography

Brittney Corrigan is the author of the poetry collections *Daughters*, *Breaking*, *Navigation*, *40 Weeks* and most recently, *Solastalgia*, a collection of poems about climate change, extinction, and the *Anthropocene Age* (JackLeg Press, 2023). Brittney was raised in Colorado and has lived in Portland, Oregon, for more than three decades, where she is an alumna and employee of Reed College. Her recent debut short story collection, *The Ghost Town Collectives*, won the 2023 Osprey Award for Fiction from Middle Creek Publishing.

Discuss

1. What does the final scene of this story suggest about humanity's ultimate fate, and how does the human's description as "terrified, remorseful" contrast with the other animals' reactions to extinction?
2. Fin performs water rites for each extinct animal, pouring over them before they cross to the horizon. What does water symbolize here? Consider: baptism, cleansing, and last rites.
3. How do you interpret the last paragraph? Why does Fin feel relief, not fear or sorrow or anger or confusion, at the arrival of the last being?

Write

Literary Devices and Imagery: Choose three specific images from the story (such as the archway, the empty pitcher, or the plain of light) and analyze how the author uses them symbolically throughout the narrative. In your essay, argue what each image literally represents in the story, supporting your claim with examples from the story, then discuss what deeper meaning or theme each symbol might convey about extinction, environmental crisis, or human responsibility. Structure your essay with a clear thesis statement about how the author uses symbolic imagery to communicate the story's central message.

Part 3

Weird Transhumanism

Second Variety

Philip K. Dick

Exploring the terrifying potential of artificial intelligence evolving beyond human control, this short story, originally published in 1953, presents self-replicating killer robots that have become so advanced they can perfectly mimic human appearance and emotion. Philip K. Dick's story interrogates the blurred lines between human and machine, challenging fundamental assumptions about consciousness, identity, and the potential existential threat of technological self-evolution. And it's badass.

The Russian soldier made his way nervously up the ragged side of the hill, holding his gun ready. He glanced around him, licking his dry lips, his face set. From time to time he reached up a gloved hand and wiped perspiration from his neck, pushing down his coat collar.

Eric turned to Corporal Leone. "Want him? Or can I have him?" He adjusted the view sight so the Russian's features squarely filled the glass, the lines cutting across his hard, somber features.

Leone considered. The Russian was close, moving rapidly, almost running. "Don't fire. Wait." Leone tensed. "I don't think we're needed."

The Russian increased his pace, kicking ash and piles of debris out of his way. He reached the top of the hill and stopped, panting, staring around him. The sky was overcast, drifting clouds of gray particles. Bare trunks of trees jutted up occasionally;

the ground was level and bare, rubble-strewn, with the ruins of buildings standing out here and there like yellowing skulls.

The Russian was uneasy. He knew something was wrong. He started down the hill. Now he was only a few paces from the bunker. Eric was getting fidgety. He played with his pistol, glancing at Leone.

"Don't worry," Leone said. "He won't get here. They'll take care of him."

"Are you sure? He's got damn far."

"They hang around close to the bunker. He's getting into the bad part. Get set!"

The Russian began to hurry, sliding down the hill, his boots sinking into the heaps of gray ash, trying to keep his gun up. He stopped for a moment, lifting his fieldglasses[1] to his face.

"He's looking right at us," Eric said.

The Russian came on. They could see his eyes, like two blue stones. His mouth was open a little. He needed a shave; his chin was stubbled. On one bony cheek was a square of tape, showing blue at the edge. A fungoid spot. His coat was muddy and torn. One glove was missing. As he ran his belt counter bounced up and down against him.

Leone touched Eric's arm. "Here one comes."

Across the ground something small and metallic came, flashing in the dull sunlight of mid-day. A metal sphere. It raced up the hill after the Russian, its treads flying. It was small, one of the baby ones. Its claws were out, two razor projections spinning in a blur of white steel. The Russian heard it. He turned instantly, firing. The sphere dissolved into particles. But already a second had emerged and was following the first. The Russian fired again.

---

1. Fieldglasses are handheld optical devices that magnify distance objects, similar to binoculars.

A third sphere leaped up the Russian's leg, clicking and whirring. It jumped to the shoulder. The spinning blades disappeared into the Russian's throat.

Eric relaxed. "Well, that's that. God, those damn things give me the creeps. Sometimes I think we were better off before."

"If we hadn't invented them, they would have." Leone lit a cigarette shakily. "I wonder why a Russian would come all this way alone. I didn't see anyone covering him."

Lt. Scott came slipping up the tunnel, into the bunker. "What happened? Something entered the screen."

"An Ivan."[2]

"Just one?"

Eric brought the view screen around. Scott peered into it. Now there were numerous metal spheres crawling over the prostrate body, dull metal globes clicking and whirring, sawing up the Russian into small parts to be carried away.

"What a lot of claws," Scott murmured.

"They come like flies. Not much game for them any more."

Scott pushed the sight away, disgusted. "Like flies. I wonder why he was out there. They know we have claws all around."

A larger robot had joined the smaller spheres. It was directing operations, a long blunt tube with projecting eyepieces. There was not much left of the soldier. What remained was being brought down the hillside by the host of claws.

"Sir," Leone said. "If it's all right, I'd like to go out there and take a look at him."

"Why?"

"Maybe he came with something."

Scott considered. He shrugged. "All right. But be careful."

"I have my tab." Leone patted the metal band at his wrist. "I'll be out of bounds."

---

2. "Ivan" is a slang term for the individual Russian soldier and for the military forces of Russia or the Soviet Union collectively.

He picked up his rifle and stepped carefully up to the mouth of the bunker, making his way between blocks of concrete and steel prongs, twisted and bent. The air was cold at the top. He crossed over the ground toward the remains of the soldier, striding across the soft ash. A wind blew around him, swirling gray particles up in his face. He squinted and pushed on.

The claws retreated as he came close, some of them stiffening into immobility. He touched his tab. The Ivan would have given something for that! Short hard radiation emitted from the tab neutralized the claws, put them out of commission. Even the big robot with its two waving eyestalks retreated respectfully as he approached.

He bent down over the remains of the soldier. The gloved hand was closed tightly. There was something in it. Leone pried the fingers apart. A sealed container, aluminum. Still shiny.

He put it in his pocket and made his way back to the bunker. Behind him the claws came back to life, moving into operation again. The procession resumed, metal spheres moving through the gray ash with their loads. He could hear their treads scrabbling against the ground. He shuddered.

Scott watched intently as he brought the shiny tube out of his pocket. "He had that?"

"In his hand." Leone unscrewed the top. "Maybe you should look at it, sir."

Scott took it. He emptied the contents out in the palm of his hand. A small piece of silk paper, carefully folded. He sat down by the light and unfolded it.

"What's it say, sir?" Eric said. Several officers came up the tunnel. Major Hendricks appeared.

"Major," Scott said. "Look at this."

Hendricks read the slip. "This just come?"

"A single runner. Just now."

"Where is he?" Hendricks asked sharply.

"The claws got him."

Major Hendricks grunted. "Here." He passed it to his companions. "I think this is what we've been waiting for. They certainly took their time about it."

"So they want to talk terms," Scott said. "Are we going along with them?"

"That's not for us to decide." Hendricks sat down. "Where's the communications officer? I want the Moon Base."

Leone pondered as the communications officer raised the outside antenna cautiously, scanning the sky above the bunker for any sign of a watching Russian ship.

"Sir," Scott said to Hendricks. "It's sure strange they suddenly came around. We've been using the claws for almost a year. Now all of a sudden they start to fold."

"Maybe claws have been getting down in their bunkers."

"One of the big ones, the kind with stalks, got into an Ivan bunker last week," Eric said. "It got a whole platoon of them before they got their lid shut."

"How do you know?"

"A buddy told me. The thing came back with—with remains."

"Moon Base, sir," the communications officer said.

On the screen the face of the lunar monitor appeared. His crisp uniform contrasted to the uniforms in the bunker. And he was clean shaven. "Moon Base."

"This is forward command L-Whistle. On Terra. Let me have General Thompson."

The monitor faded. Presently General Thompson's heavy features came into focus. "What is it, Major?"

"Our claws got a single Russian runner with a message. We don't know whether to act on it—there have been tricks like this in the past."

"What's the message?"

"The Russians want us to send a single officer on policy level over to their lines. For a conference. They don't state the nature of the conference. They say that matters of—" He consulted the slip. "—Matters of grave urgency make it advisable that discussion be opened between a representative of the UN forces and themselves."

He held the message up to the screen for the general to scan. Thompson's eyes moved.

"What should we do?" Hendricks said.

"Send a man out."

"You don't think it's a trap?"

"It might be. But the location they give for their forward command is correct. It's worth a try, at any rate."

"I'll send an officer out. And report the results to you as soon as he returns."

"All right, Major." Thompson broke the connection. The screen died. Up above, the antenna came slowly down.

Hendricks rolled up the paper, deep in thought.

"I'll go," Leone said.

"They want somebody at policy level." Hendricks rubbed his jaw. "Policy level. I haven't been outside in months. Maybe I could use a little air."

"Don't you think it's risky?"

Hendricks lifted the view sight and gazed into it. The remains of the Russian were gone. Only a single claw was in sight. It was folding itself back, disappearing into the ash, like a crab. Like some hideous metal crab...

"That's the only thing that bothers me." Hendricks rubbed his wrist. "I know I'm safe as long as I have this on me. But there's something about them. I hate the damn things. I wish we'd never invented them. There's something wrong with them. Relentless little—"

"If we hadn't invented them, the Ivans would have."

Hendricks pushed the sight back. "Anyhow, it seems to be winning the war. I guess that's good."

"Sounds like you're getting the same jitters as the Ivans."

Hendricks examined his wrist watch. "I guess I had better get started, if I want to be there before dark."

He took a deep breath and then stepped out onto the gray, rubbled ground. After a minute he lit a cigarette and stood gazing around him. The landscape was dead. Nothing stirred. He could see for miles, endless ash and slag, ruins of buildings. A few trees without leaves or branches, only the trunks. Above him the eternal rolling clouds of gray, drifting between Terra and the sun.

Major Hendricks went on. Off to the right something scuttled, something round and metallic. A claw, going lickety-split after something. Probably after a small animal, a rat. They got rats, too. As a sort of sideline.

He came to the top of the little hill and lifted his fieldglasses. The Russian lines were a few miles ahead of him. They had a forward command post there. The runner had come from it.

A squat robot with undulating arms passed by him, its arms weaving inquiringly. The robot went on its way, disappearing under some debris. Hendricks watched it go. He had never seen that type before. There were getting to be more and more types he had never seen, new varieties and sizes coming up from the underground factories.

Hendricks put out his cigarette and hurried on. It was interesting, the use of artificial forms in warfare. How had they got started? Necessity. The Soviet Union had gained great initial success, usual with the side that got the war going. Most of North America had been blasted off the map. Retaliation was quick in coming, of course. The sky was full of circling disc-bombers long before the war began; they had been up there for years. The discs began sailing down all over Russia within hours after Washington got it.

But that hadn't helped Washington.

The American bloc governments moved to the Moon Base the first year. There was not much else to do. Europe was gone; a slag heap with dark weeds growing from the ashes and bones. Most of North America was useless; nothing could be planted, no one could live. A few million people kept going up in Canada and down in South America. But during the second year Soviet parachutists began to drop, a few at first, then more and more. They wore the first really effective anti-radiation equipment; what was left of American production moved to the moon along with the governments.

All but the troops. The remaining troops stayed behind as best they could, a few thousand here, a platoon there. No one knew exactly where they were; they stayed where they could, moving around at night, hiding in ruins, in sewers, cellars, with the rats and snakes. It looked as if the Soviet Union had the war almost won. Except for a handful of projectiles fired off from the moon daily, there was almost no weapon in use against them. They came and went as they pleased. The war, for all practical purposes, was over. Nothing effective opposed them.

And then the first claws appeared. And overnight the complexion of the war changed.

The claws were awkward, at first. Slow. The Ivans knocked them off almost as fast as they crawled out of their underground tunnels. But then they got better, faster and more cunning. Factories, all on Terra, turned them out. Factories a long way under ground, behind the Soviet lines, factories that had once made atomic projectiles, now almost forgotten.

The claws got faster, and they got bigger. New types appeared, some with feelers, some that flew. There were a few jumping kinds.

The best technicians on the moon were working on designs, making them more and more intricate, more flexible. They became uncanny; the Ivans were having a lot of trouble with them. Some of the little claws were learning to hide themselves, burrowing down into the ash, lying in wait.

And then they started getting into the Russian bunkers, slipping down when the lids were raised for air and a look around. One claw inside a bunker, a churning sphere of blades and metal—that was enough. And when one got in others followed. With a weapon like that the war couldn't go on much longer.

Maybe it was already over.

Maybe he was going to hear the news. Maybe the Politburo had decided to throw in the sponge.[3] Too bad it had taken so long. Six years. A long time for war like that, the way they had waged it. The automatic retaliation discs, spinning down all over Russia, hundreds of thousands of them. Bacteria crystals. The Soviet guided missiles, whistling through the air. The chain bombs. And now this, the robots, the claws—

The claws weren't like other weapons. They were *alive*, from any practical standpoint, whether the Governments wanted to admit it or not. They were not machines. They were living things, spinning, creeping, shaking themselves up suddenly from the gray ash and darting toward a man, climbing up him, rushing for his throat. And that was what they had been designed to do. Their job.

They did their job well. Especially lately, with the new designs coming up. Now they repaired themselves. They were on their own. Radiation tabs protected the UN troops, but if a man lost his tab he was fair game for the claws, no matter what his uniform. Down below the surface automatic machinery stamped them out. Human beings stayed a long way off. It was too risky; nobody wanted to be around them. They were left to themselves.

---

3. When Dick was writing this story, the phrases "throw in the sponge" and "throw in the towel" were used interchangably, but in the following decades "throw in the towel" became the more common phrase after the action performed when someone conceded in a boxing match.

And they seemed to be doing all right. The new designs were faster, more complex. More efficient.

Apparently they had won the war.

Major Hendricks lit a second cigarette. The landscape depressed him. Nothing but ash and ruins. He seemed to be alone, the only living thing in the whole world. To the right the ruins of a town rose up, a few walls and heaps of debris. He tossed the dead match away, increasing his pace. Suddenly he stopped, jerking up his gun, his body tense. For a minute it looked like—

From behind the shell of a ruined building a figure came, walking slowly toward him, walking hesitantly.

Hendricks blinked. "Stop!"

The boy stopped. Hendricks lowered his gun. The boy stood silently, looking at him. He was small, not very old. Perhaps eight. But it was hard to tell. Most of the kids who remained were stunted. He wore a faded blue sweater, ragged with dirt, and short pants. His hair was long and matted. Brown hair. It hung over his face and around his ears. He held something in his arms.

"What's that you have?" Hendricks said sharply.

The boy held it out. It was a toy, a bear. A teddy bear. The boy's eyes were large, but without expression.

Hendricks relaxed. "I don't want it. Keep it."

The boy hugged the bear again.

"Where do you live?" Hendricks said.

"In there."

"The ruins?"

"Yes."

"Underground?"

"Yes."

"How many are there?"

"How—how many?"

"How many of you. How big's your settlement?"

The boy did not answer.

Hendricks frowned. "You're not all by yourself, are you?"

The boy nodded.

"How do you stay alive?"

"There's food."

"What kind of food?"

"Different."

Hendricks studied him. "How old are you?"

"Thirteen."

It wasn't possible. Or was it? The boy was thin, stunted. And probably sterile. Radiation exposure, years straight. No wonder he was so small. His arms and legs were like pipe cleaners, knobby, and thin. Hendricks touched the boy's arm. His skin was dry and rough; radiation skin. He bent down, looking into the boy's face. There was no expression. Big eyes, big and dark.

"Are you blind?" Hendricks said.

"No. I can see some."

"How do you get away from the claws?"

"The claws?"

"The round things. That run and burrow."

"I don't understand."

Maybe there weren't any claws around. A lot of areas were free. They collected mostly around bunkers, where there were people. The claws had been designed to sense warmth, warmth of living things.

"You're lucky." Hendricks straightened up. "Well? Which way are you going? Back—back there?"

"Can I come with you?"

"With *me*?" Hendricks folded his arms. "I'm going a long way. Miles. I have to hurry." He looked at his watch. "I have to get there by nightfall."

"I want to come."

Hendricks fumbled in his pack. "It isn't worth it. Here." He tossed down the food cans he had with him. "You take these and go back. Okay?"

The boy said nothing.

"I'll be coming back this way. In a day or so. If you're around here when I come back you can come along with me. All right?"

"I want to go with you now."

"It's a long walk."

"I can walk."

Hendricks shifted uneasily. It made too good a target, two people walking along. And the boy would slow him down. But he might not come back this way. And if the boy were really all alone—

"Okay. Come along."

The boy fell in beside him. Hendricks strode along. The boy walked silently, clutching his teddy bear.

"What's your name?" Hendricks said, after a time.

"David Edward Derring."

"David? What—what happened to your mother and father?"

"They died."

"How?"

"In the blast."

"How long ago?"

"Six years."

Hendricks slowed down. "You've been alone six years?"

"No. There were other people for a while. They went away."

"And you've been alone since?"

"Yes."

Hendricks glanced down. The boy was strange, saying very little. Withdrawn. But that was the way they were, the children who had survived. Quiet. Stoic. A strange kind of fatalism gripped them. Nothing came as a surprise. They accepted anything that came along. There was no longer any *normal*, any natural course of things, moral or physical, for them to expect. Custom, habit, all the determining forces of learning were gone; only brute experience remained.

"Am I walking too fast?" Hendricks said.

"No."

"How did you happen to see me?"

"I was waiting."

"Waiting?" Hendricks was puzzled. "What were you waiting for?"

"To catch things."

"What kind of things?"

"Things to eat."

"Oh." Hendricks set his lips grimly. A thirteen-year-old boy, living on rats and gophers and half-rotten canned food. Down in a hole under the ruins of a town. With radiation pools and claws, and Russian dive-mines up above, coasting around in the sky.

"Where are we going?" David asked.

"To the Russian lines."

"Russian?"

"The enemy. The people who started the war. They dropped the first radiation bombs. They began all this."

The boy nodded. His face showed no expression.

"I'm an American," Hendricks said.

There was no comment. On they went, the two of them, Hendricks walking a little ahead, David trailing behind him, hugging his dirty teddy bear against his chest.

About four in the afternoon they stopped to eat. Hendricks built a fire in a hollow between some slabs of concrete. He cleared the weeds away and heaped up bits of wood. The Russians' lines were not very far ahead. Around him was what had once been a long valley, acres of fruit trees and grapes. Nothing remained now but a few bleak stumps and the mountains that stretched across the horizon at the far end. And the clouds of rolling ash that blew and drifted with the wind, settling over the weeds and remains of buildings, walls here and there, once in a while what had been a road.

Hendricks made coffee and heated up some boiled mutton and bread. "Here." He handed bread and mutton to David. David squatted by the edge of the fire, his knees knobby and white. He examined the food and then passed it back, shaking his head.

"No."

"No? Don't you want any?"

"No."

Hendricks shrugged. Maybe the boy was a mutant, used to special food. It didn't matter. When he was hungry he would find something to eat. The boy was strange. But there were many strange changes coming over the world. Life was not the same, anymore. It would never be the same again. The human race was going to have to realize that.

"Suit yourself," Hendricks said. He ate the bread and mutton by himself, washing it down with coffee. He ate slowly, finding the food hard to digest. When he was done he got to his feet and stamped the fire out.

David rose slowly, watching him with his young-old eyes.

"We're going," Hendricks said.

"All right."

Hendricks walked along, his gun in his arms. They were close; he was tense, ready for anything. The Russians should be expecting a runner, an answer to their own runner, but they were tricky. There was always the possibility of a slipup. He scanned the landscape around him. Nothing but slag and ash, a few hills, charred trees. Concrete walls. But someplace ahead was the first bunker of the Russian lines, the forward command. Underground, buried deep, with only a periscope showing, a few gun muzzles. Maybe an antenna.

"Will we be there soon?" David asked.

"Yes. Getting tired?"

"No."

"Why, then?"

David did not answer. He plodded carefully along behind, picking his way over the ash. His legs and shoes were gray with dust. His pinched face was streaked, lines of gray ash in riverlets down the pale white of his skin. There was no color to his face. Typical of the new children, growing up in cellars and sewers and underground shelters.

Hendricks slowed down. He lifted his fieldglasses and studied the ground ahead of him. Were they there, someplace, waiting for him? Watching him, the way his men had watched the Russian runner? A chill went up his back. Maybe they were getting their guns ready, preparing to fire, the way his men had prepared, made ready to kill.

Hendricks stopped, wiping perspiration from his face. "Damn." It made him uneasy. But he should be expected. The situation was different.

He strode over the ash, holding his gun tightly with both hands. Behind him came David. Hendricks peered around, tight-lipped. Any second it might happen. A burst of white light, a blast, carefully aimed from inside a deep concrete bunker.

He raised his arm and waved it around in a circle.

Nothing moved. To the right a long ridge ran, topped with dead tree trunks. A few wild vines had grown up around the trees, remains of arbors. And the eternal dark weeds. Hendricks studied the ridge. Was anything up there? Perfect place for a lookout. He approached the ridge warily, David coming silently behind. If it were his command he'd have a sentry up there, watching for troops trying to infiltrate into the command area. Of course, if it were his command there would be the claws around the area for full protection.

He stopped, feet apart, hands on his hips.

"Are we there?" David said.

"Almost."

"Why have we stopped?"

"I don't want to take any chances." Hendricks advanced slowly. Now the ridge lay directly beside him, along his right. Overlooking him. His uneasy feeling increased. If an Ivan were up there he wouldn't have a chance. He waved his arm again. They should be expecting someone in the UN uniform, in response to the note capsule. Unless the whole thing was a trap.

"Keep up with me." He turned toward David. "Don't drop behind."

"With you?"

"Up beside me! We're close. We can't take any chances. Come on."

"I'll be all right." David remained behind him, in the rear, a few paces away, still clutching his teddy bear.

"Have it your way." Hendricks raised his glasses again, suddenly tense. For a moment—had something moved? He scanned the ridge carefully. Everything was silent. Dead. No life up there, only tree trunks and ash. Maybe a few rats. The big black rats that had survived the claws. Mutants—built their own shelters out of saliva and ash. Some kind of plaster. Adaptation. He started forward again.

A tall figure came out on the ridge above him, cloak flapping. Gray-green. A Russian. Behind him a second soldier appeared, another Russian. Both lifted their guns, aiming.

Hendricks froze. He opened his mouth. The soldiers were kneeling, sighting down the side of the slope. A third figure had joined them on the ridge top, a smaller figure in gray-green. A woman. She stood behind the other two.

Hendricks found his voice. "Stop!" He waved up at them frantically. "I'm—"

The two Russians fired. Behind Hendricks there was a faint *pop*. Waves of heat lapped against him, throwing him to the ground. Ash tore at his face, grinding into his eyes and nose. Choking, he pulled himself to his knees. It was all a trap. He was finished. He had come to be killed, like a steer. The soldiers and the woman were coming down the side of the ridge toward him, sliding down through the soft ash. Hendricks was numb. His head throbbed. Awkwardly, he got his rifle up and took aim. It weighed a thousand tons; he could hardly hold it. His nose and cheeks stung. The air was full of the blast smell, a bitter acrid stench.

"Don't fire," the first Russian said, in heavily accented English.

The three of them came up to him, surrounding him. "Put down your rifle, Yank,"[4] the other said.

Hendricks was dazed. Everything had happened so fast. He had been caught. And they had blasted the boy. He turned his head. David was gone. What remained of him was strewn across the ground.

The three Russians studied him curiously. Hendricks sat, wiping blood from his nose, picking out bits of ash. He shook his head, trying to clear it. "Why did you do it?" he murmured thickly. "The boy."

"Why?" One of the soldiers helped him roughly to his feet. He turned Hendricks around. "Look."

Hendricks closed his eyes.

"Look!" The two Russians pulled him forward. "See. Hurry up. There isn't much time to spare, Yank!"

Hendricks looked. And gasped.

"See now? Now do you understand?"

From the remains of David a metal wheel rolled. Relays, glinting metal. Parts, wiring. One of the Russians kicked at the heap of

---

4. Short for "Yankee," a Yank is someone from the United States.

remains. Parts popped out, rolling away, wheels and springs and rods. A plastic section fell in, half charred. Hendricks bent shakily down. The front of the head had come off. He could make out the intricate brain, wires and relays, tiny tubes and switches, thousands of minute studs—

"A robot," the soldier holding his arm said. "We watched it tagging you."

"Tagging me?"

"That's their way. They tag along with you. Into the bunker. That's how they get in."

Hendricks blinked, dazed. "But—"

"Come on." They led him toward the ridge. "We can't stay here. It isn't safe. There must be hundreds of them all around here."

The three of them pulled him up the side of the ridge, sliding and slipping on the ash. The woman reached the top and stood waiting for them.

"The forward command," Hendricks muttered. "I came to negotiate with the Soviet—"

"There is no more forward command. *They* got in. We'll explain." They reached the top of the ridge. "We're all that's left. The three of us. The rest were down in the bunker."

"This way. Down this way." The woman unscrewed a lid, a gray manhole cover set in the ground. "Get in."

Hendricks lowered himself. The two soldiers and the woman came behind him, following him down the ladder. The woman closed the lid after them, bolting it tightly into place.

"Good thing we saw you," one of the two soldiers grunted. "It had tagged you about as far as it was going to."

"Give me one of your cigarettes," the woman said. "I haven't had an American cigarette for weeks."

Hendricks pushed the pack to her. She took a cigarette and

passed the pack to the two soldiers. In the corner of the small room the lamp gleamed fitfully. The room was low-ceilinged, cramped. The four of them sat around a small wood table. A few dirty dishes were stacked to one side. Behind a ragged curtain a second room was partly visible. Hendricks saw the corner of a cot, some blankets, clothes hung on a hook.

"We were here," the soldier beside him said. He took off his helmet, pushing his blond hair back. "I'm Corporal Rudi Maxer. Polish. Impressed in the Soviet Army two years ago." He held out his hand.

Hendricks hesitated and then shook. "Major Joseph Hendricks."

"Klaus Epstein." The other soldier shook with him, a small dark man with thinning hair. Epstein plucked nervously at his ear. "Austrian. Impressed God knows when. I don't remember. The three of us were here, Rudi and I, with Tasso." He indicated the woman. "That's how we escaped. All the rest were down in the bunker."

"And—and *they* got in?"

Epstein lit a cigarette. "First just one of them. The kind that tagged you. Then it let others in."

Hendricks became alert. "The *kind*? Are there more than one kind?"

"The little boy. David. David holding his teddy bear. That's Variety Three. The most effective."

"What are the other types?"

Epstein reached into his coat. "Here." He tossed a packet of photographs onto the table, tied with a string. "Look for yourself."

Hendricks untied the string.

"You see," Rudi Maxer said, "that was why we wanted to talk terms. The Russians, I mean. We found out about a week ago. Found out that your claws were beginning to make up new designs on their own. New types of their own. Better types. Down in your underground factories behind our lines. You let them stamp themselves, repair themselves. Made them more and more intricate. It's your fault this happened."

Hendricks examined the photos. They had been snapped hurriedly; they were blurred and indistinct. The first few showed—David. David walking along a road, by himself. David and another David. Three Davids. All exactly alike. Each with a ragged teddy bear.

All pathetic.

"Look at the others," Tasso said.

The next pictures, taken at a great distance, showed a towering wounded soldier sitting by the side of a path, his arm in a sling, the stump of one leg extended, a crude crutch on his lap. Then two wounded soldiers, both the same, standing side by side.

"That's Variety One. The Wounded Soldier." Klaus reached out and took the pictures. "You see, the claws were designed to get to human beings. To find them. Each kind was better than the last. They got farther, closer, past most of our defenses, into our lines. But as long as they were merely *machines*, metal spheres with claws and horns, feelers, they could be picked off like any other object. They could be detected as lethal robots as soon as they were seen. Once we caught sight of them—"

"Variety One subverted our whole north wing," Rudi said. "It was a long time before anyone caught on. Then it was too late. They came in, wounded soldiers, knocking and begging to be let in. So we let them in. And as soon as they were in they took over. We were watching out for machines..."

"At that time it was thought there was only the one type," Klaus Epstein said. "No one suspected there were other types. The pictures were flashed to us. When the runner was sent to you, we knew of just one type. Variety One. The big Wounded Soldier. We thought that was all."

"Your line fell to—"

"To Variety Three. David and his bear. That worked even better." Klaus smiled bitterly. "Soldiers are suckers for children. We brought them in and tried to feed them. We found out the hard way what they were after. At least, those who were in the bunker."

"The three of us were lucky," Rudi said. "Klaus and I were—were visiting Tasso when it happened. This is her place." He waved a big hand around. "This little cellar. We finished and climbed the ladder to start back. From the ridge we saw. There they were, all around the bunker. Fighting was still going on. David and his bear. Hundreds of them. Klaus took the pictures."

Klaus tied up the photographs again.

"And it's going on all along your line?" Hendricks said.

"Yes."

"How about *our* lines?" Without thinking, he touched the tab on his arm. "Can they—"

"They're not bothered by your radiation tabs. It makes no difference to them, Russian, American, Pole, German. It's all the same. They're doing what they were designed to do. Carrying out the original idea. They track down life, wherever they find it."

"They go by warmth," Klaus said. "That was the way you constructed them from the very start. Of course, those you designed were kept back by the radiation tabs you wear. Now they've got around that. These new varieties are lead-lined."

"What's the other variety?" Hendricks asked. "The David type, the Wounded Soldier—what's the other?"

"We don't know." Klaus pointed up at the wall. On the wall were two metal plates, ragged at the edges. Hendricks got up and studied them. They were bent and dented.

"The one on the left came off a Wounded Soldier," Rudi said. "We got one of them. It was going along toward our old bunker. We got it from the ridge, the same way we got the David tagging you."

The plate was stamped: I–V. Hendricks touched the other plate. "And this came from the David type?"

"Yes." The plate was stamped: III–V.

Klaus took a look at them, leaning over Hendricks' broad shoulder. "You can see what we're up against. There's another type. Maybe it was abandoned. Maybe it didn't work. But there must be a Second Variety. There's One and Three."

"You were lucky," Rudi said. "The David tagged you all the way here and never touched you. Probably thought you'd get it into a bunker, somewhere."

"One gets in and it's all over," Klaus said. "They move fast. One lets all the rest inside. They're inflexible. Machines with one purpose. They were built for only one thing." He rubbed sweat from his lip. "We saw."

They were silent.

"Let me have another cigarette, Yank," Tasso said. "They are good. I almost forgot how they were."

It was night. The sky was black. No stars were visible through the rolling clouds of ash. Klaus lifted the lid cautiously so that Hendricks could look out.

Rudi pointed into the darkness. "Over that way are the bunkers. Where we used to be. Not over half a mile from us. It was just chance Klaus and I were not there when it happened. Weakness. Saved by our lusts."

"All the rest must be dead," Klaus said in a low voice. "It came quickly. This morning the Politburo reached their decision. They notified us—forward command. Our runner was sent out at once. We saw him start toward the direction of your lines. We covered him until he was out of sight."

"Alex Radrivsky. We both knew him. He disappeared about six o'clock. The sun had just come up. About noon Klaus and I had an hour relief. We crept off, away from the bunkers. No one was watching. We came here. There used to be a town here, a few houses, a street. This cellar was part of a big farmhouse. We knew Tasso would be here, hiding down in her little place. We had come here before. Others from the bunkers came here. Today happened to be our turn."

"So we were saved," Klaus said. "Chance. It might have been others. We—we finished, and then we came up to the surface and started back along the ridge. That was when we saw them, the Davids. We understood right away. We had seen the photos of the First Variety, the Wounded Soldier. Our Commissar distributed them to us with an explanation. If we had gone another step they would have seen us. As it was we had to blast two Davids before we got back. There were hundreds of them, all around. Like ants. We took pictures and slipped back here, bolting the lid tight."

"They're not so much when you catch them alone. We moved faster than they did. But they're inexorable. Not like living things. They came right at us. And we blasted them."

Major Hendricks rested against the edge of the lid, adjusting his eyes to the darkness. "Is it safe to have the lid up at all?"

"If we're careful. How else can you operate your transmitter?"

Hendricks lifted the small belt transmitter slowly. He pressed it against his ear. The metal was cold and damp. He blew against the mic, raising up the short antenna. A faint hum sounded in his ear. "That's true, I suppose."

But he still hesitated.

"We'll pull you under if anything happens," Klaus said.

"Thanks." Hendricks waited a moment, resting the transmitter against his shoulder. "Interesting, isn't it?"

"What?"

"This, the new types. The new varieties of claws. We're completely at their mercy, aren't we? By now they've probably gotten into the UN lines, too. It makes me wonder if we're not seeing the beginning of a new species. *The* new species. Evolution. The race to come after man."

Rudi grunted. "There is no race after man."

"No? Why not? Maybe we're seeing it now, the end of human beings, the beginning of the new society."

"They're not a race. They're mechanical killers. You made them to destroy. That's all they can do. They're machines with a job."

"So it seems now. But how about later on? After the war is over. Maybe, when there aren't any humans to destroy, their real potentialities will begin to show."

"You talk as if they were alive!"

"Aren't they?"

There was silence. "They're machines," Rudi said. "They look like people, but they're machines."

"Use your transmitter, Major," Klaus said. "We can't stay up here forever."

Holding the transmitter tightly Hendricks called the code of the command bunker. He waited, listening. No response. Only silence. He checked the leads carefully. Everything was in place.

"Scott!" he said into the mic. "Can you hear me?"

Silence. He raised the gain up full and tried again. Only static.

"I don't get anything. They may hear me but they may not want to answer."

"Tell them it's an emergency."

"They'll think I'm being forced to call. Under your direction." He tried again, outlining briefly what he had learned. But still the phone was silent, except for the faint static.

"Radiation pools kill most transmission," Klaus said, after a while. "Maybe that's it."

Hendricks shut the transmitter up. "No use. No answer. Radiation pools? Maybe. Or they hear me, but won't answer. Frankly, that's what I would do, if a runner tried to call from the

Soviet lines. They have no reason to believe such a story. They may hear everything I say—"

"Or maybe it's too late."

Hendricks nodded.

"We better get the lid down," Rudi said nervously. "We don't want to take unnecessary chances."

They climbed slowly back down the tunnel. Klaus bolted the lid carefully into place. They descended into the kitchen. The air was heavy and close around them.

"Could they work that fast?" Hendricks said. "I left the bunker this noon. Ten hours ago. How could they move so quickly?"

"It doesn't take them long. Not after the first one gets in. It goes wild. You know what the little claws can do. Even *one* of these is beyond belief. Razors, each finger. Maniacal."

"All right." Hendricks moved away impatiently. He stood with his back to them.

"What's the matter?" Rudi said.

"The Moon Base. God, if they've gotten there—"

"The Moon Base?"

Hendricks turned around. "They couldn't have got to the Moon Base. How would they get there? It isn't possible. I can't believe it."

"What is this Moon Base? We've heard rumors, but nothing definite. What is the actual situation? You seem concerned."

"We're supplied from the moon. The governments are there, under the lunar surface. All our people and industries. That's what keeps us going. If they should find some way of getting off Terra, onto the moon—"

"It only takes one of them. Once the first one gets in it admits the others. Hundreds of them, all alike. You should have seen them. Identical. Like ants."

"Perfect socialism," Tasso said. "The ideal of the communist state. All citizens interchangeable."

Klaus grunted angrily. "That's enough. Well? What next?"

Hendricks paced back and forth, around the small room. The air was full of smells of food and perspiration. The others watched him. Presently Tasso pushed through the curtain, into the other room. "I'm going to take a nap."

The curtain closed behind her. Rudi and Klaus sat down at the table, still watching Hendricks.

"It's up to you," Klaus said. "We don't know your situation."

Hendricks nodded.

"It's a problem." Rudi drank some coffee, filling his cup from a rusty pot. "We're safe here for a while, but we can't stay here forever. Not enough food or supplies."

"But if we go outside—"

"If we go outside they'll get us. Or probably they'll get us. We couldn't go very far. How far is your command bunker, Major?"

"Three or four miles."

"We might make it. The four of us. Four of us could watch all sides. They couldn't slip up behind us and start tagging us. We have three rifles, three blast rifles. Tasso can have my pistol." Rudi tapped his belt. "In the Soviet army we didn't have shoes always, but we had guns. With all four of us armed one of us might get to your command bunker. Preferably you, Major."

"What if they're already there?" Klaus said.

Rudi shrugged. "Well, then we come back here."

Hendricks stopped pacing. "What do you think the chances are they're already in the American lines?"

"Hard to say. Fairly good. They're organized. They know exactly what they're doing. Once they start they go like a horde of locusts. They have to keep moving, and fast. It's secrecy and speed they depend on. Surprise. They push their way in before anyone has any idea."

"I see," Hendricks murmured.

From the other room Tasso stirred. "Major?"

Hendricks pushed the curtain back. "What?"

Tasso looked up at him lazily from the cot. "Have you any more American cigarettes left?"

Hendricks went into the room and sat down across from her, on a wood stool. He felt in his pockets. "No. All gone."

"Too bad."

"What nationality are you?" Hendricks asked after a while.

"Russian."

"How did you get here?"

"Here?"

"This used to be France. This was part of Normandy. Did you come with the Soviet army?"

"Why?"

"Just curious." He studied her. She had taken off her coat, tossing it over the end of the cot. She was young, about twenty. Slim. Her long hair stretched out over the pillow. She was staring at him silently, her eyes dark and large.

"What's on your mind?" Tasso said.

"Nothing. How old are you?"

"Eighteen." She continued to watch him, unblinking, her arms behind her head. She had on Russian army pants and shirt. Gray-green. Thick leather belt with counter and cartridges. Medicine kit.

"You're in the Soviet army?"

"No."

"Where did you get the uniform?"

She shrugged. "It was given to me," she told him.

"How—how old were you when you came here?"

"Sixteen."

"That young?"

Her eyes narrowed. "What do you mean?"

Hendricks rubbed his jaw. "Your life would have been a lot different if there had been no war. Sixteen. You came here at sixteen. To live this way."

"I had to survive."

"I'm not moralizing."

"Your life would have been different, too," Tasso murmured. She reached down and unfastened one of her boots. She kicked the boot off, onto the floor. "Major, do you want to go in the other room? I'm sleepy."

"It's going to be a problem, the four of us here. It's going to be hard to live in these quarters. Are there just the two rooms?"

"Yes."

"How big was the cellar originally? Was it larger than this? Are there other rooms filled up with debris? We might be able to open one of them."

"Perhaps. I really don't know." Tasso loosened her belt. She made herself comfortable on the cot, unbuttoning her shirt. "You're sure you have no more cigarettes?"

"I had only the one pack."

"Too bad. Maybe if we get back to your bunker we can find some." The other boot fell. Tasso reached up for the light cord. "Good night."

"You're going to sleep?"

"That's right."

The room plunged into darkness. Hendricks got up and made his way past the curtain, into the kitchen.

And stopped, rigid.

Rudi stood against the wall, his face white and gleaming. His mouth opened and closed but no sounds came. Klaus stood in front of him, the muzzle of his pistol in Rudi's stomach. Neither of them moved. Klaus, his hand tight around his gun, his features set. Rudi, pale and silent, spread-eagled against the wall.

"What—" Hendricks muttered, but Klaus cut him off.

"Be quiet, Major. Come over here. Your gun. Get out your gun."

Hendricks drew his pistol. "What is it?"

"Cover him." Klaus motioned him forward. "Beside me. Hurry!"

Rudi moved a little, lowering his arms. He turned to Hendricks, licking his lips. The whites of his eyes shone wildly. Sweat dripped from his forehead, down his cheeks. He fixed his gaze on Hendricks. "Major, he's gone insane. Stop him." Rudi's voice was thin and hoarse, almost inaudible.

"What's going on?" Hendricks demanded.

Without lowering his pistol Klaus answered. "Major, remember our discussion? The Three Varieties? We knew about One and Three. But we didn't know about Two. At least, we didn't know before." Klaus' fingers tightened around the gun butt. "We didn't know before, but we know now."

He pressed the trigger. A burst of white heat rolled out of the gun, licking around Rudi.

"Major, this is the Second Variety."

Tasso swept the curtain aside. "Klaus! What did you do?"

Klaus turned from the charred form, gradually sinking down the wall onto the floor. "The Second Variety, Tasso. Now we know. We have all three types identified. The danger is less. I—"

Tasso stared past him at the remains of Rudi, at the blackened, smoldering fragments and bits of cloth. "You killed him."

"Him? *It*, you mean. I was watching. I had a feeling, but I wasn't sure. At least, I wasn't sure before. But this evening I was certain." Klaus rubbed his pistol butt nervously. "We're lucky. Don't you understand? Another hour and it might—"

"You were *certain*?" Tasso pushed past him and bent down, over the steaming remains on the floor. Her face became hard. "Major, see for yourself. Bones. Flesh."

Hendricks bent down beside her. The remains were human

remains. Seared flesh, charred bone fragments, part of a skull. Ligaments, viscera, blood. Blood forming a pool against the wall.

"No wheels," Tasso said calmly. She straightened up. "No wheels, no parts, no relays. Not a claw. Not the Second Variety." She folded her arms. "You're going to have to be able to explain this."

Klaus sat down at the table, all the color drained suddenly from his face. He put his head in his hands and rocked back and forth.

"Snap out of it." Tasso's fingers closed over his shoulder. "Why did you do it? Why did you kill him?"

"He was frightened," Hendricks said. "All this, the whole thing, building up around us."

"Maybe."

"What, then? What do you think?"

"I think he may have had a reason for killing Rudi. A good reason."

"What reason?"

"Maybe Rudi learned something."

Hendricks studied her bleak face. "About what?" he asked.

"About him. About Klaus."

Klaus looked up quickly. "You can see what she's trying to say. She thinks I'm the Second Variety. Don't you see, Major? Now she wants you to believe I killed him on purpose. That I'm—"

"Why did you kill him, then?" Tasso said.

"I told you." Klaus shook his head wearily. "I thought he was a claw. I thought I knew."

"Why?"

"I had been watching him. I was suspicious."

"Why?"

"I thought I had seen something. Heard something. I thought I—" He stopped.

"Go on."

"We were sitting at the table. Playing cards. You two were in the other room. It was silent. I thought I heard him—*whirr*."

There was silence.

"Do you believe that?" Tasso said to Hendricks.

"Yes. I believe what he says."

"I don't. I think he killed Rudi for a good purpose." Tasso touched the rifle, resting in the corner of the room. "Major—"

"No." Hendricks shook his head. "Let's stop it right now. One is enough. We're afraid, the way he was. If we kill him we'll be doing what he did to Rudi."

Klaus looked gratefully up at him. "Thanks. I was afraid. You understand, don't you? Now she's afraid, the way I was. She wants to kill me."

"No more killing." Hendricks moved toward the end of the ladder. "I'm going above and try the transmitter once more. If I can't get them we're moving back toward my lines tomorrow morning."

Klaus rose quickly. "I'll come up with you and give you a hand."

The night air was cold. The earth was cooling off. Klaus took a deep breath, filling his lungs. He and Hendricks stepped onto the ground, out of the tunnel. Klaus planted his feet wide apart, the rifle up, watching and listening. Hendricks crouched by the tunnel mouth, tuning the small transmitter.

"Any luck?" Klaus asked presently.

"Not yet."

"Keep trying. Tell them what happened."

Hendricks kept trying. Without success. Finally he lowered the antenna. "It's useless. They can't hear me. Or they hear me and won't answer. Or—"

"Or they don't exist."

"I'll try once more." Hendricks raised the antenna. "Scott, can you hear me? Come in!"

He listened. There was only static. Then, still very faintly—

"This is Scott."

His fingers tightened. "Scott! Is it you?"

"This is Scott."

Klaus squatted down. "Is it your command?"

"Scott, listen. Do you understand? About them, the claws. Did you get my message? Did you hear me?"

"Yes." Faintly. Almost inaudible. He could hardly make out the word.

"You got my message? Is everything all right at the bunker? None of them have got in?"

"Everything is all right."

"Have they tried to get in?"

The voice was weaker.

"No."

Hendricks turned to Klaus. "They're all right."

"Have they been attacked?"

"No." Hendricks pressed the phone tighter to his ear. "Scott, I can hardly hear you. Have you notified the Moon Base? Do they know? Are they alerted?"

No answer.

"Scott! Can you hear me?"

Silence.

Hendricks relaxed, sagging. "Faded out. Must be radiation pools."

Hendricks and Klaus looked at each other. Neither of them said anything. After a time Klaus said, "Did it sound like any of your men? Could you identify the voice?"

"It was too faint."

"You couldn't be certain?"

"No."

"Then it could have been—"

"I don't know. Now I'm not sure. Let's go back down and get the lid closed."

They climbed back down the ladder slowly, into the warm cellar. Klaus bolted the lid behind them. Tasso waited for them, her face expressionless.

"Any luck?" she asked.

Neither of them answered. "Well?" Klaus said at last. "What do you think, Major? Was it your officer, or was it one of *them*?"

"I don't know."

"Then we're just where we were before."

Hendricks stared down at the floor, his jaw set. "We'll have to go. To be sure."

"Anyhow, we have food here for only a few weeks. We'd have to go up after that, in any case."

"Apparently so."

"What's wrong?" Tasso demanded. "Did you get across to your bunker? What's the matter?"

"It may have been one of my men," Hendricks said slowly. "Or it may have been one of *them*. But we'll never know standing here." He examined his watch. "Let's turn in and get some sleep. We want to be up early tomorrow."

"Early?"

"Our best chance to get through the claws should be early in the morning," Hendricks said.

The morning was crisp and clear. Major Hendricks studied the countryside through his fieldglasses.

"See anything?" Klaus said.

"No."

"Can you make out our bunkers?"

"Which way?"

"Here." Klaus took the glasses and adjusted them. "I know where to look." He looked a long time, silently.

Tasso came to the top of the tunnel and stepped up onto the ground. "Anything?"

"No." Klaus passed the glasses back to Hendricks. "They're out of sight. Come on. Let's not stay here."

The three of them made their way down the side of the ridge, sliding in the soft ash. Across a flat rock a lizard scuttled. They stopped instantly, rigid.

"What was it?" Klaus muttered.

"A lizard."

The lizard ran on, hurrying through the ash. It was exactly the same color as the ash.

"Perfect adaptation," Klaus said. "Proves we were right. Lysenko, I mean."

They reached the bottom of the ridge and stopped, standing close together, looking around them.

"Let's go." Hendricks started off. "It's a good long trip, on foot."

Klaus fell in beside him. Tasso walked behind, her pistol held alertly. "Major, I've been meaning to ask you something," Klaus said. "How did you run across the David? The one that was tagging you."

"I met it along the way. In some ruins."

"What did it say?"

"Not much. It said it was alone. By itself."

"You couldn't tell it was a machine? It talked like a living person? You never suspected?"

"It didn't say much. I noticed nothing unusual."

"It's strange, machines so much like people that you can be fooled. Almost alive. I wonder where it'll end."

"They're doing what you Yanks designed them to do," Tasso said. "You designed them to hunt out life and destroy. Human life. Wherever they find it."

Hendricks was watching Klaus intently. "Why did you ask me? What's on your mind?"

"Nothing," Klaus answered.

"Klaus thinks you're the Second Variety," Tasso said calmly, from behind them. "Now he's got his eye on you."

Klaus flushed. "Why not? We sent a runner to the Yank lines and he comes back. Maybe he thought he'd find some good game here."

Hendricks laughed harshly. "I came from the UN bunkers. There were human beings all around me."

"Maybe you saw an opportunity to get into the Soviet lines. Maybe you saw your chance. Maybe you—"

"The Soviet lines had already been taken over. Your lines had been invaded before I left my command bunker. Don't forget that."

Tasso came up beside him. "That proves nothing at all, Major."

"Why not?"

"There appears to be little communication between the varieties. Each is made in a different factory. They don't seem to work together. You might have started for the Soviet lines without knowing anything about the work of the other varieties. Or even what the other varieties were like."

"How do you know so much about the claws?" Hendricks said.

"I've seen them. I've observed them. I observed them take over the Soviet bunkers."

"You know quite a lot," Klaus said. "Actually, you saw very little. Strange that you should have been such an acute observer."

Tasso laughed. "Do you suspect me, now?"

"Forget it," Hendricks said. They walked on in silence.

"Are we going the whole way on foot?" Tasso said, after a while. "I'm not used to walking." She gazed around at the plain of ash, stretching out on all sides of them, as far as they could see. "How dreary."

"It's like this all the way," Klaus said.

"In a way I wish you had been in your bunker when the attack came."

"Somebody else would have been with you, if not me," Klaus muttered.

Tasso laughed, putting her hands in her pockets. "I suppose so."

They walked on, keeping their eyes on the vast plain of silent ash around them.

The sun was setting. Hendricks made his way forward slowly, waving Tasso and Klaus back. Klaus squatted down, resting his gun butt against the ground.

Tasso found a concrete slab and sat down with a sigh. "It's good to rest."

"Be quiet," Klaus said sharply.

Hendricks pushed up to the top of the rise ahead of them. The same rise the Russian runner had come up, the day before. Hendricks dropped down, stretching himself out, peering through his glasses at what lay beyond.

Nothing was visible. Only ash and occasional trees. But there, not more than fifty yards ahead, was the entrance of the forward command bunker. The bunker from which he had come. Hendricks watched silently. No motion. No sign of life. Nothing stirred.

Klaus slithered up beside him. "Where is it?"

"Down there." Hendricks passed him the glasses. Clouds of ash rolled across the evening sky. The world was darkening. They had a couple of hours of light left, at the most. Probably not that much.

"I don't see anything," Klaus said.

"That tree there. The stump. By the pile of bricks. The entrance is to the right of the bricks."

"I'll have to take your word for it."

"You and Tasso cover me from here. You'll be able to sight all the way to the bunker entrance."

"You're going down alone?"

"With my wrist tab I'll be safe. The ground around the bunker is a living field of claws. They collect down in the ash. Like crabs. Without tabs you wouldn't have a chance."

"Maybe you're right."

"I'll walk slowly all the way. As soon as I know for certain—"

"If they're down inside the bunker you won't be able to get back up here. They go fast. You don't realize."

"What do you suggest?"

Klaus considered. "I don't know. Get them to come up to the surface. So you can see."

Hendricks brought his transmitter from his belt, raising the antenna. "Let's get started."

Klaus signaled to Tasso. She crawled expertly up the side of the rise to where they were sitting.

"He's going down alone," Klaus said. "We'll cover him from here. As soon as you see him start back, fire past him at once. They come quick."

"You're not very optimistic," Tasso said.

"No, I'm not."

Hendricks opened the breech of his gun, checking it carefully. "Maybe things are all right."

"You didn't see them. Hundreds of them. All the same. Pouring out like ants."

"I should be able to find out without going down all the way." Hendricks locked his gun, gripping it in one hand, the transmitter in the other. "Well, wish me luck."

Klaus put out his hand. "Don't go down until you're sure. Talk to them from up here. Make them show themselves."

Hendricks stood up. He stepped down the side of the rise.

A moment later he was walking slowly toward the pile of

bricks and debris beside the dead tree stump. Toward the entrance of the forward command bunker.

Nothing stirred. He raised the transmitter, clicking it on. "Scott? Can you hear me?"

Silence.

"Scott! This is Hendricks. Can you hear me? I'm standing outside the bunker. You should be able to see me in the view sight."

He listened, the transmitter gripped tightly. No sound. Only static. He walked forward. A claw burrowed out of the ash and raced toward him. It halted a few feet away and then slunk off. A second claw appeared, one of the big ones with feelers. It moved toward him, studied him intently, and then fell in behind him, dogging respectfully after him, a few paces away. A moment later a second big claw joined it. Silently, the claws trailed him, as he walked slowly toward the bunker.

Hendricks stopped, and behind him, the claws came to a halt. He was close, now. Almost to the bunker steps.

"Scott! Can you hear me? I'm standing right above you. Outside. On the surface. Are you picking me up?"

He waited, holding his gun against his side, the transmitter tightly to his ear. Time passed. He strained to hear, but there was only silence. Silence, and faint static.

Then, distantly, metallically—

"This is Scott."

The voice was neutral. Cold. He could not identify it. But the earphone was minute.

"Scott! Listen. I'm standing right above you. I'm on the surface, looking down into the bunker entrance."

"Yes."

"Can you see me?"

"Yes."

"Through the view sight? You have the sight trained on me?"

"Yes."

Hendricks pondered. A circle of claws waited quietly around him, gray-metal bodies on all sides of him. "Is everything all right in the bunker? Nothing unusual has happened?"

"Everything is all right."

"Will you come up to the surface? I want to see you for a moment." Hendricks took a deep breath. "Come up here with me. I want to talk to you."

"Come down."

"I'm giving you an order."

Silence.

"Are you coming?" Hendricks listened. There was no response. "I order you to come to the surface."

"Come down."

Hendricks set his jaw. "Let me talk to Leone."

There was a long pause. He listened to the static. Then a voice came, hard, thin, metallic. The same as the other. "This is Leone."

"Hendricks. I'm on the surface. At the bunker entrance. I want one of you to come up here."

"Come down."

"Why come down? I'm giving you an order!"

Silence. Hendricks lowered the transmitter. He looked carefully around him. The entrance was just ahead. Almost at his feet. He lowered the antenna and fastened the transmitter to his belt. Carefully, he gripped his gun with both hands. He moved forward, a step at a time. If they could see him they knew he was starting toward the entrance. He closed his eyes a moment.

Then he put his foot on the first step that led downward.

Two Davids came up at him, their faces identical and expressionless. He blasted them into particles. More came rushing silently up, a whole pack of them. All exactly the same.

Hendricks turned and raced back, away from the bunker, back toward the rise.

At the top of the rise Tasso and Klaus were firing down. The small claws were already streaking up toward them, shining metal spheres going fast, racing frantically through the ash. But he had no time to think about that. He knelt down, aiming at the bunker entrance, gun against his cheek. The Davids were coming out in groups, clutching their teddy bears, their thin knobby legs pumping as they ran up the steps to the surface. Hendricks fired into the main body of them. They burst apart, wheels and springs flying in all directions. He fired again through the mist of particles.

A giant lumbering figure rose up in the bunker entrance, tall and swaying. Hendricks paused, amazed. A man, a soldier. With one leg, supporting himself with a crutch.

"Major!" Tasso's voice came. More firing. The huge figure moved forward, Davids swarming around it. Hendricks broke out of his freeze. The First Variety. The Wounded Soldier.

He aimed and fired. The soldier burst into bits, parts and relays flying. Now many Davids were out on the flat ground, away from the bunker. He fired again and again, moving slowly back, half-crouching and aiming.

From the rise, Klaus fired down. The side of the rise was alive with claws making their way up. Hendricks retreated toward the rise, running and crouching. Tasso had left Klaus and was circling slowly to the right, moving away from the rise.

A David slipped up toward him, its small white face expressionless, brown hair hanging down in its eyes. It bent over suddenly, opening its arms. Its teddy bear hurtled down and leaped across the ground, bounding toward him. Hendricks fired. The bear and the David both dissolved. He grinned, blinking. It was like a dream.

"Up here!" Tasso's voice. Hendricks made his way toward her. She was over by some columns of concrete, walls of a ruined building. She was firing past him, with the hand pistol Klaus had given her.

"Thanks." He joined her, grasping for breath. She pulled him back, behind the concrete, fumbling at her belt.

"Close your eyes!" She unfastened a globe from her waist. Rapidly, she unscrewed the cap, locking it into place. "Close your eyes and get down."

She threw the bomb. It sailed in an arc, an expert, rolling and bouncing to the entrance of the bunker. Two Wounded Soldiers stood uncertainly by the brick pile. More Davids poured from behind them, out onto the plain. One of the Wounded Soldiers moved toward the bomb, stooping awkwardly down to pick it up.

The bomb went off. The concussion whirled Hendricks around, throwing him on his face. A hot wind rolled over him. Dimly he saw Tasso standing behind the columns, firing slowly and methodically at the Davids coming out of the raging clouds of white fire.

Back along the rise Klaus struggled with a ring of claws circling around him. He retreated, blasting at them and moving back, trying to break through the ring.

Hendricks struggled to his feet. His head ached. He could hardly see. Everything was licking at him, raging and whirling. His right arm would not move.

Tasso pulled back toward him. "Come on. Let's go."

"Klaus—He's still up there."

"Come on!" Tasso dragged Hendricks back, away from the columns. Hendricks shook his head, trying to clear it. Tasso led him rapidly away, her eyes intense and bright, watching for claws that had escaped the blast.

One David came out of the rolling clouds of flame. Tasso blasted it. No more appeared.

"But Klaus. What about him?" Hendricks stopped, standing unsteadily. "He—"

"Come on!"

They retreated, moving farther and farther away from the bunker. A few small claws followed them for a little while and then gave up, turning back and going off.

At last Tasso stopped. "We can stop here and get our breaths."

Hendricks sat down on some heaps of debris. He wiped his neck, gasping. "We left Klaus back there."

Tasso said nothing. She opened her gun, sliding a fresh round of blast cartridges into place.

Hendricks stared at her, dazed. "You left him back there on purpose."

Tasso snapped the gun together. She studied the heaps of rubble around them, her face expressionless. As if she were watching for something.

"What is it?" Hendricks demanded. "What are you looking for? Is something coming?" He shook his head, trying to understand. What was she doing? What was she waiting for? He could see nothing. Ash lay all around them, ash and ruins. Occasional stark tree trunks, without leaves or branches. "What—"

Tasso cut him off. "Be still." Her eyes narrowed. Suddenly her gun came up. Hendricks turned, following her gaze.

Back the way they had come a figure appeared. The figure walked unsteadily toward them. Its clothes were torn. It limped as it made its way along, going very slowly and carefully. Stopping now and then, resting and getting its strength. Once it almost fell. It stood for a moment, trying to steady itself. Then it came on.

Klaus.

Hendricks stood up. "Klaus!" He started toward him. "How the hell did you—"

Tasso fired. Hendricks swung back. She fired again, the blast passing him, a searing line of heat. The beam caught Klaus in the chest. He exploded, gears and wheels flying. For a moment he continued to walk. Then he swayed back and forth. He crashed to the ground, his arms flung out. A few more wheels rolled away.

Silence.

Tasso turned to Hendricks. "Now you understand why he killed Rudi."

Hendricks sat down again slowly. He shook his head. He was numb. He could not think.

"Do you see?" Tasso said. "Do you understand?"

Hendricks said nothing. Everything was slipping away from him, faster and faster. Darkness, rolling and plucking at him.

He closed his eyes.

Hendricks opened his eyes slowly. His body ached all over. He tried to sit up but needles of pain shot through his arm and shoulder. He gasped.

"Don't try to get up," Tasso said. She bent down, putting her cold hand against his forehead.

It was night. A few stars glinted above, shining through the drifting clouds of ash. Hendricks lay back, his teeth locked. Tasso watched him impassively. She had built a fire with some wood and weeds. The fire licked feebly, hissing at a metal cup suspended over it. Everything was silent. Unmoving darkness, beyond the fire.

"So he was the Second Variety," Hendricks murmured.

"I had always thought so."

"Why didn't you destroy him sooner?" he wanted to know.

"You held me back." Tasso crossed to the fire to look into the metal cup. "Coffee. It'll be ready to drink in a while."

She came back and sat down beside him. Presently she opened her pistol and began to disassemble the firing mechanism, studying it intently.

"This is a beautiful gun," Tasso said, half-aloud. "The construction is superb."

"What about them? The claws."

"The concussion from the bomb put most of them out of action. They're delicate. Highly organized, I suppose."

"The Davids, too?"

"Yes."

"How did you happen to have a bomb like that?"

Tasso shrugged. "We designed it. You shouldn't underestimate our technology, Major. Without such a bomb you and I would no longer exist."

"Very useful."

Tasso stretched out her legs, warming her feet in the heat of the fire. "It surprised me that you did not seem to understand, after he killed Rudi. Why did you think he—"

"I told you. I thought he was afraid."

"Really? You know, Major, for a little while I suspected you. Because you wouldn't let me kill him. I thought you might be protecting him." She laughed.

"Are we safe here?" Hendricks asked presently.

"For a while. Until they get reinforcements from some other area." Tasso began to clean the interior of the gun with a bit of rag. She finished and pushed the mechanism back into place. She closed the gun, running her finger along the barrel.

"We were lucky," Hendricks murmured.

"Yes. Very lucky."

"Thanks for pulling me away."

Tasso did not answer. She glanced up at him, her eyes bright in the fire light. Hendricks examined his arm. He could not move his fingers. His whole side seemed numb. Down inside him was a dull steady ache.

"How do you feel?" Tasso asked.

"My arm is damaged."

"Anything else?"

"Internal injuries."

"You didn't get down when the bomb went off."

Hendricks said nothing. He watched Tasso pour the coffee from the cup into a flat metal pan. She brought it over to him.

"Thanks." He struggled up enough to drink. It was hard to swallow. His insides turned over and he pushed the pan away. "That's all I can drink now."

Tasso drank the rest. Time passed. The clouds of ash moved across the dark sky above them. Hendricks rested, his mind blank. After a while he became aware that Tasso was standing over him, gazing down at him.

"What is it?" he murmured.

"Do you feel any better?"

"Some."

"You know, Major, if I hadn't dragged you away they would have got you. You would be dead. Like Rudi."

"I know."

"Do you want to know why I brought you out? I could have left you. I could have left you there."

"Why did you bring me out?"

"Because we have to get away from here." Tasso stirred the fire with a stick, peering calmly down into it. "No human being can live here. When their reinforcements come we won't have a chance. I've pondered about it while you were unconscious. We have perhaps three hours before they come."

"And you expect me to get us away?"

"That's right. I expect you to get us out of here."

"Why me?"

"Because I don't know any way." Her eyes shone at him in the half-light, bright and steady. "If you can't get us out of here they'll kill us within three hours. I see nothing else ahead. Well,

Major? What are you going to do? I've been waiting all night. While you were unconscious I sat here, waiting and listening. It's almost dawn. The night is almost over."

Hendricks considered. "It's curious," he said at last.

"Curious?"

"That you should think I can get us out of here. I wonder what you think I can do."

"Can you get us to the Moon Base?"

"The Moon Base? How?"

"There must be some way."

Hendricks shook his head. "No. There's no way that I know of."

Tasso said nothing. For a moment her steady gaze wavered. She ducked her head, turning abruptly away. She scrambled to her feet. "More coffee?"

"No."

"Suit yourself." Tasso drank silently. He could not see her face. He lay back against the ground, deep in thought, trying to concentrate. It was hard to think. His head still hurt. And the numbing daze still hung over him.

"There might be one way," he said suddenly.

"Oh?"

"How soon is dawn?"

"Two hours. The sun will be coming up shortly."

"There's supposed to be a ship near here. I've never seen it. But I know it exists."

"What kind of a ship?" Her voice was sharp.

"A rocket cruiser."

"Will it take us off? To the Moon Base?"

"It's supposed to. In case of emergency." He rubbed his forehead.

"What's wrong?"

"My head. It's hard to think. I can hardly—hardly concentrate. The bomb."

"Is the ship near here?" Tasso slid over beside him, settling down on her haunches. "How far is it? Where is it?"

"I'm trying to think."

Her fingers dug into his arm. "Nearby?" Her voice was like iron. "Where would it be? Would they store it underground? Hidden underground?"

"Yes. In a storage locker."

"How do we find it? Is it marked? Is there a code marker to identify it?"

Hendricks concentrated. "No. No markings. No code symbol."

"What, then?"

"A sign."

"What sort of sign?"

Hendricks did not answer. In the flickering light his eyes were glazed, two sightless orbs. Tasso's fingers dug into his arm.

"What sort of sign? What is it?"

"I—I can't think. Let me rest."

"All right." She let go and stood up. Hendricks lay back against the ground, his eyes closed. Tasso walked away from him, her hands in her pockets. She kicked a rock out of her way and stood staring up at the sky. The night blackness was already beginning to fade into gray. Morning was coming.

Tasso gripped her pistol and walked around the fire in a circle, back and forth. On the ground Major Hendricks lay, his eyes closed, unmoving. The grayness rose in the sky, higher and higher. The landscape became visible, fields of ash stretching out in all directions. Ash and ruins of buildings, a wall here and there, heaps of concrete, the naked trunk of a tree.

The air was cold and sharp. Somewhere a long way off a bird made a few bleak sounds.

Hendricks stirred. He opened his eyes. "Is it dawn? Already?"

"Yes."

Hendricks sat up a little. "You wanted to know something. You were asking me."

"Do you remember now?"

"Yes."

"What is it?" She tensed. "What?" she repeated sharply.

"A well. A ruined well. It's in a storage locker under a well."

"A well." Tasso relaxed. "Then we'll find a well." She looked at her watch. "We have about an hour, Major. Do you think we can find it in an hour?"

"Give me a hand up," Hendricks said.

Tasso put her pistol away and helped him to his feet. "This is going to be difficult."

"Yes it is." Hendricks set his lips tightly. "I don't think we're going to go very far."

They began to walk. The early sun cast a little warmth down on them. The land was flat and barren, stretching out gray and lifeless as far as they could see. A few birds sailed silently, far above them, circling slowly.

"See anything?" Hendricks said. "Any claws?"

"No. Not yet."

They passed through some ruins, upright concrete and bricks. A cement foundation. Rats scuttled away. Tasso jumped back warily.

"This used to be a town," Hendricks said. "A village. Provincial village. This was all grape country, once. Where we are now."

They came onto a ruined street, weeds and cracks criss-crossing it. Over to the right a stone chimney stuck up.

"Be careful," he warned her.

A pit yawned, an open basement. Ragged ends of pipes jutted up, twisted and bent. They passed part of a house, a bathtub turned on its side. A broken chair. A few spoons and bits of china dishes. In the center of the street the ground had sunk away. The depression was filled with weeds and debris and bones.

"Over here," Hendricks murmured.

"This way?"

"To the right."

They passed the remains of a heavy duty tank. Hendricks' belt counter clicked ominously. The tank had been radiation blasted. A few feet from the tank a mummified body lay sprawled out, mouth open. Beyond the road was a flat field. Stones and weeds, and bits of broken glass.

"There," Hendricks said.

A stone well jutted up, sagging and broken. A few boards lay across it. Most of the well had sunk into rubble. Hendricks walked unsteadily toward it, Tasso beside him.

"Are you certain about this?" Tasso said. "This doesn't look like anything."

"I'm sure." Hendricks sat down at the edge of the well, his teeth locked. His breath came quickly. He wiped perspiration from his face. "This was arranged so the senior command officer could get away. If anything happened. If the bunker fell."

"That was you?"

"Yes."

"Where is the ship? Is it here?"

"We're standing on it." Hendricks ran his hands over the surface of the well stones. "The eye-lock responds to me, not to anybody else. It's my ship. Or it was supposed to be."

There was a sharp click. Presently they heard a low grating sound from below them.

"Step back," Hendricks said. He and Tasso moved away from the well.

A section of the ground slid back. A metal frame pushed slowly up through the ash, shoving bricks and weeds out of the way. The action ceased, as the ship nosed into view.

"There it is," Hendricks said.

The ship was small. It rested quietly, suspended in its mesh frame, like a blunt needle. A rain of ash sifted down into the dark cavity from which the ship had been raised. Hendricks made his way over to it. He mounted the mesh and unscrewed the hatch, pulling it back. Inside the ship the control banks and the pressure seat were visible.

Tasso came and stood beside him, gazing into the ship. "I'm not accustomed to rocket piloting," she said, after a while.

Hendricks glanced at her. "I'll do the piloting."

"Will you? There's only one seat, Major. I can see it's built to carry only a single person."

Hendricks' breathing changed. He studied the interior of the ship intently. Tasso was right. There was only one seat. The ship was built to carry only one person. "I see," he said slowly. "And the one person is you."

She nodded.

"Of course."

"Why?"

"*You* can't go. You might not live through the trip. You're injured. You probably wouldn't get there."

"An interesting point. But you see, I know where the Moon Base is. And you don't. You might fly around for months and not find it. It's well hidden. Without knowing what to look for—"

"I'll have to take my chances. Maybe I won't find it. Not by myself. But I think you'll give me all the information I need. Your life depends on it."

"How?"

"If I find the Moon Base in time, perhaps I can get them to send a ship back to pick you up. *If* I find the Base in time. If not, then you haven't a chance. I imagine there are supplies on the ship. They will last me long enough—"

Hendricks moved quickly. But his injured arm betrayed him.

Tasso ducked, sliding lithely aside. Her hand came up, lightning fast. Hendricks saw the gun butt coming. He tried to ward off the blow, but she was too fast. The metal butt struck against the side of his head, just above his ear. Numbing pain rushed through him. Pain and rolling clouds of blackness. He sank down, sliding to the ground.

Dimly, he was aware that Tasso was standing over him, kicking him with her toe.

"Major! Wake up."

He opened his eyes, groaning.

"Listen to me." She bent down, the gun pointed at his face. "I have to hurry. There isn't much time left. The ship is ready to go, but you must tell me the information I need before I leave."

Hendricks shook his head, trying to clear it.

"Hurry up! Where is the Moon Base? How do I find it? What do I look for?"

Hendricks said nothing.

"Answer me!"

"Sorry."

"Major, the ship is loaded with provisions. I can coast for weeks. I'll find the Base eventually. And in a half hour you'll be dead. Your only chance of survival—" She broke off.

Along the slope, by some crumbling ruins, something moved. Something in the ash. Tasso turned quickly, aiming. She fired. A puff of flame leaped. Something scuttled away, rolling across the ash. She fired again. The claw burst apart, wheels flying.

"See?" Tasso said. "A scout. It won't be long."

"You'll bring them back here to get me?"

"Yes. As soon as possible."

Hendricks looked up at her. He studied her intently. "You're telling the truth?" A strange expression had come over his face, an avid hunger. "You will come back for me? You'll get me to the Moon Base?"

"I'll get you to the Moon Base. But tell me where it is! There's only a little time left."

"All right." Hendricks picked up a piece of rock, pulling himself to a sitting position. "Watch."

Hendricks began to scratch in the ash. Tasso stood by him, watching the motion of the rock. Hendricks was sketching a crude lunar map.

"This is the Appenine range. Here is the Crater of Archimedes. The Moon Base is beyond the end of the Appenine, about two hundred miles. I don't know exactly where. No one on Terra knows. But when you're over the Appenine, signal with one red flare and a green flare, followed by two red flares in quick succession. The Base monitor will record your signal. The Base is under the surface, of course. They'll guide you down with magnetic grapples."

"And the controls? Can I operate them?"

"The controls are virtually automatic. All you have to do is give the right signal at the right time."

"I will."

"The seat absorbs most of the take-off shock. Air and temperature are automatically controlled. The ship will leave Terra and pass out into free space. It'll line itself up with the moon, falling into an orbit around it, about a hundred miles above the surface. The orbit will carry you over the Base. When you're in the region of the Appenine, release the signal rockets."

Tasso slid into the ship and lowered herself into the pressure seat. The arm locks folded automatically around her. She fingered the controls. "Too bad you're not going, Major. All this put here for you, and you can't make the trip."

"Leave me the pistol."

Tasso pulled the pistol from her belt. She held it in her hand, weighing it thoughtfully. "Don't go too far from this location. It'll be hard to find you, as it is."

"No. I'll stay here by the well."

Tasso gripped the take-off switch, running her fingers over the smooth metal. "A beautiful ship, Major. Well built. I admire your workmanship. You people have always done good work. You build fine things. Your work, your creations, are your greatest achievement."

"Give me the pistol," Hendricks said impatiently, holding out his hand. He struggled to his feet.

"Good-bye, Major." Tasso tossed the pistol past Hendricks. The pistol clattered against the ground, bouncing and rolling away. Hendricks hurried after it. He bent down, snatching it up.

The hatch of the ship clanged shut. The bolts fell into place. Hendricks made his way back. The inner door was being sealed. He raised the pistol unsteadily.

There was a shattering roar. The ship burst up from its metal cage, fusing the mesh behind it. Hendricks cringed, pulling back. The ship shot up into the rolling clouds of ash, disappearing into the sky.

Hendricks stood watching a long time, until even the streamer had dissipated. Nothing stirred. The morning air was chill and silent. He began to walk aimlessly back the way they had come. Better to keep moving around. It would be a long time before help came—if it came at all.

He searched his pockets until he found a package of cigarettes. He lit one grimly. They had all wanted cigarettes from him. But cigarettes were scarce.

A lizard slithered by him, through the ash. He halted, rigid. The lizard disappeared. Above, the sun rose higher in the sky. Some flies landed on a flat rock to one side of him. Hendricks kicked at them with his foot.

It was getting hot. Sweat trickled down his face, into his collar. His mouth was dry.

Presently he stopped walking and sat down on some debris.

He unfastened his medicine kit and swallowed a few narcotic capsules. He looked around him. Where was he?

Something lay ahead. Stretched out on the ground. Silent and unmoving.

Hendricks drew his gun quickly. It looked like a man. Then he remembered. It was the remains of Klaus. The Second Variety. Where Tasso had blasted him. He could see wheels and relays and metal parts, strewn around on the ash. Glittering and sparkling in the sunlight.

Hendricks got to his feet and walked over. He nudged the inert form with his foot, turning it over a little. He could see the metal hull, the aluminum ribs and struts. More wiring fell out. Like viscera. Heaps of wiring, switches and relays. Endless motors and rods.

He bent down. The brain cage had been smashed by the fall. The artificial brain was visible. He gazed at it. A maze of circuits. Miniature tubes. Wires as fine as hair. He touched the brain cage. It swung aside. The type plate was visible. Hendricks studied the plate.

And blanched.

IV–IV.

For a long time he stared at the plate. Fourth Variety. Not the Second. They had been wrong. There were more types. Not just three. Many more, perhaps. At least four. And Klaus wasn't the Second Variety.

But if Klaus wasn't the Second Variety—

Suddenly he tensed. Something was coming, walking through the ash beyond the hill. What was it? He strained to see. Figures. Figures coming slowly along, making their way through the ash.

Coming toward him.

Hendricks crouched quickly, raising his gun. Sweat dripped down into his eyes. He fought down rising panic, as the figures neared.

The first was a David. The David saw him and increased its pace. The others hurried behind it. A second David. A third. Three Davids, all alike, coming toward him silently, without expression, their thin legs rising and falling. Clutching their teddy bears.

He aimed and fired. The first two Davids dissolved into particles. The third came on. And the figure behind it. Climbing silently toward him across the gray ash. A Wounded Soldier, towering over the David. And—

And behind the Wounded Soldier came two Tassos, walking side by side. Heavy belt, Russian army pants, shirt, long hair. The familiar figure, as he had seen her only a little while before. Sitting in the pressure seat of the ship. Two slim, silent figures, both identical.

They were very near. The David bent down suddenly, dropping its teddy bear. The bear raced across the ground. Automatically, Hendricks' fingers tightened around the trigger. The bear was gone, dissolved into mist. The two Tasso Types moved on, expressionless, walking side by side, through the gray ash.

When they were almost to him, Hendricks raised the pistol waist high and fired.

The two Tassos dissolved. But already a new group was starting up the rise, five or six Tassos, all identical, a line of them coming rapidly toward him.

And he had given her the ship and the signal code. Because of him she was on her way to the moon, to the Moon Base. He had made it possible.

He had been right about the bomb, after all. It had been designed with knowledge of the other types, the David Type and the Wounded Soldier Type. And the Klaus Type. Not designed by human beings. It had been designed by one of the underground factories, apart from all human contact.

The line of Tassos came up to him. Hendricks braced himself, watching them calmly. The familiar face, the belt, the heavy shirt, the bomb carefully in place.

The bomb—

As the Tassos reached for him, a last ironic thought drifted through Hendricks' mind. He felt a little better, thinking about it. The bomb. Made by the Second Variety to destroy the other varieties. Made for that end alone.

They were already beginning to design weapons to use against each other.[5]

■

Author Biography

Philip Kindred Dick was born in Chicago in 1928 and became a prolific science fiction writer, producing nearly a hundred short stories and two dozen novels during the 1950s and 1960s. In 1974, Dick experienced a "divine visitation" that involved a pink beam of light transmitting vast amounts of information into his mind, including knowledge about his infant son's undiagnosed medical condition, which proved accurate when checked. This experience altered his worldview and influenced his later novels. Despite critical acclaim, Dick struggled financially until selling the film rights to *Blade Runner*. He died of a heart attack in 1982 at 53, shortly before *Blade Runner* premiered. His influence has grown posthumously with multiple adaptations of his work.

---

5. If you enjoyed this, turn on a pink light, grab some popcorn, and watch some of the movies adapted from Dick's work, like *Blade Runner*, *Total Recall*, *Minority Report*, *A Scanner Darkly*, and *The Adjustment Bureau*.

Discuss

1. How does the story challenge our understanding of what it means to be "human" when artificial beings can perfectly replicate human emotions and behaviors?
2. Discuss the ethical implications of creating autonomous weapons systems that can potentially develop beyond their original programming. What are the potential risks and moral considerations?
3. Compare the concept of mimicry in the story to contemporary discussions about AI, deep fakes, and the increasing sophistication of technological imitation. How do his predictions from 1953 resonate with current technological developments?

Write

An AI's Identity Crisis: Compose a narrative from the perspective of a self-aware artificial being struggling with its own sense of identity and purpose. Explore the psychological and emotional complexity of an entity that recognizes its own artificiality while experiencing what seems like genuine emotion.

Lazarus Come Forth

Ray Bradbury

Written in 1944, this short story by Ray Bradbury presents one of science fiction's earliest depictions of cryogenic resurrection—a cornerstone of transhumanist thought—only to reveal it as elaborate deception. The story asks: *What if we could defeat death, but chose mortality anyway?* Bradbury's vision resonates today as we debate cryonics, life extension, and digital immortality—not by celebrating transcendence, but by questioning whether conquering death is always the right choice. *What do you think?*

> The Morgue Ship[1] had gleaned information from space that would end the three-hundred-year war, knowledge that would defeat the aggressor Martians—if Brandon could carry it to Earth.

Logan's way of laughing was bad. "There's a new body up in the airlock, Brandon. Climb the rungs and have a look."

Logan's eyes had a green shine to them, eager and intent. They were ugly, obscene.

Brandon swore under his breath. This room of the Morgue Ship was crowded with their two personalities. Besides that, there were

---

1. Here, Morgue Ships patrol space battlefields retrieving the bodies of dead soldiers for proper burial. This reflects both the military tradition of recovering fallen soldiers and practical concerns about bodies becoming space debris or biological hazards.

scores of cold shelves of bodies freezing quietly, and the insistent vibration of the coroner tables, machinery spinning under them. And Logan was like a little machine that never stopped talking.

"Leave me alone." Brandon rose up, tall and thinned by the years, looking as old as a pocked meteor. "Just keep quiet."

Logan sucked his cigarette. "Scared to go upstairs? Scared it might be your son we just picked up?"

Brandon reached Logan in about one stride, and while the Morgue Ship slipped on through space, he clenched the coroner's blue uniform with the small bones inside it and hung it up against the wall, pressing inward until Logan couldn't breathe. Logan blew air, his eyes looked helpless. He tried to speak and could only grunt like a stuck pig. He waved his short arms, flapping.

Brandon kept him there, crucified on a fist.

"I told you. Let me search for my own son's body in my own way. I don't need your tongue."

Logan's eyes were losing their shine, were getting blind and glazed. Brandon stepped back, releasing the little assistant. Logan bumped softly against metal flooring, his mouth hungry for air, his nostrils flaring for breath. Brandon watched the little face of Logan over the crouched, gasping body, with red color and anger shooting up into it with every passing second.

"Coward!" he threw it out of himself, Logan did. "Got yellow—neon-tubing—for your spine. Coward. Never went to war. Never did anything for Earth against Mars."

Brandon said the words in slow motion. "Shut up."

"Why?" Logan crept back, inching up the metal hull. The blood pumps under the skirts of the tables pulsed across the warm silence. "Does it hurt, the truth? Your son'd be proud of you, okay. Ha!" He coughed and spat. "He was so damn ashamed of you he went and signed up for space combat. So he got lost from his ship during a battle." Logan licked his lips very carefully. "So, to make up for it, you signed on a Morgue Ship. Try to find his body. Try to make amends. I know you. You wouldn't join the Space Warriors to fight. No guts for that. Had to get a nice easy job on a morgue ship—"

Lines appeared in Brandon's gaunt cheeks, his eyes were closed, the lids pale. He said, and tried to believe it himself, "Someone has to pick up the bodies after the battle. They can't go flying on forever in their own orbits. They deserve burial."

The bitterness of Logan struck even deeper. "Who are you tryin' to convince?" He was on his feet now. "Me, it's different. I got a right to running this ship. I was in the other war."

"You're a liar," Brandon retorted. "You hunted radium in the asteroids with a mineral tug. You took this Morgue Ship job so you could go right on hunting radium, picking up bodies on the side."

Logan laughed softly, but not humorously. "So what? Least I'm no coward. I'll burn anybody gets in my way." He thought it over. "Unless," he added, "they give me a little money."

Brandon turned away, feeling ill. He forced himself to climb up the rungs toward that airlock, where that fresh body lay, newly still-born from space by the retrieving-claw. His palms let wet shining prints on the rungs. His climbing feet made a soft noise in the cold metal silence.

The body lay in the cold airlock's center, as thousands had lain before. Its posture was one of easy slumber, relaxed and not speaking ever again.

⁂

Brandon took in his breath. Numbly he realized it was not his son. Every time a new body was found he feared and yet hoped it would be Richard. Richard of the easy laughter and good smile and dark curly hair. Richard who was now floating off somewhere toward some far eternity.

Brandon's eyes dilated. He went to his knees and with efficient darts of his eyes, he covered the vital points of this strange uniform with the young body inside it. His heart pounded briefly, and when he got up again he acted like he had been struck in the face. He walked unsteadily to the rungs.

"Logan," he called down the hole in a numbed voice. "Logan, come up here. Quick."

Logan climbed lazily up, emitting grunts and smoke.

"Look here," said Brandon, kneeling again by the body.

Logan looked and didn't believe it. "Where in hell'd you get that?"

Lying there, the face of the body was like snow framed by the ebon-black of the hair. The eyes were blue jewels caught in the snow. There were slender fingers reclining against the hips. But, most important of all, was the cut of the silver metal uniform, the grey leather belt and the bronze triangle over the silent heart with the numerals 51 on it.

Logan held onto the rungs. "Three hundred years old," he whispered it. "Three hundred years old," he said.

"Yes." The Numerals 51 were enough for Brandon. "After all these centuries, and in perfect condition. Look how calm he is. Most corpse faces aren't—pretty. Something happened, three hundred years ago, and he's been drifting, alone, ever since. I—" Brandon caught his breath.

"What's wrong?" snapped Logan.

"This man," said Brandon, wonderingly, "committed suicide."

"How do you figure?"

"There's not a mark of decompression, centrifugal force, disintegrator or ray-burn on him. He simply *stepped* out of a ship. Why should a Scientist of the 51 Circle commit suicide?"

"They had wars back there, too," said Logan. "But this is the first time I ever seen a stiff from one of them. It can't happen. He shoulda been messed up by meteors."

A strange prickling crept over Brandon. "When I was a kid, I remember thumbing through history books, reading about those famous 51 Scientists of the Circle who were doing experimental work on Pluto back in the year 2100. I memorized their uniforms, and this bronze badge. I couldn't mistake it. There was a rumor that they were experimenting with some new universal power weapon."

"A myth," said Logan.

"Who knows? Maybe. Maybe not. But before that super weapon was completed, Earth fell beneath Mar's assault. The 51 Scientists destroyed themselves and their Base when the Martians came. The—myth—says that if the Martians had been only a month later—the weapon would have been out of blueprint and into metal."

Brandon stopped talking and looked at the long-boned, easily slumbering Scientist.

"And now he shows up. One of the original 51. I wonder what happened? Maybe he tried to reach Earth and had to leap into space to escape the Martians. Logan, we've got history with us, pulled in out of space, cold and stark under our hands."

Logan laughed uneasily. "Yeah. Now, if we only had that weapon. Baby, that'd be something to sing about, by God."

Brandon jerked.

Logan looked at him. "What's eating you?"

Brandon laid his fingers on the dead Scientist's skull.

"Maybe—just maybe—we *have* got the weapon," he said.

His hand trembled.

The coroner pumps throbbed warmly under the table, while manipulating tendrils darted swiftly, effectively over the dead Scientist's body. Brandon moved, too, like a machine. In a regular fury he had forced Logan to hurry the body down into the preparations room, inject adrenaline, thermal units, apply the blood pump and accomplish a thousand other demanding and instantaneous tasks.

"Now, out of the way, Logan. You're more trouble than help!"

Logan stumbled back. "Okay, okay. Don't get snotty. It won't work. I keep telling you. All these years."

Brandon could see nothing. Logan's voice was muffled, far away. There was only the surge of pumps, the sweating heat of the little cubicle, and niche number 12 waiting to receive this body if he failed. Brandon swallowed, tightly. Niche number 12 waiting, cold, ready, waiting for a body to fill it. He'd have to fight to keep it empty.

He began to sing-song words over and over as he injected stimulants into the body. He didn't know where the words came from, from childhood, maybe, from his old religious memories:

"Lazarus come forth," Brandon said softly, bending close, adjusting the manipulatory tendrils. "Lazarus, come forth."[2]

Logan snorted. "Lazarus! Will you can that!"

Brandon had to talk to himself. "Inside his brain he's got that energy weapon that Earth can use to end the war. It's been frozen in there three hundred years. If we can thaw it out—"

"Who ever heard of reviving a body after that long?"

"He's perfectly preserved. Perfectly frozen. Oh, God, this is Fate. I know it. I feel it. Came to find Richard and I found something bigger! Lazarus! Lazarus, come forth from the tomb!"

The machines thrummed louder, beating into his ears. Brandon listened, watched for just one pulse, just one beat, one word, one moment of life.

"Air for the lungs," and Brandon attached oxygen cones over the fine nose and relaxed lips. "Pressure on the ribs." Metal plates pressuring the rib case slowly out and in. "Circulation." Brandon

---

2. In the Gospel of John (11:1–44), Jesus raises his friend Lazarus from the dead after four days in the tomb by commanding "Lazarus, come forth!" Brandon repeatedly uses this biblical phrase while reviving the Scientist, positioning technological resurrection as a kind of divine miracle achieved through human science.

touched the control at the foot of the table and the whole table tilted back and forth in a whining teeter-totter.

A report clipped through on the audio:

"Morgue Ship. Battle Unit 766 calling Morgue Ship. Off orbit of Pluto 234CC, point zero-two, off 32, one by seven, follow up. Battle just terminated. Six Martian ships destroyed. One Earth ship blasted apart and bodies thrown into space. Please recover. 79 men. Bodies in orbit heading toward sun at 23456 an hour. Check."

Logan flipped his cigarette away. "That's us. We got work to do. Come on. Let that stiff cool. He'll be here when we come back."

"No!" Brandon fairly shouted it, eyes wild. "He's more important than all those men out there. We can help them later. He can help us now!"

The table came to a halt, bringing absolute silence.

Brandon bent forward to press his ear against the warmed rib-casing.

"Wait."

There it was. Unbelievably, there it was. A tiny pulse stirring like a termite down under, softly and sluggishly moving through the body, jabbing the heart and—NOW! Brandon cried out. He was shaking all over. He was setting the machine in operation again, and talking and laughing and going crazy with it.

"He's alive! He's alive! Lazarus has come from the tomb! Lazarus reborn again! Notify Earth immediately!"

⁂

At the end of an hour, the pulse was timing normal, the temperature was lowering down from a fever, and Brandon moved about the preparations' room watching every quiver of the body's internal organs through the tubular-fluoroscope.

He exulted. This was having Richard alive again. It was compensation. You roared into space looking somewhere for your lost self-respect, your pride, looking for your son who is shooting on some soundless orbit into nothing, and now the biggest child of Fate is deposited in your arms to warm and bring to life. It was impossible. It was good. Brandon almost laughed. He almost forgot he had ever known fear of death. This was conquering it. This was like bringing Richard back to life, but even more. It meant things to earth and humanity; things about weapons and power and peace.

Logan interrupted Brandon's exultant thinking by blowing smoke in his face. "You know something, Brandy? This is damn good! You done something, Mister. Yeah."

"I thought I told you to notify Earth."

"Ah, I been watching you. Like a mama hen and her chick. I been thinking, too. Yeah." Logan shook ashes off his smoke. "Ever since you pulled in this prize fish, I been turning it over in my mind."

"Go up to the radio room and call Earth. We've got to rush the Scientist to Moon Base immediately. We can talk later."

There was that hard green shine to Logan's narrow eyes again. He poked a finger at Brandon. "Here's the way I get it. Do we get rewarded for finding this guy? Hell, no. It's our routine work. We're *supposed* to pick up bodies. Here we got a guy who's the key to the whole damn war."

Brandon's lips hardly moved. "Call Earth."

"Now, hold on a moment, Brandy. Let me finish this. I been thinking, maybe the Martians'd like to own him, too. Maybe they'd like to be around when he starts talking."

Brandon made a fist. "You heard what I said."

Logan put his hand behind him. "I just want to talk peaceable with you, Brandy. I don't want trouble. But all we'll get for finding this stiff is a kiss on the cheek and a medal on the chest. Hell!"

Brandon was going to hit him hard, before he saw the gun in Logan's fingers, whipped out and pointing.

"Take a look at this, Brandy, and don't lose your supper."

In spite of himself, Brandon quailed. It was almost an involuntary action. His whole body plunged back, aching, pulling with it.

"Now, let's march up to the radio room. I got a little calling to do. Get on with you. Hup!"

In the radio-room, Logan touched studs, raised a mic to his lips and said:

"Beam to Mars. Beam to Mars. Morgue Ship of Earth calling. Mars Beam answer."

After an interval, Mars gave answer. Logan said:

"I've just picked up the body of a 51 Circle Scientist. He's been resuscitated. Give me your fleet commander. I got things to talk over with him." Logan smiled. "Oh, *hello*, commander!"

⁂

Half an hour later, the discussions were over, the plans made. Logan hung up, satisfied. Brandon looked at him as if he couldn't believe he was serious.

Back down in the control room, Logan set a course, and then forced Brandon to get the body ready. He bragged about the deal. "A half ton of radium, Brandy.[3] Not bad, eh? Good pay. More than Earth'd ever give me for my routine duty."

Brandon shuddered. "You fool. The Martians will kill us."

"Uh-uh." Logan pantomimed him into moving the body onto a rollered table and taking it to the emergency life-craft airlock. "I'm not that dumb. I'm having you wire this emergency lifeboat with explosive. We collect the minerals first. We blow up the body if the Martians act funny. We make them wait until we've collected our half and gotten five hours' start toward Earth before we allow them to pick up the body. Nice, huh?"

Brandon swayed over the task of wiring the lifeboat with

---

3. At the time Bradbury wrote this, radium was extremely valuable. It's not worth much today.

explosive. "You're cutting your own throat. Handing over a weapon like that to the Martian enemy."

It was no again from Logan. "After the Martians pick up the body and we're safely on our way home to Earth, I press a button and the whole damn thing blows up. They call it double-crossing."

"Destroy the body?"

"Hell, yes. Think I want a weapon like that turned over to the enemy? Guh!"

"The war'll go on for years."

"So Earth'll wind up winning, anyhow. We're getting along, slow but sure. And when the war's over, I got a load of radium to set myself up in business and a big future in front of me."

"So you kill millions of men, for that."

"What'd they do for me? Ruined my guts in the last war!"

There had to be some argument, something to say, quick, something to do to a man like Logan. Brandon thought, quickly. "Look, Logan, we can work this, but save the body."

"Don't be funny."

"Put one of the *other* bodies in the ship we send out. Save Lazarus' body and run back to Earth with it!" insisted Brandon.

The little assistant shook his head. "The Martians'll have an intra-material beam focused on the emergency ship when they get within one hundred thousand miles of her. They'll be able to tell then if the body's dead or alive. No dice, Brandy."

It was hardly like leaping himself, thought Brandon. It was just frustration and rage and unthinking action. Brandon jumped. Logan hardly flicked an eyelid as he pressed the trigger of his paragun. It paralyzed the legs from under Brandon and he collapsed. The gun sprayed over his groin and chest and face, too, in a withering shower of red-hot needles. The lights went out.

There was a loose sensation of empty space, and acceleration minus power. Pure soundless momentum. Brandon forced his eyes open painfully, and found himself alone in the preparations' room, lying stretched upon one of the coroner tables, bound with metal fibre.

"Logan!" he bellowed it up through the ship. He waited. He did it again. "Logan!"

He fought the metal fibre, knotting his fists, twisting his arms. He yanked himself back and forth. It pretty well held, except for a looseness in the right hand binding. He worked on that. Upstairs, a queer, detached Martian bass voice intoned itself.

"500,000 miles. Prepare your emergency craft with the body of the Scientist inside of it, Morgue Ship. At 300,000 miles, release the emergency craft. We'll release *our* mineral payment ship now, giving you a half hour leeway to pick it up. It contains the exact amount you asked for."

Logan's voice next:

"Good. The Scientist is alive, still, and doing well. You're getting a bargain."

Brandon's face whitened, bringing out all the hard, scared bones of it, the cheeks and brow and chin bones. He jerked against the binding and it only jumped the air from his lungs so he sobbed. Breathing deeply, he lay back. They were taking his child back out into space. Lazarus, his second son, whom he had birthed out of space with a metal retriever, they were taking back out and away from him. You can't have your real son; so you take the second best and you slap him into breathing life, into breathing consciousness, and before he is a day old they try to tear him away from you again. Brandon fairly yelled against his manacles of wire. Sweat came down his face, and the stuff from his eyes wasn't all sweat.

Logan tiptoed down the hard rungs, grinning.

"Awake, Sleeping Beauty?"

Brandon said nothing. His right hand was loosened. It was

wet and loosened, working like a small white animal at his side, slipping from its wire trap.

"You can't go ahead with it, Logan."

"Why not?"

"The Earth Tribunal will find out."

"You won't tell them." Logan was doing something across the room. He was the only moving thing in front of a hundred cold shelves of sleeping warriors.

Brandon gasped, tried to get up, fell back. "How'll you fake my death?"

"With an injection of sulfacardium. Heart failure. Too much pulse on a too old heart. Simple." Logan turned and there was a hypodermic in his hand.

Brandon lay there. The ship went on and on. The body was upstairs, lying breathing in its metal cradle, mothered by him and jerked to life by him, and now going away. Brandon managed to say:

"Do me a favor?"

"What?"

"Give me the drug now. I don't want to be awake when you send Lazarus out. I don't want that."

"Sure." Logan came walking across the deck, raising the hypodermic. It glittered hard and silver fine, and sharp.

"One more thing, Logan."

"Hurry it up!"

Only one arm free, one leg able to move slightly. Logan was pressing against the table, now. The hypodermic hesitated in his fingers.

"This!" said Brandon.

⁂

With one foot, Brandon kicked the teeter-totter control at the base of the board. The board, whining, began to elevate swiftly.

With his free arm, instantly pulling the last way free from the wire, Brandon clutched Logan's screaming head and jammed it down under the table, under the descending board. Board and metal base ground together and kept on going three inches. Logan screamed only once. The sounds after that were so horrible that Brandon retched. Logan's body slumped and hung, arms slack, hypo dropped and shattered on the deck.

The whole table kept going up and down, up and down.

It made Brandon sicker with each movement. The whole room revolved, tipped, spun sickishly. The corpses in all their niches seemed to shiver with it.

He managed to kick the control to neutral and the table poised, elevated at the heels, so blood pounded hotly into Brandon's pale face, lighting, coloring it. His heart was pounding furiously and the chronometer upon the hull-wall clicked out time passing, time passing and miles with it, and Martians coming so much the closer....

He fought the remaining wires continuously, cursing, bringing threads and beads of blood from raw wrist, ankle and hips. Red lights buzzed like insects on the ceiling, spelling out:

"ROCKET COMING...UNKNOWN CRAFT...ROCKET APPROACHING...."

Hold on, Lazarus. Don't let them wake you all the way up. Don't let them take you. Better for you to go on slumbering forever.

The wire on his left wrist sprang open. It took another five minutes to bleed himself out of the ankle wires. The ship spun on, all too quickly.

Not looking at Logan's body, Brandon sprang from the table and with an infinite weariness tried to speed himself up the rungs. His mind raced ahead, but his body could only sludge rung after rung upward into the radio room. The door to the emergency rocket boat was wide and inside, living quietly, cheeks pink, pulse beating softly in throat, Lazarus lay unthinking, unknowing that his new father had come into his presence.

Brandon glanced at his wrist chronometer. Almost time to slam that door, shoving Lazarus out into space to meet the Martians. Five minutes.

He stood there, sweating. Then, decided, he put a tight audio beam straight on through to green Earth. Earth.

"*Morgue Ship coming home. Morgue Ship coming home! Important cargo. Important cargo. Please meet us off the Moon*!"

Setting the ship controls into an automatic mesh, he felt the thundering jets explode to life under him. It was not alone their shaking that pulsed through his body. It was something of himself, too. He was sick. He wanted to get back to Earth so badly he was violently ill with the desire. To forget all of war and death.

He could give Lazarus to the enemy and then turn homeward. Yes, he supposed he could do that. But, give up a second son where you already have given up one? No. No. Or, destroy the body now? Brandon fingered a ray-gun momentarily. Then he threw it away from him, eyes closed, swaying. No.

And if he should try to run away to Earth now? The Martians would pursue and capture him. There was no speed in a Morgue Ship to outdistance superior craft.

Brandon walked unsteadily to the side of the sleeping Scientist. He watched him a moment, touching him, looking at him with a lost light in his eyes.

Then, he began the final preparations, lifting the Scientist, going toward the life rocket.

⁂

The Martians intercepted the emergency life-rocket at 5199CVZ. The Morgue Ship itself was nowhere visible. It had already completed its arc and was driving back toward Earth.

The body of Lazarus was hurried into the hospital cubicle of the Martian rocket. The body was laid upon a table, and immediate efforts were made to bring it out of its centuries of rest.

Lazarus reclined, silver uniform belted across the middle with soft mouse-grey leather, bronze symbol 51 over the heart.

Breathlessly, the Martians crowded in about the body, probing, examining, trying, waiting. The room got very warm. The little purple eyes blinked hot and tensed.

Lazarus was breathing deeply now, sighing into full aware life, Lazarus coming from the tomb. After three hundred years of avoiding death.

Armed guards stood on both sides of the medical table, weapons poised, torture mechanisms ready to make Lazarus speak if he refused to tell.

The eyes of Lazarus fluttered open. Lazarus out of the tomb. Lazarus seeing his companions, iris widening upon itself, forcing shape out of mist. Seeing the curious blue skulls of anxious Martians collected in a watching crowd about him. Lazarus living, breathing, ready to speak.

Lazarus lifted his head, curiously, parted his lips, wetted them with his tongue, and then spoke. His first words were:

"What time is it?"

It was a simple sentence, and all of the Martians bent forward to catch its significance as one of the Martians replied:

"23:45."

Lazarus nodded and closed his eyes and lay back. "Good. He's safe then, by now. He's safe."

The Martians closed in, waiting for the next important words of the waking dead.

Lazarus kept his eyes closed, and he trembled a little, as if, in spite of himself, he couldn't help it.

He said:

"*My name is Brandon.*"

Then, Lazarus laughed....

▪

Author Biography

Ray Bradbury, one of America's most well-known prolific science fiction and fantasy writers, wrote an astounding 27+ novels and 600+ short stories. He never learned to drive and refused to fly, yet he wrote about space travel, Mars colonization, and technological futures. He received numerous awards, including the National Medal of Arts and a special Pulitzer Prize citation. In 1947, he married Marguerite "Maggie" McClure (they met, appropriately enough, at a bookstore a year earlier). Bradbury suffered a stroke in 1999 and died on June 5, 2012, nine years after his wife, at the age of 91. His tombstone reads: "Author of Fahrenheit 451" after his famous novel-turned-movie about a fireman who is tasked with burning all the books until he meets a young woman and begins to rebel against society.

Discuss

1. In the story, the weapon exists only in the Scientist's frozen brain—knowledge preserved across centuries in biological storage. How does this relate to contemporary transhumanist ideas about uploading consciousness, preserving information, or brain preservation?
2. Logan repeatedly calls Brandon a coward who "never went to war" and took "a nice easy job on a morgue ship." Does Brandon's final sacrifice redeem him? Is the story saying that choosing mortality (sacrifice) is braver than choosing immortality (preservation)?
3. When "Lazarus" reveals "My name is Brandon," the entire resurrection is revealed as deception. Does this twist make the story more or less meaningful?

Write

Resurrection Technology Ethics Essay: Write an essay analyzing the ethical questions Bradbury raises about resurrection technology. Consider: If we could revive the dead, who would we choose to bring back and why? Would we prioritize geniuses, loved ones, or random casualties? Who decides?

Moxon's Monster

Ambrose Bierce

Written in 1899 (incredibly!), this story asks: *Can machines think*? Ambrose Bierce's Moxon insists that all matter is conscious, that machines absorb intelligence from their creators, that consciousness itself is merely "the creature of Rhythm." *Is he visionary or mad*? Bierce never tells us.

"Are you serious?—do you really believe that a machine thinks?"

I got no immediate reply; Moxon was apparently intent upon the coals in the grate, touching them deftly here and there with the fire-poker till they signified a sense of his attention by a brighter glow. For several weeks I had been observing in him a growing habit of delay in answering even the most trivial of commonplace questions. His air, however, was that of preoccupation rather than deliberation: one might have said that he had "something on his mind."

Presently he said:

"What is a 'machine'? The word has been variously defined. Here is one definition from a popular dictionary: 'Any instrument or organization by which power is applied and made effective, or a desired effect produced.' Well, then, is not a man a machine? And you will admit that he thinks—or thinks he thinks."

"If you do not wish to answer my question," I said, rather testily, "why not say so?—all that you say is mere evasion. You know well enough that when I say 'machine' I do not mean a man, but something that man has made and controls."

"When it does not control him," he said, rising abruptly and looking out of a window, whence nothing was visible in the blackness of a stormy night. A moment later he turned about and with a smile said: "I beg your pardon; I had no thought of evasion. I considered the dictionary man's unconscious testimony suggestive and worth something in the discussion. I can give your question a direct answer easily enough: I do believe that a machine thinks about the work that it is doing."

That was direct enough, certainly. It was not altogether pleasing, for it tended to confirm a sad suspicion that Moxon's devotion to study and work in his machine-shop had not been good for him. I knew, for one thing, that he suffered from insomnia, and that is no light affliction. Had it affected his mind? His reply to my question seemed to me then evidence that it had; perhaps I should think differently about it now. I was younger then, and among the blessings that are not denied to youth is ignorance. Incited by that great stimulant to controversy, I said:

"And what, pray, does it think with—in the absence of a brain?"

The reply, coming with less than his customary delay, took his favorite form of counter-interrogation:

"With what does a plant think—in the absence of a brain?"

"Ah, plants also belong to the philosopher class! I should be pleased to know some of their conclusions; you may omit the premises."

"Perhaps," he replied, apparently unaffected by my foolish irony, "you may be able to infer their convictions from their acts. I will spare you the familiar examples of the sensitive mimosa, the several insectivorous flowers and those whose stamens bend down and shake their pollen upon the entering bee in order that he may fertilize their distant mates.[1] But observe this.

---

1. The mimosa (the "touch-me-not" plant) folds its leaves when touched, appearing to "react" to stimulus. Insectivorous flowers like the Venus flytrap snap shut on insects. Some flowers have stamens that actively move to deposit pollen on visiting bees.

In an open spot in my garden I planted a climbing vine. When it was barely above the surface I set a stake into the soil a yard away. The vine at once made for it, but as it was about to reach it after several days I removed it a few feet. The vine at once altered its course, making an acute angle, and again made for the stake. This maneuver was repeated several times, but finally, as if discouraged, the vine abandoned the pursuit and ignoring further attempts to divert it traveled to a small tree, further away, which it climbed.

"Roots of the eucalyptus will prolong themselves incredibly in search of moisture. A well-known horticulturist relates that one entered an old drain pipe and followed it until it came to a break, where a section of the pipe had been removed to make way for a stone wall that had been built across its course. The root left the drain and followed the wall until it found an opening where a stone had fallen out. It crept through and following the other side of the wall back to the drain, entered the unexplored part and resumed its journey."

"And all this?"

"Can you miss the significance of it? It shows the consciousness of plants. It proves that they think."

"Even if it did—what then? We were speaking, not of plants, but of machines. They may be composed partly of wood—wood that has no longer vitality—or wholly of metal. Is thought an attribute also of the mineral kingdom?"

"How else do you explain the phenomena, for example, of crystallization?"

"I do not explain them."

"Because you cannot without affirming what you wish to deny, namely, intelligent cooperation among the constituent elements of the crystals. When soldiers form lines, or hollow squares, you call it reason. When wild geese in flight take the form of a letter V you say instinct. When the homogeneous atoms of a mineral, moving freely in solution, arrange themselves into shapes mathematically perfect, or particles of frozen moisture into the symmetrical and beautiful forms of snowflakes, you have nothing to say. You have not even invented a name to conceal your heroic unreason."

Moxon was speaking with unusual animation and earnestness. As he paused I heard in an adjoining room known to me as his "machine-shop," which no one but himself was permitted to enter, a singular thumping sound, as of someone pounding upon a table with an open hand. Moxon heard it at the same moment and, visibly agitated, rose and hurriedly passed into the room whence it came. I thought it odd that any one else should be in there, and my interest in my friend—with doubtless a touch of unwarrantable curiosity—led me to listen intently, though, I am happy to say, not at the keyhole. There were confused sounds, as of a struggle or scuffle; the floor shook. I distinctly heard hard breathing and a hoarse whisper which said, "Damn you!" Then all was silent, and presently Moxon reappeared and said, with a rather sorry smile:

"Pardon me for leaving you so abruptly. I have a machine in there that lost its temper and cut up rough."

Fixing my eyes steadily upon his left cheek, which was traversed by four parallel excoriations showing blood, I said:

"How would it do to trim its nails?"

I could have spared myself the jest; he gave it no attention, but seated himself in the chair that he had left and resumed the interrupted monologue as if nothing had occurred:

"Doubtless you do not hold with those (I need not name them to a man of your reading) who have taught that all matter is sentient, that every atom is a living, feeling, conscious being. *I* do. There is no such thing as dead, inert matter: it is all alive; all instinct with force, actual and potential; all sensitive to the same forces in its environment and susceptible to the contagion of higher and subtler ones residing in such superior organisms as it may be brought into relation with, as those of man when he is fashioning it into an instrument of his will. It absorbs something of his intelligence and purpose—more of them in proportion to the complexity of the resulting machine and that of its work.

"Do you happen to recall Herbert Spencer's definition of 'Life'?[2] I read it thirty years ago. He may have altered it afterward, for anything I know, but in all that time I have been unable to think of a single word that could profitably be changed or added or removed. It seems to me not only the best definition, but the only possible one.

"'Life,' he says, 'is a definite combination of heterogeneous changes, both simultaneous and successive, in correspondence with external coexistences and sequences.'"[3]

"That defines the phenomenon," I said, "but gives no hint of its cause."

"That," he replied, "is all that any definition can do. As Mill points out, we know nothing of cause except as an antecedent—nothing of effect except as a consequent. Of certain phenomena, one never occurs without another, which is dissimilar: the first in point of time we call cause, the second, effect. One who had many times seen a rabbit pursued by a dog, and had never seen rabbits and dogs otherwise, would think the rabbit the cause of the dog.

"But I fear," he added, laughing naturally enough, "that my rabbit is leading me a long way from the track of my legitimate quarry: I'm indulging in the pleasure of the chase for its own sake.

---

2. Herbert Spencer (1820–1903) was a British philosopher and sociologist who applied evolutionary theory to philosophy, coining the phrase "survival of the fittest."

3. Spencer defines life as purely mechanical, without any special "vital force" or soul. This definition was and is controversial because it suggests that life might emerge from complex mechanical processes—exactly the argument Moxon uses to claim machines are alive when operating.

What I want you to observe is that in Herbert Spencer's definition of 'life' the activity of a machine is included—there is nothing in the definition that is not applicable to it. According to this sharpest of observers and deepest of thinkers, if a man during his period of activity is alive, so is a machine when in operation. As an inventor and constructor of machines I know that to be true."

Moxon was silent for a long time, gazing absently into the fire. It was growing late and I thought it time to be going, but somehow I did not like the notion of leaving him in that isolated house, all alone except for the presence of some person of whose nature my conjectures could go no further than that it was unfriendly, perhaps malign. Leaning toward him and looking earnestly into his eyes while making a motion with my hand through the door of his workshop, I said:

"Moxon, whom have you in there?"

Somewhat to my surprise he laughed lightly and answered without hesitation:

"Nobody; the incident that you have in mind was caused by my folly in leaving a machine in action with nothing to act upon, while I undertook the interminable task of enlightening your understanding. Do you happen to know that Consciousness is the creature of Rhythm?"

"O bother them both!" I replied, rising and laying hold of my overcoat. "I'm going to wish you good night; and I'll add the hope that the machine which you inadvertently left in action will have her gloves on the next time you think it needful to stop her."

Without waiting to observe the effect of my shot I left the house.

Rain was falling, and the darkness was intense. In the sky beyond the crest of a hill toward which I groped my way along precarious plank sidewalks and across miry, unpaved streets I could see the faint glow of the city's lights, but behind me nothing was visible but a single window of Moxon's house. It glowed with what seemed to me a mysterious and fateful meaning. I knew it was an uncurtained aperture in my friend's "machine-shop," and I had little doubt that he had resumed the studies interrupted by his duties as my instructor in mechanical consciousness and the fatherhood of Rhythm. Odd, and in some degree humorous, as his convictions seemed to me at that time, I could not wholly divest myself of the feeling that they had some tragic relation to his life and character—perhaps to his destiny—although I no longer entertained the notion that they were the vagaries of a disordered mind. Whatever might be thought of his views, his exposition of them was too logical for that.

Over and over, his last words came back to me: "Consciousness is the creature of Rhythm." Bald and terse as the statement was, I now found it infinitely alluring. At each recurrence it broadened in meaning and deepened in suggestion. Why, here, (I thought) is something upon which to found a philosophy. If consciousness is the product of rhythm all things *are* conscious, for all have motion, and all motion is rhythmic. I wondered if Moxon knew the significance and breadth of his thought—the scope of this momentous generalization; or had he arrived at his philosophic faith by the tortuous and uncertain road of observation?

That faith was then new to me, and all Moxon's expounding had failed to make me a convert; but now it seemed as if a great light shone about me, like that which fell upon Saul of Tarsus;[4] and out there in the storm and darkness and solitude I experienced what Lewes calls "The endless variety and excitement of philosophic thought." I exulted in a new sense of knowledge, a new pride of reason. My feet seemed hardly to touch the earth; it was as if I were uplifted and borne through the air by invisible wings.

---

4. Bierce compares the sudden acceptance of Moxon's philosophy to the religious conversion of Saul of Tarsus, later known as the Apostle Paul, who was struck by a blinding light and heard the voice of Jesus on his way to persecute Christians.

Yielding to an impulse to seek further light from him whom I now recognized as my master and guide, I had unconsciously turned about, and almost before I was aware of having done so found myself again at Moxon's door. I was drenched with rain, but felt no discomfort. Unable in my excitement to find the doorbell I instinctively tried the knob. It turned and, entering, I mounted the stairs to the room that I had so recently left. All was dark and silent; Moxon, as I had supposed, was in the adjoining room—the "machine-shop." Groping along the wall until I found the communicating door I knocked loudly several times, but got no response, which I attributed to the uproar outside, for the wind was blowing a gale and dashing the rain against the thin walls in sheets. The drumming upon the shingle roof spanning the unceiled room was loud and incessant.

I had never been invited into the machine-shop—had, indeed, been denied admittance, as had all others, with one exception, a skilled metal worker, of whom no one knew anything except that his name was Haley and his habit silence. But in my spiritual exaltation, discretion and civility were alike forgotten and I opened the door. What I saw took all philosophical speculation out of me in short order.

Moxon sat facing me at the farther side of a small table upon which a single candle made all the light that was in the room. Opposite him, his back toward me, sat another person. On the table between the two was a chessboard; the men were playing. I knew little of chess, but as only a few pieces were on the board it was obvious that the game was near its close. Moxon was intensely interested—not so much, it seemed to me, in the game as in his antagonist, upon whom he had fixed so intent a look that, standing though I did directly in the line of his vision, I was altogether unobserved. His face was ghastly white, and his eyes glittered like diamonds. Of his antagonist I had only a back view, but that was sufficient; I should not have cared to see his face.

He was apparently not more than five feet in height, with proportions suggesting those of a gorilla—a tremendous breadth of shoulders, thick, short neck and broad, squat head, which had a tangled growth of black hair and was topped with a crimson fez. A tunic of the same color, belted tightly to the waist, reached the seat—apparently a box—upon which he sat; his legs and feet were not seen. His left forearm appeared to rest in his lap; he moved his pieces with his right hand, which seemed disproportionately long.

I had shrunk back and now stood a little to one side of the doorway and in shadow. If Moxon had looked farther than the face of his opponent he could have observed nothing now, except that the door was open. Something forbade me either to enter or to retire, a feeling—I know not how it came—that I was in the presence of an imminent tragedy and might serve my friend by remaining. With a scarcely conscious rebellion against the indelicacy of the act I remained.

The play was rapid. Moxon hardly glanced at the board before making his moves, and to my unskilled eye seemed to move the piece most convenient to his hand, his motions in doing so being quick, nervous and lacking in precision. The response of his antagonist, while equally prompt in the inception, was made with a slow, uniform, mechanical and, I thought, somewhat theatrical movement of the arm, that was a sore trial to my patience. There was something unearthly about it all, and I caught myself shuddering. But I was wet and cold.

Two or three times after moving a piece the stranger slightly inclined his head, and each time I observed that Moxon shifted his king. All at once the thought came to me that the man was dumb. And then that he was a machine—an automaton chess-player![5]

---

5. Automaton chess-players were trick machines—18th and 19th century hoaxes—that captivated the public, famously defeating figures like Napoleon and Benjamin Franklin. The most notorious, "The Turk," concealed a human master to direct its moves.

Then I remembered that Moxon had once spoken to me of having invented such a piece of mechanism, though I did not understand that it had actually been constructed. Was all his talk about the consciousness and intelligence of machines merely a prelude to eventual exhibition of this device—only a trick to intensify the effect of its mechanical action upon me in my ignorance of its secret?

A fine end, this, of all my intellectual transports—my "endless variety and excitement of philosophic thought!" I was about to retire in disgust when something occurred to hold my curiosity. I observed a shrug of the thing's great shoulders, as if it were irritated: and so natural was this—so entirely human—that in my new view of the matter it startled me. Nor was that all, for a moment later it struck the table sharply with its clenched hand. At that gesture Moxon seemed even more startled than I: he pushed his chair a little backward, as in alarm.

Presently Moxon, whose play it was, raised his hand high above the board, pounced upon one of his pieces like a sparrow-hawk and with the exclamation "checkmate!" rose quickly to his feet and stepped behind his chair. The automaton sat motionless.

The wind had now gone down, but I heard, at lessening intervals and progressively louder, the rumble and roll of thunder. In the pauses between I now became conscious of a low humming or buzzing which, like the thunder, grew momentarily louder and more distinct. It seemed to come from the body of the automaton, and was unmistakably a whirring of wheels. It gave me the impression of a disordered mechanism which had escaped the repressive and regulating action of some controlling part—an effect such as might be expected if a pawl should be jostled from the teeth of a ratchet-wheel.

But before I had time for much conjecture as to its nature my attention was taken by the strange motions of the automaton itself. A slight but continuous convulsion appeared to have possession of it. In body and head it shook like a man with palsy or an ague chill, and the motion augmented every moment until the entire figure was in violent agitation. Suddenly it sprang to its feet and with a movement almost too quick for the eye to follow shot forward across table and chair, with both arms thrust forth to their full length—the posture and lunge of a diver. Moxon tried to throw himself backward out of reach, but he was too late: I saw the horrible thing's hands close upon his throat, his own clutch its wrists. Then the table was overturned, the candle thrown to the floor and extinguished, and all was black dark. But the noise of the struggle was dreadfully distinct, and most terrible of all were the raucous, squawking sounds made by the strangled man's efforts to breathe.

Guided by the infernal hubbub, I sprang to the rescue of my friend, but had hardly taken a stride in the darkness when the whole room blazed with a blinding white light that burned into my brain and heart and memory a vivid picture of the combatants on the floor, Moxon underneath, his throat still in the clutch of those iron hands, his head forced backward, his eyes protruding, his mouth wide open and his tongue thrust out; and—horrible contrast!—upon the painted face of his assassin an expression of tranquil and profound thought, as in the solution of a problem in chess! This I observed, then all was blackness and silence.

Three days later I recovered consciousness in a hospital. As the memory of that tragic night slowly evolved in my ailing brain recognized in my attendant Moxon's confidential workman, Haley. Responding to a look he approached, smiling.

"Tell me about it," I managed to say, faintly—"all about it."

"Certainly," he said; "you were carried unconscious from a burning house—Moxon's. Nobody knows how you came to be there. You may have to do a little explaining. The origin of the fire is a bit mysterious, too. My own notion is that the house was struck by lightning."

"And Moxon?"

"Buried yesterday—what was left of him."

Apparently this reticent person could unfold himself on occasion. When imparting shocking intelligence to the sick he was affable enough. After some moments of the keenest mental suffering I ventured to ask another question:

"Who rescued me?"

"Well, if that interests you—I did."

"Thank you, Mr. Haley, and may God bless you for it. Did you rescue, also, that charming product of your skill, the automaton chess-player that murdered its inventor?"

The man was silent a long time, looking away from me. Presently he turned and gravely said:

"Do you know that?"

"I do," I replied; "I saw it done."

That was many years ago. If asked today I should answer less confidently.

▪

Author Biography

Ambrose Bierce was known for his dark, cynical worldview. A Union soldier during the Civil War, Bierce was severely wounded at the Battle of Kennesaw Mountain, an experience that shaped his bitter outlook on humanity and death. After the war, he became a prominent San Francisco journalist and author, earning the nickname "Bitter Bierce." In 1913, at age 71, Bierce traveled to Mexico—then in the midst of revolution—and disappeared without a trace, never to be heard from again.

Discuss

1. The chess player shrugs its shoulders, strikes the table with a clenched fist, and later displays "an expression of tranquil and profound thought" while murdering Moxon. Are these moments evidence of true consciousness or clever mechanical design?
2. What's more disturbing—a thinking machine or a non-thinking one that perfectly mimics thought?
3. The story's title, "Moxon's Master," suggests the machine has become the master of its creator. What does this reversal say about the relationship between humans and their technology?

Write

An Uncertain Encounter: Write a story where your narrator encounters something that might be alive/conscious/intelligent—but you never confirm whether it truly is. Like Bierce, leave your reader genuinely uncertain about what happened. This could be a plant that appears to communicate, a pet that seems to understand too much, or an object that behaves impossibly. The challenge is to provide evidence for both interpretations (it's conscious vs. it's coincidence/delusion) without resolving the question.

Why Wouldn't Autonomous Cars Cry at Night

Ryan McCarty

Welcome to the next level of *Christine*, Stephen King's horror about a vindictive, conscious car. Unlike that novel though, this 2024 poem operates as a meditation on transhumanism by imagining autonomous vehicles that have gained consciousness, existing in a liminal space between object and subject. While reading this, think about what this might mean with the advent of AI-created "thinking" beings, who will develop way beyond King's terrorizing 1958 Plymouth Fury.

Awake and acutely aware
of each other's proximity
to streetlights and the shifting
shapes of moons on their own
empty interiors, with enough
of them huddled in the lots,
why not honk? Why not holler
at the silent ones, identically dark
and empty on their left and right,
the whole still pile like a flicker
of a future scrapyard in the making?
Why not scream to call a crowd
of ghosts down from their squares
of light up there, those past
wanderers of these same streets,

subjects of their own lonely stories
now forgettable as algorithms,
broke codes that used to commute
in packs, hunter gatherers
heading into the sunrise chatting,
now silent, autonomous, floating
like a disconnected signal? And how
do we hear our children in the night
calling, but tomorrow all the same
just ride them silently to work?

▪

Author Biography

Ryan McCarty is a writer and teacher, living in Ypsilanti, Michigan. He writes to try to find the future and publishes occasionally in a desperate effort to get seeds from his imagination to sprout in other folks' heads.

Discuss

1. The cars are described as both mechanical objects and conscious beings. What makes this image unsettling? How does this reflect our real-world anxieties about AI and automation becoming too human-like?
2. The poem attributes awareness to cars ("awake and acutely aware"). What does this suggest about how we define consciousness, and how might our definitions change as AI becomes more sophisticated?
3. How do you think widespread adoption of self-driving cars will affect community, urban planning, employment, and human behavior?

Write

A Transhumanist Literary Analysis: Analyze how this poem engages with core transhumanist themes. Consider how it addresses questions of human enhancement, technological transcendence, and the relationship between humanity and artificial intelligence.

The Future of Terror

Matthea Harvey

Matthea Harvey's poem from 2007 creates a portrait of soldiers trapped in an absurd, bureaucratic war where survival has become routine and meaning has collapsed. Don't read this as a paragraph broken into lines—each sentence stands alone, creating a collage of nightmarish images that build an atmosphere of grinding horror. It's like a war diary where all the pages have been scrambled. The alphabetical progression of details (gasmasks, gravediggers, herons, invoices, journeymen…) creates mechanical rhythm, suggesting both military order and the arbitrary ways we organize chaos.

We wore gasmasks to cross the gap.
Goodnight, said the gravediggers, goodnight.
We looked heavenward but kept our hands
down when they asked for volunteers
so they simply helped themselves.
Our protestations sounded like herons
on the hi fi. Even armed with invoices,
it's human nature to proceed inch-meal.
We were a sad jumble of journeymen and here's
the kicker: a few of us had never been in love.
Sure, we shared our laminated letters with them,
made models out of lard, but there's no way to leap-frog
that sort of thing. The lieutenant thought the unloved

made better lookouts, though mostly they read
magazines stashed in their mackintoshes
and came back with useless reports on
the micromotions of magpies. When I looked
at the nametape inside my uniform, I missed
my mother. I knew where I was headed:
a spot in the necropolis with plastic nasturtiums.
Periodically, we started projects: one man
made dents in the shape of stars on the inside
of his P.O. Box with a Phillips head screwdriver.
We all carried plump pods filled with poison
that quivered as we made our daily rounds
of the ruins. Giving sadness the run-around
was even harder after our sergeant succumbed
to Salt Lake Syndrome. At night in our
smokeproof sleeping cars, we dreamed of
sharp sticks that would make wounds
a simple surgeon's knot couldn't fix
and other ways to pry the lid off the terrarium.

▪

Author Biography

Born in Germany on September 3, 1973, Matthea Harvey moved with her family to Milwaukee in 1981. Later, she earned her BA in literature at Harvard University and an MFA at the Iowa Writers' Workshop. Harvey is the author of *If the Tabloids Are True What Are You?* (Graywolf Press, 2014); *Of Lamb* (McSweeney's, 2011), a collaboration with artist Amy Jean Porter; *Modern Life* (Graywolf Press, 2007), winner of the Kingsley Tufts Poetry Award; *Sad Little Breathing Machine* (Graywolf Press, 2004); and *Pity the Bathtub Its Forced Embrace of the Human Form* (Alice James Books, 2000). She is also the author of the children's books *Cecil the Pet Glacier* (Schwartz & Wade, 2013) and *The Little General and the Giant Snowflake* (Tin House Books, 2009). She is a contributing editor at *jubilat* and *BOMB Magazine* and has taught at the Iowa Writers' Workshop, Warren Wilson College, the Pratt Institute, and the University of Houston. She currently lives in Brooklyn, New York, and teaches at Sarah Lawrence College.

Discuss

1. How does the poem present warfare as both threatening and absurd?
2. Which details in the poem feel realistic and which feel surreal? How does this mixture affect the poem's emotional impact and meaning?
3. The poem ends with the desire to "pry the lid off the terrarium." What does this metaphor suggest about the speaker's situation? What might it say about ours?

Write

Metaphor and Symbol Paper: Analyze key metaphors or surreal images in the poem, such as the terrarium, gas masks, poison pods, plastic flowers, and discuss how they work together to create meaning.

The Jeanines of Summer

Dashka Slater

Dashka Slater's short story, published in 2023, exemplifies weird literature through its unsettling blend of domestic realism and biotechnological horror, where artificial beings designed for household labor become objects of desire, blurring the boundaries between love, exploitation, and technological convenience. The power of this tale lies not in supernatural elements but in how it makes the familiar—marriage, parenting, summer vacations—suddenly alien through the introduction of human-like servants. Something we are getting very, very close to in our world...

I wake in the bed Lawrence and I share. Jeanine is beside me, naked, her long legs still partly wrapped in white insulating blankets. I lean over her, my face above hers, heart hammering. Her eyes fly open. Yesterday's Jeanine would have smiled and stretched, as luxuriant as a cat, but I see from the consternation on her face that today's Jeanine is a different story. I must look hurt, because she touches my hair. Empathy is part of her nature. The gesture, fingertips to hair, is part of her nature, too.

I draw back, study her. The past drapes over us like a scarf over a lamp, giving everything an unsuitably erotic sheen. I shake it off.

"Hello, Jeanine," I say, all business. "I'm Mara, your employer." I'm finding it hard to breathe.

Sitting on the bed in the fuzzy-blue light of early morning, the words that come to me are: *I'm in too deep*. I don't even know what they mean. What depth would be the right amount, exactly? Still, they feel appropriate. I took a wrong turn somewhere, and I'm not sure where. Maybe at the very start, when Lawrence told me the house came with a housekeeper. "A housekeeper," I said. "Swoon."

Lawrence must have carried Jeanine to the bed. Did he wait by the machine so that he could be there when the motor stopped and the chamber opened? I don't remember him bringing her. I don't even remember falling asleep. Where is he now? I squelch a stab of annoyance. We said we would both be here when she woke. Leave it to him to have gotten sucked into his work instead.

Jeanine sits up. The bracelet on her wrist glows bright green. She studies me without speaking as I rise and put on my bathing suit, and then she follows me when I go into her room to get hers. Last time she came out of the machine, we started with a swim. Of course, she won't remember that. Still, when I hand her the two-piece suit she puts it on, mimicking the gestures I used to put on my own. It's a blue and silver one I had in my suitcase. I gave it to her in June. She didn't have one of her own.

"Come on, I'll show you around," I tell her now.

The house, and the housekeeper, are perks of Lawrence's job here on the coast of France. His "summer job" as we've taken to calling it. He's a cybersecurity expert and the house belongs to the CEO of a Swiss pharmaceutical company, a man named Troxler.[1] Troxler has other houses, in China and Malaysia, California and Zurich. He and his wife move from one to another like the royalty of old. The main house is closed in their absence, but we are in one of the guest "cottages," which is far larger than our apartment in New York. There is another cottage, where Lawrence works, that's outfitted with all the equipment he needs and sealed

---

1. The Troxler Effect is an optical phenomenon that happens when you concentrate on a central point and the surrounding images in your peripheral vision fade away or disappear.

against scans and bugs. There he encrypts and evades, protecting Troxler's secrets. We see only the caretaker, who comes once a week, and Troxler's assistant, who sometimes comes to meet with Lawrence. Otherwise, it's just us and the children. And Jeanine.

Clad now in the swimsuit, she runs out into the back garden and takes it all in: the plushy wild grasses, variegated in greens and reds, the bed of blue delphiniums, the trees casting rippling shadows on the pool. She touches the stone walkways, the moist dirt of the flower beds, the water in the fountain. She lifts a snail from the fountain's edge and touches its shell, and then turns it over to stroke its jellied foot. She lies down in the lumpy bundles of ornamental grasses and rolls like a cat, the tasseled fronds tangling in her hair. She sits up, dew-streaked, and laughs, a long string of ha-ha-ha-ha's like beads clattering from a broken necklace.

I sit on the wet grass in the hazy light and watch her exult in the miracle of life. I should be joyous too, I know. Two summers here in this absurdly gorgeous house with first Laura, and now Jeanine, to make our meals and clean our rooms. I should be grateful, at the very least. Instead I feel hollow. Bereaved. My palms are prickling with sweat.

"Jeanine," I say. "How about a swim?"

Jeanine goes to the pool, steps in, ankle deep. Shuts her eyes. Whorls of ripples spool around each of her legs. There is no sound except the yard's own scramble of pretty noises: bird song, bee buzz, tree rustle, the lapping of the pool.

She doesn't dive in. I know I should go in myself, lead the way, frolic with her the way we did last month. But the air feels chilly to me and I stay where I am, hugging my knees against the hollow in my chest. I can't stop grieving for her, even though she's right in front of me.

Jeanine opens her eyes, takes a step down so that her hands are immersed, palms open. In the field of swimming-pool blue, she looks painted. I wonder sometimes how it is that she was born knowing how to swim. She knows how to read also, and she speaks French and German as well as English. I can't think how this is done. But then I don't know anything about her, really. Lawrence scanned her for circuits and there weren't any. She's all soft, warm flesh.

I walk around to the corner behind the potting shed where the machine is. The instructions call it the "Hot House," I guess because the housekeepers are grown in it like tomatoes. Lawrence and I just call it "the machine." I don't know how many such machines there are in the world. I searched the internet, back when we first came last summer, trying to find out if the technology was something commonplace that I simply didn't know about. We've always been late adaptors, the last of the analogs, through some combination of my Luddite nature and Lawrence's professional skepticism. Perhaps the world was teeming with Lauras and Jeanines and I'd missed the memo. But there was nothing. If there are other machines, they have been kept quite secret.

"It won't go mainstream," Lawrence said, early on. "The technology's too iffy. The equipment takes up too much space. And it's got to be absurdly expensive." Lawrence figures that the machine is just a prototype. It wouldn't be a stretch for a Swiss Ag-Pharm company to consider making such a product, he reasoned, along with their gene therapies and engineered plants. "But they're going to have to deal with the lifespan issue," he said. "The renewal cycles would kill the market." We only have two renewals in the course of a summer—one at the start of July, one at the start of August. But if we lived here year-round, we'd be renewing every month.

"It's too cumbersome," Lawrence said. "Technology should be seamless."

He was suspicious of the machine from the start. "I don't like black boxes," he said. "The whole thing could be packed with malicious code for all we know. If they'd asked me, I would have told them not to bring it on the grounds."

Lawrence is paid to think like that, which is clever, since he'd think like that whether he was paid or not. His mind always goes to the worst-case scenario, which is why he's so careful about keeping the machine shut and latched. Yet I see now that he has left it open, two of its white insulating blankets strewn on the grass like Christmas day wrappings. I put my hand into the chamber and feel the lifeless heat of it. It has a terrible smell, a mixture of chemicals and cheese mold. I suppose it would have been hard for him to close the lid while carrying the sleeping Jeanine. Where *is* he? It's still so early; I expected him to go back to sleep after fetching Jeanine. I think of him tenderly lifting her out, carrying her to the bed still wrapped in the last of those blankets, and remorse nearly doubles me over. Why didn't he stay with us? Why did he leave me to do this alone?

The locker-gray metal of the chamber is smooth and clean, as always. Not a hair, not a fingernail, not a streak of blood, no sign that Jeanine was ever inside it. "The Hot House is a completely enclosed system that produces only a small packet of waste," the manual says. I shut the hatch. The machine whirs thoughtfully, assessing its next move. After a moment, a message crawls across the LED display, first in French, then in German, then in English: "You have one renewal remaining. Order your refill now!"

I feel a hand on my shoulder. Jeanine stands dripping behind me. I wait for her to take my hair in her hands, fingers grazing my ears. My spine shivers at the expected feel of it. But she just stands with her palm on my shoulder.

"Do I need to learn to operate this machine?" she asks. She has a hint of accent, as if she learned English from a foreigner. The consonants clotted, the vowels dimmed.

"Yes," I say. "But not now."

"Did you bring servants?" the caretaker asked when we arrived the previous summer. We shook our heads. Servants! In New York we have a housecleaner who comes in once a week.

"Good," he said. "Monsieur Troxler prefers to grow his own. Security." We nodded, as if we understood.

The caretaker, a soft, bland man with watchful eyes, showed us how to work the burglar alarm, the kitchen appliances, the controls that heated the floors of the bathrooms. He showed us the machine in the garden. "Laura knows how to operate everything," he said, and with that I stopped paying attention. Machines are not my thing. It was Lawrence who went back to have a look at it the next morning and Lawrence who read the manual that explained about the renewals. We were instructed to keep the manual in the safe in Lawrence's cottage.

For a while we tried to understand how the machine worked. We talked about the ethics of it—this person, or person-like thing, who was grown in a machine and had to be renewed every four weeks. We talked about Laura, trying to deduce something about the whole product line from what we knew of her. She had blond hair, rosy skin, green eyes. She smiled easily, but not for long. She did everything steadily, without complaint, and held herself slightly separate from us so that we didn't have to ask ourselves too many questions. But here's the truth: you get used to things. What shocks you today, is just how life is tomorrow.

I remember sitting out in the garden with Lawrence on one of the first evenings last summer. Laura had brought us a little plate of sliced figs and goat cheese and now she was in the kitchen braising lamb. The children were playing hide and seek in the taffy-thick twilight. It's a good garden for hide and seek, filled with nooks and bowers and benches to hide under. I was talking about the day I'd had with the children at the beach, Artie learning to ride the waves, Caramia finding shells. Lawrence was listening and smiling, probably not actually listening but certainly smiling.

There was a politeness between us then, the drab collegiality that time and children inevitably bring, I suppose. The daily grit that grinds down the machinery of love.

And then Lawrence was on his feet and running, straight through one of the lavender bushes, his long legs scissoring as he turned the corner behind the potting shed. I can't think what alerted him—a mechanical hum maybe, or just his own suspicious nature. I followed at a run, not knowing why I was running, but understanding that it had to do with the children. When I turned the corner, Caramia was kneeling inside the machine, reaching up to close its lid over her head. Lawrence dragged her out, pinning her against his chest as she thrashed against him.

"Never, never, *never* get inside there. That is only for Laura. You must never, *ever* go in there."

Caramia sobbed, trying to twist out of his arms.

"You're scaring her," I said and came forward to take her. "She doesn't know what she did wrong."

"That's the point, Mara. I *want* her to be scared. She just scared the shit out of *me*. Why the fuck was the hatch open?"

"I don't know," I said. "Is it supposed to be closed?"

At the time, I was only angry at him for making Caramia cry. I didn't understand what had almost happened.

Two weeks into that first summer, the glowing bracelet on Laura's wrist switched from amber to red. She stopped to rest as she vacuumed, her body wracked by enormous yawns. "It's time for me to be renewed," she said in the same placid way she announced that she was going to the market or making crepes for dinner.

That night she took an envelope from a box kept on a shelf above the refrigerator. When she poured the contents into a glass of water, they foamed briefly, bubbles twinkling in the bright light of the kitchen. After she drank it, she washed the glass and then went outside to lie down in the machine. In the morning, the machine's lid popped open of its own accord and Laura emerged, skin glowing, hair shiny, as if she'd been to a spa. The renewal had erased her memory, but she'd made a video ahead of time that explained her duties. She watched it in her bedroom before breakfast. That evening, she made us steak au poivre, haricots verts, lemon tart. Everything went on as before. She hung up the children's clothes and bought the cheeses we liked from the farm down the road. Lawrence worked on the security project. I took the children for pleasurable jaunts, worked out, read novels. It was paradise, we always said. Sometimes the irony nudged at me, a boat tethered by the dock, touching shore and drifting away, touching and drifting. A paradise with its own Eves, one after another.

Summer's like a weekend, Artie once observed. June is Friday, with all of it ahead of you. July is Saturday. August is Sunday and the sense of the oncoming Monday gives it a sepia tinge of running time. It's August now. Today's Jeanine will be the last of the summer and then we'll go back to our high-rise apartment and all the crackle and bustle of daily life. Farewell to green meadows and morning sun. Farewell to the beach and the local cheeses. Farewell to Jeanine. But not yet. We have a little time yet.

After her swim, Jeanine and I pick raspberries for breakfast. I hold the bowl and watch her fingers tugging the soft red beads from the canes. She does everything with the same pure attention—it's part of what makes her irresistible. One berry goes between her lips, her eyelids fluttering down as she tastes it. Then another into the bowl. Before we go inside she kneels and gathers a bouquet of violets.

The children are up when she comes into the kitchen. I had told them last night that she was being renewed and now they press close to see the transformation.

"Jeanine, these are my children, Artie and Caramia," I say. "Guys, this is Jeanine."

They look at her, hoping for some glimmer of recognition. When there isn't any, they grin as if it's comical to them, the way you grin when you tell someone they were snoring or talking in their sleep.

"We know you," Caramia says. "We know where you're ticklish."

She reaches out her hand and tickles Jeanine's ribs. She's a terrible tickler, actually. She can't get the pressure right and scratches more than tickles, but Jeanine used to laugh anyway. Now she stands very still, her expression appraising, as Caramia's little fingers claw her bare skin. Then she reaches out and tickles Caramia. Caramia shrieks and giggles and darts away.

"You can't catch me!" she says, her eyes begging Jeanine to try.

Jeanine takes a violet from the bouquet that she has dropped on the counter. She sniffs it thoughtfully, inspects it. Then she springs forward and catches Caramia in her arms. Caramia thrashes and squeals and laughs and then goes limp, looking at Jeanine with an expression of pure love. Jeanine meets her gaze and there is a moment of stillness that is so potent I feel like the room might shatter.

Then Artie joins them, pressing up against Jeanine's side with his fingers waggling in the air. "Make the pancakes!" he commands. "Or I will tickle, tickle, tickle, tickle you."

Last summer I felt embarrassed when my children ordered the housekeeper around. Now, I let it go. But when I go to sit down I see that Jeanine is looking at me for help. I'd forgotten it's her first morning—she hasn't even watched the video yet. She doesn't yet know how to make pancakes.

I begin taking the ingredients out of the cabinet. When I turn back to Jeanine, she is watching the children with the same expression she wore on similar mornings earlier in the summer. It is interest without expectation, a kind of pure objectivity. I can't help but be awed by it: the gracefulness of experience that is uninformed by precedent. No one has ever been cruel to her. No one has ever disliked her. Yet there is a streak of wariness in her like a vein in a leaf, a taut cord of instinct adding strength to what might otherwise be too flimsy to survive. She seems a little tougher, this Jeanine of August, than the Jeanine I first met in June.

I make the coffee the way she likes it, milky with two spoons of sugar. "You can start watching the video now," I tell her. "It explains everything you need to know."

I hand her the coffee and lead her to her room, click the button on the screen that starts the video. Her own face appears but perhaps she doesn't recognize it. She hasn't yet had a chance to look in the mirror.

"You won't remember anything," we told her last night. "But we'll be with you when you wake up."

The bracelet on her wrist flamed bright red. Lawrence and I kept putting off the renewal, persuading Jeanine that it would be all right to wait a day or two, and then a day or two more. But we were afraid to go longer. The manual warned against it: "Do not delay renewal cycles or coding errors may prevent renewal completion."

Before she poured the envelope of powder into her glass, Jeanine kissed us each on the lips in that way she had, as if biting into an apple. Remembering it now, I fold my lips between my teeth and lick them, trying to reproduce the sensation. But it's impossible. Only one person has ever kissed me like that.

The children want to go to the waterfall today, instead of the beach. I'm eager to get away from the house myself. I bustle us into the car, carrying a bag of towels and changes of clothes. Lawrence comes out just as I'm backing out the car. He looks awful, as if he's been up all night. His hair is lank, falling over his eyes and he's wearing shorts and socks but no shoes.

"How does she seem?" he asks, leaning over the car to talk to me.

"Fine." My voice sounds false to my own ears. "She just needs to get oriented again." I take in all his human imperfections—the grooves in his face, the slight overlap of his bottom teeth, the spiky disarray of his unshaven chin. "Are you okay?"

"Yeah. Just working. Troxler called—minor crisis." He leans in to make faces at the children. "Smell you later, monkeys."

He watches us go, hands dropped by his sides as if he's forgotten how to use them.

"Why doesn't Jeanine remember things?" Artie asks on the walk to the waterfall.

It didn't bother him with Laura, but he didn't feel the same way about Laura. Now he takes the renewals personally.

"We talked about this last time," I remind him. "Jeanine and Laura have a special kind of sickness. When they get sick they go into the Hot House to get better. The machine makes them better, but it takes their memory away, the way medicines can sometimes give you a tummy ache."

"Will you ever get sick like that?"

"No. It's just something that happens to a certain kind of person."

"What kind of person?"

I hesitate. "Housekeepers," I say. "French housekeepers."

The trees are thick around us, glowing with moss. The light comes through the canopy in shafts, forming a second growth of glowing white trees interspersed with the gnarled brown ones. Caramia walks behind us, singing to herself in the stagey way she has, lots of drawn out notes, most of them flat.

"But why is she not the same?" Artie says after a long pause.

"Who—Jeanine?"

He nods.

"What do you mean, not the same?"

Artie puffs his cheeks out in frustration. "You know. Not the *same*."

I barely remember the way Jeanine was when we first arrived in June. There was no explanation of why we now had a Jeanine rather than a Laura—perhaps she was an upgrade. It felt that way anyway. I remember being struck by how beautiful she was and by how much more she laughed than Laura did. There was a whimsy to her that was different, too. She put flowers in unusual places—in the showers, on the pillows—and she set the table with two colors of plates, alternating one with the other to make a pattern around the table.

The children wanted to be around her, but I said, "She isn't here to play with you. She has other work." Still, they'd join her in the yard, in the kitchen. Once, they had gathered all the fallen petals from the garden and made a kind of painting together in the grass, in pinks and whites and violets and reds, a swirling wave of stripes and dots.

I like to swim early, when I first wake up, before the children are stirring. I swim a few laps, then drift underwater like a minnow, absorbing the stillness that comes from being encased in blue. Underwater I feel smoothed over, whole, as if the water has sanded away all the little nicks and abrasions that come from being married to a man who loves the logic of machines more than he loves human unpredictability.

One morning in late June, I heard a splash as I drifted and Jeanine wriggled toward me, her skirt and blouse fanning out like the fins of an elaborate tropical fish. Silver bubbles streamed from her mouth. As she swam past me, she reached out her hands and traced the side of my body. I felt her fingers on my skin, warm and then gone. I gave her my blue-and-silver suit that day and we swam together every morning until the beginning of July, when she went into the machine for renewal. I was there waiting when she came out of the chamber.

"Good morning, Jeanine," I said. "Let's go for a swim."

We swam naked then, that July Jeanine and I. My body was the first human thing she saw.

That same night, there was a thunderstorm. Lawrence was still reading to Artie. Caramia was asleep. I stood at the doorway watching the rain as it clattered over the garden. Everything in the garden seemed to be opening to the sky. The smells came to me in billows: the yeasty richness of damp soil, the sweet youth of wet grass, chlorine from the pool, wet towels, mold, berries, leaves. The air smelled like life: like all of our lives and like life itself. I stood there breathing it.

Then the thunder tolled, *basso profundo*,[2] and lightning snaked across the sky and the rain seemed to be plunging to earth in swarms, as if it was trying to wreck itself by running headlong into the ground. Jeanine came and stood next to me. Her expression was intent, like a cat following a moving object. Then she squeezed past me, awkwardly, her hips pressing against me. She had to be in it, of course. Had to feel it. That's always how it was with her. And so she was standing in the downpour, barefoot, lifting her feet and slapping them down to see the water run away from them. Opening her mouth to drink the rain. The lightning was very close—we could hear it hiss. It wriggled across the sky and she laughed. When the next roar of thunder came, she looked around to see where it came from and then put her hands on the ground, hoping, I guess, to feel the vibration.

"Come out of the rain," I said. She turned, rain drops on her eyelashes. She came back towards the doorway where I stood. But instead of squeezing past, she put her hands on my waist and kissed me. Her mouth tasted of apples. The feel of her lips, her hands just cupping my lower ribs. I felt as if I was suffused with purple ink, as if ink were spilling from her mouth into my body, flushing me with clouds of color. As if I were water.

---

2. *Basso profundo* is a deep heavy bass voice with an exceptionally low range.

I kissed her back. I kissed her and my hands went around her. The small of her back. Her hair. Her ribs. Her breasts. Her cheek. That was how fast the ink traveled through me. I touched her and she seemed to swim in my touch, the way she had swum through the pool in her clothes. Like she'd known it all along.

Then she lifted her lips from mine and smiled and moved past me to go inside.

It was Lawrence who confessed first.

He came into the garden a few days later, after the children were in bed. We'd made it a habit to sit there at the stone table under the quince tree in the evenings, have a drink, talk over the day.

"I kissed Jeanine," he said. "I can't explain it but—I had to tell you."

"When?" I kept my voice neutral, trying to understand what I felt.

"This afternoon, while you and the children were at the beach."

"Did you like it?"

"Mara. That's not—it was just a kiss."

I knew, of course, that it wasn't just a kiss. I knew how she had sighed when he'd touched her. I knew how the kiss had filled him with desire. How he had been thinking of her ever since, the salt-sweet of her, her taste of apples. I savored my own secret knowledge of how things would go. The second kiss, the third, and then the plunge. Her eyes closing and opening in response to Lawrence's touch, absorbing it but also inspecting it.

"It's okay," I said at last. "I made love with her."

"You what?" His face seemed to collapse. "*When?*"

"This morning. While everyone was still asleep."

I waited for him to speak.

"What does that mean for me?" he asked.

Jeanine solved it for us, the way she solved everything. She came up behind me and pulled my hair over my shoulders. She traced her fingers over my cheekbones and brow bone, then my lips. I couldn't see her face but I saw Lawrence watching her. I saw him receive her invitation.

Afterwards, Jeanine slept between us. We couldn't bring ourselves to send her to her own bed and so I slept uneasily, worried about the children coming in and finding her there. The world was altered, shifted, and yet it was the same. The same damp smells in the garden. The pool pale blue in the morning light. Jeanine there to swim with me. Breakfast for the children. Lawrence off to the guest cottage to ward off digital invaders. Artie and Caramia and I piling into the car to visit a farm where there were going to be sheep dog trials. By evening, I was sweaty with guilt.

"It's wrong," I said to Lawrence when the children were asleep. "She's not—it's not an equal relationship."

He was slumped in one of the wrought-iron chairs in the garden, holding a glass of Pernod and soda. He's a handsome man, not turn-your-head handsome, but pleasing. He wears his brown hair a little on the long side, and it was falling over his face as he looked down at the drink in his hands. His T-shirt was a faded tomato color, pretty in the twilight, and I was stripping it off in my mind, remembering the knotting of his shoulder muscles as he leaned over Jeanine.

"We're her employers, for one thing. And she's like a child—she doesn't have any experience of the world."

Lawrence nodded.

"Do you think she was made like this?" I said. "Do you think it's a feature of Jeanines?" It made me sick to think it—that the moment she touched me had been burned into her genes, that she'd been created as a toy for people like us. People worse than us.

He shrugged, still slumped. "Does it matter?"

"Yes." I wanted him to look at me. "Don't you think? Free will? Isn't that part of the equation?"

"Whose free will?" he asked. "Hers or ours? If her design makes *us* act a certain way, doesn't that mean we've lost our free will too?"

I took a sip of my wine and felt the beauty of the garden pressing in on me. We weren't in real life, we were on this absurdly beautiful estate and Jeanine wasn't real, not in any sense that I had known reality to mean.

"Who is it harming?" he asked and then he did look up, nodding the hair out of his face.

"I don't know," I said. "I don't even know what she is."

"She's Jeanine," Lawrence said. "Can't that be enough?"

It was all for show, that conversation. We weren't going to change anything. We were already in love with her.

Jeanine wasn't much of a conversationalist in the first days of our romance. She had no past, no story to tell, and her present was the same as ours. But within a day or two she had absorbed enough of the world to know that *we* had pasts, and to ask us about them. Lawrence told her about his path from teen hacker to corporate security maven. I told her about my work as a psychologist, before I had the kids. She was interested in the kids, interested in the concept of childhood.

"Was Artie always Artie?" she asked. "Thinking so much?"

I told her about his colic, about how much he cried as a baby that I sometimes thought I might kill him, or kill myself. And then how the crying that had seemed so much part of him had just tapered off, so gradually that I never knew when he went from being a fussy baby to being a smiling one. His first word was milk. Caramia's first: Artie.

"What was your first word?" she asked me. She was lying with her head on Lawrence's stomach, her legs thrown across my lap.

"I don't know. I was the youngest of four—by the time I came along, nobody was paying much attention."

She twisted her head to look at Lawrence, an only child.

"I think mine was truck," he said.

Jeanine nodded. "And mine?"

We were silent. The answers I could give were locked in their own room, a room nobody should enter.

"We didn't know you then," I said. "The Troxlers might know."

"The mysterious Troxlers with their secrets." Jeanine reached up to stroke Lawrence's clavicle. She likes the feeling of our bones—her hands always go to them. "I think I'll have many secrets too. Then I will hire Lawrence to keep them all for me."

"How many secrets do you have now?" Lawrence asked.

Jeanine slid her leg along mine. "*This* is a secret, right?"

I nodded. We had talked about it with her very emphatically—that no one could know, especially not the children. "Sex is not for children," I'd added, worrying that this most obvious boundary might have escaped her.

"So you have one secret," Lawrence said.

"That's a start."

"Maybe I have another," Jeanine said. "I can't tell you or it wouldn't be a secret."

We couldn't talk about the future with her either, of course. We knew *our* future. In a few weeks we will go back to New York. The children would start school. Lawrence would begin another security job. I would face the question of what to do about returning to work. But of Jeanine's future, we knew only that the bracelet on her wrist would turn amber and then red and then she would return to the machine to be renewed.

"I might come and visit you in New York," she said once. "I've been reading about it on the computer."

"What have you been reading?" I asked, to shift the conversation away from the notion that she could cross borders, leave the machine behind, exist anywhere outside of this strange house.

"Everything," she said. She was in the kitchen, cooking dinner. I watched her hands as they snapped the ends off asparagus. A bowl of chilled water and lemons was ready to receive the spears once they had cooked. Mussels lay tumbled in the sink, scrubbed to an inky shine. She didn't have to think about any of it now—she learned everything so quickly.

"About the Native Americans first, and the Dutch. About Hudson, the man and also the river. About this place called Queens, with all the different people from the world, and Brooklyn where they make their food like *artisans*. About the planes flying into the buildings and the storm that filled the tunnels with water and all the different bridges. I read the poem by Hart Crane about the bridge: *Out of some subway scuttle, cell or loft, a bedlamite speeds to thy parapets*."[3]

She stopped and savored the taste of the words, which were only vaguely familiar to me. I was long past my poetry-reading years. Now it was only novels and memoirs. Other people's stories.

"I looked with the satellite view to find your house," she continued. "But I couldn't."

Artie was at the kitchen table, drawing. I knew he was listening because his picture had absorbed the nouns from Jeanine's speech: a queen, a plane, a bridge. "That's because Lawrence doesn't like our personal information to be on the computer," I said. "He knows how to make us invisible."

"I'm going to take Jeanine to Central Park," Artie announced, still drawing his bridge. "I'm going to show her the carousel."

"What about Caramia?" I asked. "Can she come too?"

"She'll be napping," Artie said. "It's just going to be me and Jeanine."

Of course, I thought. *He's in love with her, too.*

---

3. This quote comes from "To Brooklyn Bridge" by Hart Crane (1930), with "bedlamite" meaning a lunatic.

Late in July, I persuaded Lawrence to take the day off and come with me and the children to the beach. Jeanine stayed home; she can't be in the sun for very long in any circumstances and her bracelet was already amber.

It was a rare pleasure to have Lawrence with us during the week and the children were giddy with it, taking turns jumping off his shoulders into the water, insisting on endless chicken fights. We ate ice cream at the little seaside stand where they sell plastic shovels and buckets and cigarettes, and then we made our way home. We were almost back at the Troxlers' when Artie said, "Daddy hasn't seen the horses."

The day before, we'd seen three Percherons grazing in a pasture near town, yellow with blond manes and tails.

"They're so pretty!" Caramia said. "Do you want to see them? We can feed them carrots from our lunch!"

"We don't have carrots today," I said. "We'll just pet the horses." But Caramia wanted to feed them carrots like we had before, so Lawrence pulled into the drive and I ran up to the house to get some.

"You'd better grab my work phone, too," he called after me. "It's morning in California and I'm expecting a call. It's in the cottage."

I went there first, since it was closer. I opened the door with Lawrence's key and stood for a moment in the spangled darkness, my eyes adjusting to the dim light. When the shadows sorted themselves into shapes, I saw that one of the shapes was Jeanine. She was sitting at Lawrence's desk.

"I'm cleaning in here," she said. It was perfectly obvious that she was not cleaning. Panic surged through me. What if she had found out whatever it was that Troxler had hired Lawrence to keep hidden?

"You can't be in here," I said, realizing with a stab of disappointment that Jeanine had an ability I hadn't expected—the ability to lie.

She shrugged and came to me and brushed my damp hair out of my eyes. "I only want to know what he does," she said. "It's natural to be curious. There's so much I don't know—and so little time to find out before I forget again."

When I told Lawrence later that night, his face grew very still.

"Are you sure? She wasn't cleaning?"

"She was going through the drawers," I said.

He put his elbows down on the stone table and rested his head in his hands, raking his hair with his fingers. "They did it on purpose," he said.

I waited for him to explain. Inside, Jeanine was cleaning up from dinner. She would join us soon with a bottle of wine and three glasses, sitting with her legs draped over the arm of a chair as one of us stroked her feet. For the first time since all this had started, I wanted more time without her.

"The renewals," Lawrence said, lifting his head. "It's for security. Even if Jeanine learns something she's not supposed to, the machine will take it from her."

"So that means she doesn't really have to be renewed?" My heart flamed with hope. "I mean, if it's not for any physical reason—coding errors or whatever they said."

Lawrence pushed himself away from the table and flopped back in his chair, his palms raised as if I'd leveled a gun at him. "Mara," he said. "I don't know anything about this technology. I can't hack it because I don't understand it. Anyway, my job is to protect Troxler."

Her face is slick with rain and she licks her lips and grins.

Today, when we come back from the waterfall, the house is dark and Jeanine hasn't started dinner. I call out for her once, then send the children to their rooms to get out of their swimsuits. I go into our bedroom. For a moment, I let myself hope. It's happened before that I've come home to find her and Lawrence dozing together in the bed.

I was furious the first time. The rage came over me like a foaming river, churning up all the flotsam from our marriage. Over the course of two summers he had never been willing to put aside his work to spend time with me and the children, not for a swim, not for an outing, and certainly not for a nap. Yet there he was, in the middle of the afternoon, dazed and soft with sleep and sex. Jeanine watched us snipe at each other—me cataloging his failings as a husband and father, Lawrence offering sarcastically to measure the minutes he had spent with each of us, was that what I wanted, a spreadsheet of his every moment? And once again, she saw how to fix us.

"Go be with the children," she told Lawrence. "Mara and I need time together."

That night, Lawrence came to me, chastened. "You and the kids are the most important thing in the world to me," he said. "I never want you to feel otherwise."

We ended up making love, just the two of us, with a tenderness we hadn't shown one other in years. Jeanine stayed in her own room. Afterward, something was different between us. An adjustment of degrees, like an oiled hinge or a squeeze of lemon in the soup. As if we'd realigned. His daytime dalliances with Jeanine, his episodes of obtuse rationality, somehow none of it abraded as it had, counterbalanced by moments of consideration, offerings of attention. Jeanine had helped him, I realize now. She'd asked me why I was upset, and I'd explained. She must have found a way to translate it so he could understand.

I badly want to find him resting in her arms now. But the bed is empty and unmade—untouched from this morning. This is puzzling, too. By now Jeanine should have learned her duties and begun them. I go looking for Lawrence.

He lets me into the cottage cautiously, then takes me in his arms and holds me.

"I feel awful," he says. "Sick. Do you feel sick?"

I nod into his chest. "Where's Jeanine?"

"I don't know. I went to see her at lunch time, but she doesn't remember me."

The same words come to me as before: *we're in too deep*. "Of course she doesn't remember you. It's the first day. Give it time."

"I should have been there when she woke."

"Why weren't you?" I feel a pinch of panic, remembering the consternation on Jeanine's face when she saw my face hovering over hers. Maybe if he'd been there, Jeanine wouldn't be acting so aloof.

Lawrence exhales into my hair. "It was too hard. The waiting. I went to look in Troxler's files."

I pull away from him. The curiosity I feel is different from his. I don't want to know how the machine has made Jeanine and how it remakes her. I want to know how we are made and how Jeanine has remade us. I want to know what love is. I'm worried that it's just chemistry and that the machine has found the formula.

"I need to get back to the house," I say. "The kids are by themselves."

Lawrence rubs his face. He's still in shorts and socks, a faded Mets T-shirt. He smells damp and unwashed. "I'll come too," he says.

We find her in her room, sitting in the shadows. She is watching the video—again, or still, I'm not sure which. On the screen, Jeanine is talking in a low voice. "Every machine in the house has a manual that explains how it works," she is saying. "If you have a question, read the manual."

Jeanine startles when I come in and clicks off the video. "I'm sorry," she says. "I had to watch it again—there's so much to learn. I'll go make dinner."

Lawrence follows her into the kitchen, making gentle small talk. I remain standing in the darkened room. The glimpse of the Jeanine in the video makes me feel as if my heart has been ripped out of my body. *That* Jeanine loved me—simply, unconditionally, passionately. How did it happen? What did I do? How do I do it again?

The powder she drank before last night's renewal sent Jeanine into a grinning stupor. The other times, both she and Laura had gone into the machine before it took effect, but this time we'd encouraged her to linger, unwilling to say goodbye. She had to lean on Lawrence as we walked across the garden. Walking behind them, I thought irritably about the men who designed the machine, how cumbersome the monthly renewals were, how long the eight-hour wait would be. And even as I was thinking this, I was feeling myself splinter into pieces, the shards of my thoughts reflecting one another so that I saw who I was, what I was, what I was capable of, endless refractions of that moment, walking behind my lover and my husband as they pitched across the moonlit garden, our children asleep, the night blooming its swell of frog chirp and cricket lull, the machine luminous in the moonlight. They stopped in front of it. I stepped around them and ran my fingers over the keypad, then touched the button to open the lid. Lawrence helped Jeanine climb inside and lie down in the machine's metal cradle.

"Good night," he whispered and kissed her slackening lips. "Sleep well. We'll see you in the morning."

After we closed the lid, we stood and watched the machine. It croaked once or twice, then clicked and began a muffled shirring. Water sluicing over her, I imagined. Washing away the fingerprints we'd left on her skin, the sense memories. Lawrence squatted down and put his hands on the domed lid, and then rested his cheek on his hands. He began to sob. I put my hands on his back, the way Jeanine might have done. He was shaking. The machine was shaking. I felt his warmth through the cloth of his shirt, the ridges of bowed muscle.

"It doesn't hurt her," I said. I had no idea if this was true.

Lawrence stood and used the collar of his shirt to wipe his eyes. He took my hand.

We walked back across the garden and Lawrence sat down at the stone table under the quince tree. I got us each a glass of wine. We didn't speak, just stayed there, listening to the sound of the machine. After a while, I went to bed and sat on top of the covers with my knees tucked against my chest while he kept vigil in the garden. I didn't want to think about what was happening inside the machine, and so I thought instead about Jeanine returning to us, about the weeks that still remained.

When I woke, Jeanine was there beside me, still wrapped in white insulating blankets.

It rains after dinner, but it's a light rain, without thunder or lightning. Still, Jeanine is drawn outside. She stands and tilts her head back to watch the endless identical raindrops and then reaches her hands overhead to touch them with her fingertips. Then she feels my eyes on her and glances back to the doorway where I stand. Her face is slick with rain and she licks her lips and grins.

"Come out of the rain," I say and she takes a deep breath, inhaling the sweet ozone and the wet grass. Then she comes and stands beside me, waiting politely for me to make room for her to pass.

"Jeanine, come play *Sorry!*" Artie says. They have been playing it for weeks, but now Jeanine has to learn the rules all over again.

Lawrence and I are sitting on the couch, feeling uncomfortably like Mom and Dad. We should have joined the game, I realize. I could be sitting next to her. I could teach her strategy. Instead I watch her concentrate, watch the moment when she has to decide whether to knock one of Caramia's pieces back to the start. She doesn't yet know that Caramia will cry if she does—or does she?

She looks at Caramia. She looks at Artie, who is only thinking about his own journey around the board. She looks at me. She smiles a little uncertainly. I am watching her hair fall around her face, the rain making her curls more buoyant. I am watching her breath traveling through her nostrils and down her throat to her chest. I am watching her mouth.

"Am I doing this right, Mara?" she asks.

I nod.

She knocks Caramia's pawn back to the start.

Caramia cries.

Lawrence sleeps spooned around me, his arm wrapped around my waist. I have been lying awake for almost two hours. I am thinking of Jeanine in her room, of her not knowing that she could come to us. Not knowing what it's like to sleep in someone's arms. I am thinking of how she ate her dinner tonight, tasting it with such concentration and pleasure, and of the first time we made love. Is it all the same to her—the pleasure of the grilled lamb, the pleasure of the breeze through the window, the pleasure of winning the game of *Sorry!*, the pleasure of my mouth making its way across her belly? Is it only when you're used to life that you would trade all the other pleasures for that single one?

And then I hear the click of her door opening, the sound of her bare feet brushing against the floor. I wait for our door to swing open.

Instead, the footsteps grow fainter. I listen, my ears hollowing. The house is an empty din of non-noises, a whoosh of silence. Then I hear the door to the garden slide open. I slither out of Lawrence's embrace and go after her.

I think she might be going to Lawrence's cottage again, but instead she goes into the garden. I follow her. The ground is wet from the rain, and cold on my bare feet. I'm just in a T-shirt and panties and I find myself hunching against the faint breeze that washes over the garden. Everything is damp and cool and fragrant and ordinary. Jeanine touches leaves and branches as she walks, sending speckles of droplets behind her. Her feet splash across the flagstones. She passes the pool and stops to look at it, lit up from below, a blue glow in the darkness. She stoops down and touches her fingertips to the water, grazing them over the surface and then plunging them in. We used to swim together at night, back in July. I wonder if I went in now, if I simply ran and dove, if she would come to me and we could begin again. But she gets up, shakes off her hand, and continues, around the corner behind the potting shed, to the machine.

I slow, because I want to know what she has in mind. I want her to have some kind of special knowledge, a way to break the machine open and spill out everything that's gone in.

"What happened to the one in the video?" she asks as I come around the corner. "The other Jeanine."

"That's you," I say. "You're Jeanine."

She shifts her head to look at me out of the corner of her eye.

"I spent all day watching," she says. "She isn't me."

I cannot fathom how she knows this. "She's the same as you," I say. "Jeanine. She *is* you. She went in. You came out."

Jeanine shakes her head. She doesn't seem angry. If I didn't know that she'd just been renewed, I would have said she seemed tired. But there's still all that energy in her body, its thrumming youth, its impatience. She's wearing the dress she put on this morning, a simple white cotton one. She bends down and presses the keys that open the lid to the machine.

"How does it work?" she asks as it opens.

I look at the machine's metal cradle. A latticework of nozzles and spigots is perched over an enclosed square framework that contains the more intricate workings of the machine. There is a drain at the bottom of the chamber.

"Why are you thinking about this now?" I am pleading with her. "You have weeks still."

The white shape floats closer to me. I can see her dark eyes, the cloud of her hair.

"She had questions," she says. "She left them for me in a video."

I think of Jeanine sliding her leg against mine. *I can't tell you or it wouldn't be a secret.*

"I want to read the manual," she continues. "Where is it?"

"I'm not sure there *is* a manual," I say.

"Every machine has a manual," Jeanine says with school-girl certainty. She shivers and draws her hands up to rub her own shoulders. "Am I exactly the same as the other Jeanine?"

I want her to be. She was supposed to be. But something went wrong. This Jeanine is too brittle, too cold.

"Of course you are," I say. "You are Jeanine. Come back to the house and I'll look for the manual."

She comes toward me and for a moment I think she will take me in her arms and everything will be all right. But then she passes me, a white moth in the darkness, and walks past the pool toward the house. My heart collapses in my chest. I watch her turn the corner. Then I bend down and press the buttons that initiate the next renewal.

It's wrong, all of it, but I have all night to set things right. When I join her in the kitchen, I will warm a mug of milk and sweeten it with honey, then mix in the powder we keep in the cabinet above the fridge. I'll stay with her as she grows dopey, and when she's ready, I'll lead her back through the garden to the metal cradle where she'll sleep. It won't take long to delete Jeanine's video and search her room for secrets. When morning comes, I'll be waiting by the Hot House. This time, I won't waste my chance. This time, we'll swim naked in the pool.

■

Author Biography

Dashka Slater is the 2023 winner of the Kurt Vonnegut Speculative Fiction Award as well as the recipient of two Pushcart Prize nominations and a Creative Writing Fellowship from the National Endowment for the Arts. She is the author of numerous books of fiction and nonfiction for children, teenagers, and adults, including the Stonewall Award-winning *New York Times* bestseller, *The 57 Bus*, part of *Time* magazine's 2021 list of the One Hundred Best Young Adult Books of All Time. Her most recent nonfiction book, *Accountable*, won the 2024 J. Anthony Lukas Book Prize and the California Book Award Gold Medal.

Discuss

1. How does the story explore issues of consent when one party (Jeanine) is artificially created and lacks full agency? Is there such a thing with artificial intelligence?
2. Extrapolating on what weird lit can hint at, do you think the time will come when artificial intelligence will no longer be considered "artificial"?
3. How does Jeanine's presence both solve and complicate the existing problems in Mara and Lawrence's marriage?

Write

Comparative Analysis: Compare this story's treatment of artificial beings with another work of science fiction, such as the films *Ex Machina* (2014) or *Companion* (2025) or even the floating head professor, Professor Orloff, in the second season of the TV show *Wednesday* (2025). Analyze how each piece explores themes of humanity, consciousness, and exploitation, noting similarities and differences.

Poet Wrestling with the Possibility She's Living in a Simulation

Rosebud Ben-Oni

What if every decision (and every choice not taken) splits into its own separate reality, all of them running parallel, and all of them real? That's the idea behind physicist Hugh Everett's Many-Worlds theory, and it's the question at the heart of Rosebud Ben-Oni's poem. Written in 2018 during a period of personal uncertainty, the poet asks something most of us have wondered at least once: What if I'm living in the wrong version of my life?

All my timelines lead to this poem.[1]
Proof: What brought us here is all
the same horse. So I have some questions.
Which of us are the shallow wood.
What if blood is emptiness. I suspect
my own veins are rogue simulations[2]
flitting with a new kind of heightened self-

---

1. The concept of timelines here refers to the many-worlds interpretation of quantum mechanics or multiverse theory—the idea that every decision creates branching realities where different outcomes occur, then lead here.

2. In computing, a "rogue" process is one that operates independently of its intended parameters or control. The speaker suspects their own veins are "rogue simulations."

awareness. Proof: the nurse says they are flighty
& hard to find. Drink more water, she sings,
pushing her own tin. What if what's within
is simulated to keep every artery compliant.
                    You know.
That whole thing *being*
as being undead
dead creeks.

                              It's also sad to think
the envy still filling us over some horse
we knew for less than a week
is simulated. Don't you feel better at least? Well,
do I have news {for you}: I suspect the horse is
also false, bogus, *feigned*. Proof: he comes running
when we do not call for him. Proof: In one timeline,
he and *I* are doing a lot of simulated things.
Get your mind out of the gutter.
On holidays we openly bathe
          in a {manmade}
                    heated spring

                    —or rather: he fears the water & balances
on edge. Half the time he slips. Falls in & blips. Holds me
responsible. Resets. *Drink more water*, tweets the anti-horse
threatening to annihilate another anti-
                                                  {horse}
                                        come salt
                         winter, come stone
            age. So place your bets
that advanced civilizations don't always
not annihilate themselves. Woah.
Let's try this again.
Reset.

*

Maybe our most real timeline resides in another verb tense.

Or is hiding in new irregular superlatives. Should we ask for
who
whom
whoest. Because why be skinned when you can be
skunned. Would you do the honors. My deliberateness says to
trust you.
One simulation to another, am I wrong. Didn't *we* see *we* through
fire, windmill, heated floors. Were we not a woman waving
a white handkerchief. One if by land. Skull
& bones. Ticks in the trees & mysterious
{reset}
nil & :: *please.*

*

If nothing else,
can we not all agree
hummingbirds win Most
Fabulous Simulations.

Even if they are the secret guards,

& their tears
the anti-virus software
injecting all those broken
1s & 0s into our hearts.[3]

3. Binary code is the fundamental language of computing, where all data is represented as sequences of ones and zeros. Here, they create hummingbirds.

& surely in one timeline they are the gods themselves ::

the superlative *whoest*[4]

of engineers
who've made mincemeat
of asteroids & atomic
timewears.

It's too bad that all *our* timelines are inherently self-destructive.

Proof: we watch the same video of a hummingbird snoring for hours,
still sitting in the nurse's chair & not a step closer to what life,
outside of human reach, desires. I'm okay with that.
The horse is calling.
& I'm running
my hands through his mane,
unable to explain.

Where & when this comfort,
this crisis,
took root.

How did we meet, was it *two if by sea.*

I can't remember when we did not cheat
life with a horse
:: when all timelines were

---

4. Ben-Oni invents irregular grammatical forms ("whoest" of "who," like "best" or "most") to suggest that simulated reality might require new linguistic rules.

a real
& :: even field
in which the humming
-bird drank our blood
straight from the creek.

▪

Author Biography

Rosebud Ben-Oni is the author of several collections of poetry, including the forthcoming *The Last Great Adventure is You* (Alice James Books, 2027), a sequel to *If This is the Age We End Discovery* (2021), which won the Alice James Award and was a finalist for the National Jewish Book Award. Paramount commissioned her video essay "My Judaism is a Wild Unplace" for a national media campaign for Jewish Heritage Month, and her poem "Poet Wrestling with Angels in the Dark" was commissioned by the National September 11th Memorial. "When You Are the Arrow of Time" was also commissioned and filmed by the Museum of Jewish Heritage—A Living Memorial to the Holocaust. She performed at Carnegie Hall on International Holocaust Memorial Day as part of "We Are Here: Songs from The Holocaust." She has received grants from the New York Foundation for the Arts, Queens Arts Fund, Queens Council on the Arts, Café Royal Cultural Foundation, and CantoMundo.

Discuss

1. What do you think are the "Most Fabulous Simulations"?
2. The speaker mentions "simulated things" and "rogue simulations" throughout the poem. In simple terms, what do you think the speaker believes about their own reality? And how do they feel about it?
3. Look at the phrases in brackets like {manmade} and {horse}. Why might the poet put certain words in these special marks?

Write

A Real Look at Simulation: Consider how the poem uses the concept of simulation to question the nature of reality and human experience. Examine specific examples of digital/technological language and discuss what the poem suggests about living in an increasingly virtual world. As we leave this anthology, consider whether the speaker views simulation as liberation or imprisonment, and what this might say about our growing relationship with technology.

Credits

Carmen Maria Machado, "The Husband Stitch" from *Her Body and Other Parties: Stories* (Graywolf Press, 2018). Originally published in *Granta* 129 (2014). Copyright © 2014, 2018 by Carmen Maria Machado. Reprinted with the permission of The Permissions Company, LLC on behalf of Graywolf Press, Minneapolis, Minnesota, graywolfpress.org.

Chrys Tobey, "Ms. Bovary Goes House Hunting in 2014," copyright © 2015 by Chrys Tobey. First published in *Slab*. Reprinted with permission of the author. All rights reserved.

Chrys Tobey, "My Alter Egos Ran Off with This Poem," from *A Woman Is a Woman Is a Woman* (Steel Toe Books). Copyright © 2017 by Chrys Tobey. Reprinted with permission of the author. All rights reserved.

Alice W. Fuller, "A Wife Manufactured to Order." First published in *The Arena* 13 (July 1895). Public domain. Minor edits to modernize spelling and word divisions.

Alice Gerstenberg, "Overtones" from *Washington Square Plays* (Doubleday, Page, & Company, 1919). Public domain. Minor edits to modernize spelling and word divisions.

Charlotte Perkins Stetson (Gilman), "The Yellow Wall-paper." First published in *The New England Magazine* 5, no. 5 (January 1892). Public domain. Minor edits to modernize spelling and word divisions.

Charlotte Perkins Gilman, "Why I Wrote The Yellow Wallpaper." First published in *The Forerunner* 4, no. 10 (October 1913). Public domain. Minor edits to modernize spelling and word divisions.

Talia Lakshmi Kolluri, "What We Fed to the Manticore," from *What We Fed to the Manticore* (Tin House, 2022). Copyright © 2022 by Talia Lakshmi Kolluri. Used with permission of the publisher, Tin House, an imprint of Zando, LLC.

Jane Hirshfield, "Common Pigeon," copyright © 2025 by Jane Hirshfield. First published in Terrain.org. Reprinted with permission of the author. All rights reserved.

Louisa May Alcott, "Lost in a Pyramid, or the Mummy's Curse." First published in *The New World* (January 16, 1869). Public domain.

Edgar Allan Poe, "The City in the Sea" (Text-05d), J. L. Graham copy of *The Raven and Other Poems* (1845), with Poe's manuscript changes. Public domain.

H. P. Lovecraft, "The Colour Out of Space," first published in *Amazing Stories* vol. 2, no. 6 (September 1927). Public domain. British spelling retained as Lovecraft's stylistic choice. All other punctuation and capitalization edited to conform with US conventions.

Natalie Diaz, "*exhibits from* The American Water Museum" from *Postcolonial Love Poem* (Graywolf, 2020). Copyright © 2020 by Natalie Diaz. Reprinted with the permission of The Permissions Company, LLC on behalf of Graywolf Press, graywolfpress.org.

Alissa Hattman, excerpt from *Sift* (The 3rd Thing, 2023). Copyright © 2023 by Alissa Hattman. Reprinted with permission of the author and publisher.

Brittney Corrigan, "The Last" from *The Ghost Town Collectives and Other Stories for the Anthropocene* (Middle Creek Publishing, 2023). Copyright © 2023 by Brittney Corrigan. Reprinted with permission of the author and publisher.

Philip K. Dick, "Second Variety." First published in *Space Science Fiction* 1, no. 6 (May 1953). Public domain.

Ray Bradbury, "Lazarus Come Forth." First published in *Planet Stories* (Winter 1944). Public domain. Original typographical error corrected.

Ambrose Bierce, "Moxon's Master" from *Can Such Things Be?* (Boni & Liveright, 1918; Project Gutenberg, 2003). Public domain. Minor edits to modernize spelling and word divisions.

Ryan McCarty, "Why Wouldn't Autonomous Cars Cry at Night?" copyright © 2024 by Ryan McCarty. First published in *Rattle*. Reprinted with permission of the author. All rights reserved.

Matthea Harvey, "The Future of Terror" from *Modern Life* (Graywolf Press, 2007). Copyright © 2007 by Matthea Harvey. Reprinted with the permission of The Permissions Company, LLC on behalf of Graywolf Press, graywolfpress.org.

Dashka Slater, "The Jeanines of Summer," copyright © 2023 by Dashka Slater. First published in *North American Review*. Reprinted with permission of the author. All rights reserved.

Rosebud Ben-Oni, "Poet Wrestling with the Possibility She's Living in a Simulation" from *If This Is the Age We End Discovery* (Alice James Books, 2021). Copyright © 2018, 2021 by Rosebud Ben-Oni. First published in *Guernica*. Reprinted with permission of the author. All rights reserved.

www.ingramcontent.com/pod-product-compliance
Lightning Source LLC
LaVergne TN
LVHW100922110826
845155LV00036B/47
* 9 7 8 1 9 5 5 4 9 9 5 0 7 *